DOING W

By the same author:
The Hot Line
Signs and Blunders

Doing
What Comes
Supernaturally

PETER H LAWRENCE

Terra Nova Publications Ltd
Bristol

First published 1992 by Kingsway Publications
Reprinted 1993

This Terra Nova Publications Ltd edition 1997

Cover photo: The Image Bank

British Library Cataloguing in Publication Data
A catalogue record for this book is available
from the British Library.

ISBN 0 9522688 4 1

Published by Terra Nova Publications Ltd
Registered office: 21 St Thomas Street,
Bristol, BS1 6JS, Great Britain.

Produced for the publishers
by Bookprint Creative Services
P.O. Box 827, BN21 3YJ, England.
Printed in Great Britain.

Contents

Acknowledgements

I am indebted to David Smith for the title of this book.
When David has used it in the past, Christians have asked
him whose side he is on. David and I would like you to
know we are both definitely on Jesus' side. I am thrilled
Margaret Shaw was able to find time in a difficult year to
type the manuscript and correct all the spelling and gram-
mar. If you find any mistakes, be assured it was originally
much worse. I am delighted David Pytches helped to edit
this book. He would have liked you to know he doesn't
agree with everything I've said. I haven't let him write
the Foreword this time.

I am grateful to all the many people who gave permission for their stories to be included, checked the
details and offered constructive comments. I have occasionally changed their names when it seemed appropriate
to do so.

If you like the content of this book it is almost certainly because it is about God, who is a bit special. If you
don't like what's written it's probably because I wrote it.

That leaves my wife, Carol, to whom I have dedicated
this book, as I could not have done it without her.

To you all, a very big thank you.

Peter H. Lawrence

To Carol

Preface

This book is intended for those who don't think they can minister in the power of the Holy Spirit but would rather like to try. It is written to help beginners begin and is aimed at answering the question, 'Where do we start?' These pages will let you know where we started. I preach and teach the Bible but I share experience. This is a sharing book. It is not about the best way to do it—it may not even be a good way to do it—it is about the way we did it.

One of the difficulties of sharing our story and the way we minister is that some people always say, 'Ah, but it wouldn't work here.' With these people in mind I have included a number of accounts of what happened when we took our teaching to other places. We are a small inner-city Anglican church where I am the vicar, but from time to time I have been privileged to go into different cultures and settings, and I have found God to be willing to come in each one.

As I write I have been a Christian for nearly thirty years. For the first twenty-four years I loved Jesus, I loved worshipping God, I loved the Bible and reading books about exciting things which happened to other

believers in other places at other times. I always hoped
and prayed that one day such things would happen to me.

Six years ago I went to a conference led by John
Wimber and his friends. I was impressed by the effective
preaching of God's word and the accompanying signs of
God's power and grace. But this conference was different
from others I had attended. This time I was taught
methods of procedure and I returned home not only
grateful to God for the way he uses other men and
women to advance his kingdom, but believing he could
actually use me. For the first time in my life I began to
think I too could do it.

In the last six years nothing has happened to change
my mind. We have begun to minister in the power of the
Holy Spirit at Christ Church and I feel sure as we have
managed to start, anyone can. Just as it was passed on to
me, so my aim is to pass it on to others. Equipping the
saints to do God's work for his sake and glory is very
dear to my heart and I long to give away everything
which has been given to me.

It is my desire and prayer that all who want to be like
Jesus and minister as he did, might find some help in
these pages.

Peter H. Lawrence
Vicar of Christ Church, Burney Lane, Birmingham

1

Come, Holy Spirit

I like to sleep on planes. Economy seats are built to fit economy-sized people and, being a little larger than most, the less time I am conscious of my crumpled state during a flight the better. But on our journey to Malawi I was grateful to the captain for waking us as we flew over Mount Kilimanjaro, the highest mountain in Africa. There below us not far from the equator, clearly visible through wispy clouds, lay snow sprinkled over the summit of a majestic and isolated peak, which dominated an otherwise brown and barren world.

I was on my way to a clergy conference in the Diocese of Southern Malawi in the company of Canon Tom Walker, the main speaker, who had asked me to do 'healing and deliverance'.[1] Many months earlier I had felt confident in saying 'yes' because of the style of ministry we'd seen God exercising among us in the previous three years. I believed the way God's Spirit was beginning to touch a number of lives had given me something positive to share with others, even through an interpreter. Now, somewhat unsure and feeling fearful, I was grateful for the spectacular new sights which distracted my mind from myself and my insecurity as I marvelled from my window seat over God's creation below.

We stepped from the plan at Lilongwe, the country's capital, into a warm, balmy atmosphere and enjoyed the sight of an unexpectedly green and pleasant land before catching another plane to Blantyre. This flight took us along the edge of Lake Malawi, an area of water the size of England, which feeds the Zambesi River. The shore was peppered with pinpoints of light as darkness began to fall. Not, as I first thought, street lights or home lights, but the backyard fires over which every meal was cooked. People in Malawi do not live in houses as we do but use them merely for shelter or sleep.

After two days' rest at Blantyre we were driven along a breathtaking route to Chilema. Travelling along the southern end of the Great Rift Valley, we found ourselves surrounded by mountains similar to the Scottish Highlands (only twice as high and bathed in continual sunshine). The conference centre itself nestled among the trees at the foot of the mighty Zomba plateau where the Bishop of Southern Malawi also had his residence. When we arrived, he and his wife along with the diocesan clergy and their wives were waiting for us in the garden amid blue, purple and bright red trees. We dined that evening with Bishop Nathaniel.

'Peter,' he asked, 'if you met a lion when you left my home tonight, would you know what to do?'

'Well, Bishop,' I replied, 'we don't meet too many lions in Birmingham. I don't think I would.'

'One evening,' he continued, 'I left this house on foot with some members of my family and came face to face with a lion.'

I made some suitably astonished noises and he continued: 'I knew,' he said, 'that whatever I did I must not turn and run. I told everyone else to keep still, stared back at him and eventually he turned and walked away.'

Must be a sermon there, I thought, *even if it wasn't a roaring lion* (1 Pet 5:8–9). 'Are there many lions around here?' I asked, trying to sound nonchalant.

'No,' he replied, obviously enjoying his subject, 'there are more leopards than lions around here.'

'Oh,' I said, 'and what do I do if I meet one of those?'

'You won't see a leopard,' he reassured me. 'They live in trees and leap on you from behind. You'd have no chance with a leopard.'

'Right,' I said, 'I won't waste my time looking for a leopard. Are there any snakes in Chilema?'

'You've come at a bad time for snakes,' he said. 'We've had a lot of rain lately and they've all been washed out of their holes. There's a lot of them about and they're very angry.' As an afterthought he added, 'Sleep well. We're looking forward to hearing from you tomorrow.'

Yes, I thought, *if I'm still here.*

As it turned out, the lack of hot water, absence of plugs in the bath and sink, wobbly loo seat and most of all no mosquito net were far more serious threats to my wellbeing than the wild night-life of central Africa. Despite the heat I shut all windows and doors firmly, covered myself with anti-mosquito spray—several times—and went to sleep counting spotted sheep with manes and forked tongues.

After my first teaching session about thirty Anglican clergy and twenty wives stood before me, eyes closed, hands held out expectantly as I prayed, 'Come, Holy Spirit.' I too was expecting great things. 'It's easy to minister in Africa,' some had told me. 'They're so open to things of the Spirit.' Tom laid hands on a tall, elderly white English missionary who beamed all over his face before sliding gracefully to the floor where God continued to bless him, but it would have needed a very experienced and sensitive eye to see the Holy Spirit moving on anyone else. Later Tom assured me that he thought some good things were beginning to happen, and that I should repeat the process in the afternoon.

Conversation over lunch was very interesting. I had

shared a number of stories and they had witnessed the
'falling in the Spirit' of a highly-respected and well-loved
but reserved English priest. They asked a couple of
questions English clergy and laity often ask as well:

1. Isn't 'Come, Holy Spirit' something of a technique?

Many people's first experience of this ministry is as a
spectator, and lying behind this question is often the fear
of manipulation.

If I see someone who has a physical illness shake all
over and then testify to being healed, I can understand it
and be glad. If a bereaved friend who has never cried
suddenly bursts into tears, I will feel positive about what
is taking place. If I see an unbeliever collapse to the floor,
as Saul did, and come up later saying, 'Jesus is Lord!' I
will rejoice with the angels in heaven. But if something
takes place beyond my own experience or understanding
as I look on from the side I will want to ask a few
questions.

Who is this person at the front? Where is he coming
from and what is he doing? Why did the Englishman fall
on the floor? What is the speaker trying to do and, most
important of all, what is he trying to get me to do? I did
my best to answer.

My aim is to invite the Lord to be the Lord, to have his
own way among us and do whatever he wants to do. In
our services at home we meet to worship God, preach
Christ crucified and invite the Holy Spirit to come and
minister to us. In this way we seek his face, long to know
more of his truth, and ask to share in his risen life—not
for our own sakes but that the love of God in us may
overflow to the world, and the kingdom of praise for our
God be extended.

Often in our churches different people take it in turns

to play at being God. The organist says, 'You won't have any clap-hands-here-comes-Charlie choruses in this church while I'm in charge of the music.' The treasurer says, 'If you waste money we don't have on a sound amplification system (people could hear George White-field a mile away) then I'm resigning.' Even the vicar might say, 'Let's keep the ship on an even keel and try not to do anything which will upset anyone.'

It is so refreshing sometimes to let God be God in his own church; he invariably waits to be invited. Far from being a 'technique' which strives to twist God's arm or to manipulate the congregation into particular responses, praying, 'Come, Holy Spirit,' has become for us a way of giving God his church back and inviting him to do whatever he wants to do.

There was an understandable response: 'But if God wants his church back so he can do what he wants to do in our meetings, why is there any need to pray, 'Come, Holy Spirit?'

In the last century people said to would-be missionaries like David Livingstone, who brought Christianity to Malawi, 'If God wants to convert Africa he'll do it without your help.' Thankfully a number of missionaries knew better. God has given us responsibility. We are not yet the perfect bride of Christ for there is much we still need to let God do for us, with us, in us and through us. What we do affects what he does because God the Father has given his children freedom and revealed his mind to us in the Bible. We are commanded to ask, seek and knock, and in the context of this teaching Jesus assures us God will give the Holy Spirit to those who ask him (Lk 11:9–13). God has given us the responsibility of letting our requests be made known to him (Phil 4:6).

My dictionary says that 'technique' means 'the method of procedure...any method of doing a thing'. As far as I can tell, praying, 'Come, Holy Spirit,' is a good method for asking God to come and do whatever he wants to do. Not that one technique is the only one or even the best. I visited a church where, before the vicar experienced someone praying, 'Come, Holy Spirit,' at a conference, they used to wait in silence without saying anything. He shared with me how the same manifestations occurred then as those he witnessed at the conference and subsequently when praying, 'Come, Holy Spirit.' God was apparently doing it before the vicar learned a new technique.

My Catholic friends often speak of the 'real presence' of Jesus in the Eucharist. Sister Briege McKenna writes about an outdoor mass in a mountainous Latin American country where a seriously ill child was placed under the altar. As the priest consecrated the elements she saw Jesus in her imagination with his hands held out, and the child was miraculously healed.[2]

If praying, 'Come, Holy Spirit,' or silence, or a particular moment in the mass can raise people's expectations and faith to receive whatever God wants to do, then so be it, and to him be all the glory. I simply share how I have found asking God to come in services while waiting in silence has moved us further on in things of the Spirit at Burney Lane, and become a way for us of letting God be God in his own church.

2. Why do you ask us to stand?

Sometimes people suspect that I invite congregations to stand so that I can have the thrill of seeing them all fall over. There is no advantage in falling over. I often speak and write about this phenomenon simply because it is a good example of seeing with our natural eyes when God is doing something.

In experience—and the Jews whom Jesus taught would be accustomed to praying standing up—I have found five advantages in encouraging people to stand at the beginning of a time of ministry:

(a) More seems to happen. We prayed, 'Come, Holy Spirit,' in small groups weekly for a year, with very few signs and testimonies of God's power coming on people. When we stood instead of remaining seated, more people looked open to the Holy Spirit and there was an appreciable increase in the power we received, not only externally visible to the onlooker, but internally experienced by the participant.

(b) Practically, if people sit in church pews and rows it is harder for ministry team members to reach them and lay on hands: heads are slumped forward and knees seem to stick out more.

(c) Because of the atoning work of Jesus all Christians can stand in the presence of God. It seems right to kneel when confessing sins, and to sit when listening to sermons or the Bible being read, but in the intimate exchange when we his children wait upon Father God to send his Spirit among us, it seems appropriate to stand in his presence through the blood of Jesus. Body language can so often help us to express and be what we know in our minds is true.

(d) Psychiatrists tell us that we think while sitting and feel while lying down. I find standing to be a more neutral position, when Christians are often less defensive, less cerebral and less religious.

(e) I once asked the Holy Spirit to come on a group of people seated comfortably in a warm lounge, and within five minutes four of them had fallen asleep. I am sure there are times when standing can help us to stay awake and to concentrate.

But having said all that, with the invitation to stand I frequently tell people to sit if they become uncomfortable, and to feel free at all times to adopt their own position. Some elderly and physically handicapped people obviously cannot stand and need to be put at ease.

I was delighted that some of the Malawi clergy wanted to think a few things through before committing themselves to new ideas and practices. After such helpful and meaningful discussions I tried again in the afternoon.

'Come, Holy Spirit,' I prayed.

We waited in silence and this time there were more obvious signs of God touching people's lives. One person's hands began to shake; another had to sit down as power made him unsteady; one or two wives began to weep; and generally there was a more relaxed and receptive atmosphere which allowed challenging ministry to take place. It is never the outward and dramatic signs and wonders we seek, but the inner sanctifying work of God's grace. It is our experience that such visible signs are often accompanied by testimonies of feeling God's love, knowing him and his mercy more deeply, or receiving greater power to serve him more effectively.

During the course of the week, everyone became more and more open to the gentle waves of God's Spirit bringing to the surface a few problems, allowing some grief to be expressed and encouraging many with feelings of warmth, love, forgiveness and acceptance.

Following these general sessions, individuals asked for private ministry. During these times Tom heard several confessions, cast demons out of one and led another into the gift of tongues. Several came to me determined to change sinful aspects of their lives and I particularly remember one who came seeking healing.

He was a clergyman with poor mobility in his legs. He was in constant discomfort and on some days could hardly stagger more than a few yards. He shared some personal sins, repented, accepted forgiveness and I prayed over him, 'Come, Holy Spirit.' His face became hot, his hands began to shake and after a little while he slid to the floor where he remained for about fifteen minutes with signs of power all over him.

'I felt power,' he said, 'slowly working its way down my body, removing the pain, taking it down my legs and out through my toes.' He certainly looked and walked better when God had finished with him.

Those who came to see us especially seeking spiritual gifts, healing or deliverance were encouraged to do so because of the ministry they experienced in our communal times together. In public worship people with needs and problems are often making decisions about whether to come to us for help privately. In my first five years at Burney Lane hardly anyone asked to see me for counselling or private prayer, even though there were many I believe I could have helped. From the moment I began regularly to ask the Holy Spirit to come upon us I have been inundated with requests for private prayer and am now having to say 'no' to the majority. It is a way of praying which seems to open us up to God and to one another, facilitating more biblical activity and deeper relationships.

More surprisingly to me, only the Englishman fell over in the Spirit in general sessions, and no demon manifested itself at our public meetings. All manifestations of God doing things with us were gentle and gradual, but real and well received. I was delighted to be asked before we parted to teach the clergy how to do this kind of ministry in their own churches. It went something like this, based on notes I give out when teaching at home, where I would normally have a team with their own leader available to help me.

Come, Holy Spirit

I often find it helpful to stand with eyes closed, preferably after times of worship and preaching which have helped us to centre our thoughts upon Jesus.

1. Depending on their past experience, I frequently spend a brief time preparing the people. I may say, packaged with a little humour, something like this:

(a) It is not a time to say our prayers or speak in tongues initially.

(b) It is a time to be quiet and receive.

(c) We try not to resist or be afraid.

(d) We try not to be too conscious of others, or curious.

(e) We wait for God to give, not trying too hard to receive.

(f) We welcome the Holy Spirit and thank him for coming.

2. I use a *short* prayer asking the Holy Spirit to come. A long prayer often communicates lack of faith, nervousness and a desire to tell God what to do.

3. Some people need help over the initial silence. I may say, 'We wait—no need to panic—some will be engaged by the Holy Spirit more quickly than others.' I try to maintain mostly silence, punctuated with occasional words encouraging people to relax and be comfortable.

4. If at this stage I feel panicky, I try to resist the temptation to speak too much too soon as it can take time before people can let go and let God.

5. As soon as I see the Holy Spirit on people, I say so. People like to know if he has come.

6. I comment on anything happening which may disturb people, for example, falling over, shrieking or loud weeping, by making comments like, 'Don't worry, someone is with him, it's only God,' or, 'It's all right, just let God do with you what he wants to do.'

7. If by natural observation or direct 'words' I think I know what God is doing in a particular 'wave', I say so— preferably as it is happening or just after, to prevent manipulation. Often if God comes in a certain 'wave', I feel or experience the same as everyone else.

8. If 'words' come to me for small groups or individuals direct from God or via others, I find it is normally best to wait until God's waves appear to be over before giving them.

9. The team leader deals in the early part with people who obviously need assistance, such as those who are shrieking, falling or weeping. In extreme cases a person may be taken out for more private help and prayer.

10. At an appropriate moment I normally ask the team to go and minister.

11. Before closing I ask if anyone would like prayer for any need. I ask them to raise their hands so the team can move alongside, providing there are enough members available. If not, I will invite them to come forward and wait until we can offer help.

12. I always try to have an official closing prayer at the expected time, while still encouraging people to go on receiving until God has finished.

Undoubtedly the hardest part, and probably the most important, is the silence. A ministerial friend said to me the other day, 'Peter, thirty seconds of silence is an awfully long time.' Recently my wife attended a main session at a large conference where a well-known speaker announced, 'We'll now have five minutes' silence while we wait upon the Holy Spirit,' and then talked all the way through it. He simply could not do what he sensed he should be doing. In fairness to him, what seems like five seconds to those in the congregation can feel like five minutes when up at the front, but waiting patiently, perhaps with watch in hand, can be of vital importance.

At a Brighton conference in 1989 the Spirit of God moved powerfully among 5,000 people after which several hundred came forward to make a commitment to Christ.[3] John Wimber was at the microphone and said nothing for twenty minutes. If I want to make sure it is God's Holy Spirit and not my flesh, soul or spirit dictating proceedings, then I need to shut up for at least the first few minutes.

In the early days I learned a lot by watching Rick Williams, now Pastor at the Riverside Vineyard, Teddington in Middlesex. He wasn't dynamic—he didn't give a lot of 'words' from God—he was simply very good at waiting and encouraging others to wait. Sometimes after fifteen minutes hardly anything was happening; I would have given up and gone home long ago. Then with relaxed patience Rick would begin to comment on a few things he saw, others would relax, feeling no pressure—and the second fifteen minutes would be as fast-flowing as the first fifteen were apparently stagnant.

If I am likely to be nervous after I have asked God to come, I find things to do. I might take my watch off, sip a glass of water, ask God to give me 'words' to be used later, concentrate on people's faces to see if I can detect what, if anything, is beginning to happen, and so on. Being relaxed, non-dominating, trusting and silent can sometimes be very hard work, especially for preachers.

Our conference in Malawi finished officially with a party at the Bishop's residence on the Saturday night, but most of us attended the local Anglican church in Chilema on the Sunday morning and stayed on for lunch. Word of our presence and the work of the Holy Spirit among the clergy and their wives had obviously reached the locals because after the service I was asked if I would pray with a number of people who needed healing. The rest of the clergy disappeared for lunch while I was left on my own with a queue of about forty people, all hoping to be healed.

I have personally never found the model of the typical healing evangelist to be a very helpful one, with its queues of sick people down the aisle waiting for the one with the gift of healing to lay hands on each one for ten seconds. I know God gives ministries to certain people and some are obviously better channels of his love and healing power than others, but I am unhappy using this model on most occasions myself for five reasons:

1. Practically, one person cannot pray with very many people for very long.

2. Many sicknesses are merely the surface symptoms of deeper personal problems or sins which need time and discernment to solve.

3. Some who receive a ten-second ministry are not helped or healed and then either pretend they have been, or leave disillusioned.

4. There is a great danger of people looking to the minister rather than to Jesus for healing.

5. This model will not encourage people to believe all Christians can pray with the sick (Jn 14:12; Jas 5:16).

I looked at the forty people waiting to be healed, realised I would probably never see them again and sensed what I should do. I invited them to line up across the front of the church and taught them briefly through an interpreter the principles I was going to adopt which they could follow on their own or with one another afterwards. I invited them all to stand upright, close their eyes, and hold out their hands while I prayed, 'Come, Holy Spirit.'

As with the clergy, progress was initially slow, but eventually signs of God's Spirit began to appear on their faces or in their bodies. Some began to beam, one to shake, and another to weep. I continued to encourage them all to relax, explaining how it often takes time, and during the next twenty minutes, while still speaking occasionally to all forty, I went along the line and managed to lay hands briefly on each one. By now I could see what God was doing in most cases and was able to speak to each condition as I saw things naturally or felt God giving me a 'word'. Normally I would have preferred other members of the team to do this, but as they were not there and the numbers involved were not great, this seemed the most appropriate action to adopt at the time.

I concluded the session and still managed to be in time for lunch. By the end everyone had felt God's Spirit for about twenty minutes and those who did not feel physically better—and some did—generally expressed feelings of blessing, power and love. One or two people stayed with friends or relatives and where God appeared to be highlighting a few problems I was able to advise how to proceed further. It was not a very dramatic time but I was happy that, given just thirty minutes, everyone present felt at least a touch of God's love and power, some felt better or improved, and all were encouraged to pray for one another after I left. However well or badly I did, I thought by the end this particular model gave God maximum chance, with the maximum number of people, to do what he desired, while not shirking my own responsibility or failing to use the faith I sensed within me at the time.

After lunch the remaining clergy were returning to their parishes so I was pleased to try to answer two more questions of a practical nature:

1. Who may pray, 'Come, Holy Spirit'?

This is a question I have puzzled over many times. Here are some of my thoughts:

(a) You must be born again (Jn 3:7)

Luke 11:1–13 seems to suggest that God will always give the Holy Spirit to his children when they ask him. We are encouraged to ask and go on asking, as a child asks his father for food whenever he is hungry.

Who then are God's children?

John said of Jesus, 'To all who received him, to those who believed in his name, he gave the right to become children of God—children born not of natural descent, nor of human decision or a husband's will, but born of God' (Jn 1:12–13).

Our faith in Jesus gives us the right 'to become children of God'.

Jesus said, 'I tell you the truth, unless a man is born again, he cannot see the kingdom of God... unless a man is born of water and the Spirit, he cannot enter the kingdom of God' (Jn 3:3,5).

To become God's children we need to be born again of water and the Spirit.

Having preached Jesus, Peter said, 'Repent and be baptised, every one of you, in the name of Jesus Christ so that your sins may be forgiven. And you will receive the gift of the Holy Spirit' (Acts 2:38).

To be born again we need to repent, be baptised in the name of Jesus and receive the Holy Spirit.

Paul wrote:

But when the time had fully come, God sent his Son, born of a woman, born under law, to redeem those under law, that we might receive the full rights of sons. Because you are sons, God sent the Spirit of his Son into our hearts, the Spirit who calls out, 'Abba, Father.' So you are no longer a slave, but a son; and since you are a son, God has made you also an heir (Gal 4:4–7).

Once we have responded with faith in Jesus—been

born again of water and Spirit by repenting, being baptised and receiving the Holy Spirit—then the Holy Spirit
within us enables us to call God our Father.

It is my impression from the New Testament that not
everyone can call God Father, but only those who have
been born again. On the basis of this I do believe everyone who prays, 'Come, Holy Spirit,' in a meeting needs
to be born again. Naturally, those who have experienced
the power of the Holy Spirit in their own lives are those
best qualified to ask him to come on others.

(b) 'The prayer of a righteous man is powerful and effective' (Jas 5:16)

It is very dangerous to judge ministers on the signs which
accompany their ministries (Mt 7:21–23). 'By their fruit
you will recognise them' (Mt 7:20) and not by the free,
unmerited spiritual gifts God gives to them. Nevertheless, I believe a born-again person seeking first the kingdom of God will not be lacking in any good gift God
wishes to bestow and will more likely have the trust of a
Christian congregation. Ministering in the power of the
Holy Spirit is always done by grace and not by works—
we can never earn God's favour—and yet our unrepen-
tant sin can grieve the Holy Spirit and cause his face to be
hidden from us. Consequently, I would say that a person
'worthy of respect, sincere, not indulging in much wine,
and not pursuing dishonest gain', and keeping 'hold of
the deep truths of the faith with a clear conscience' (1 Tim
3:8–9) is a good candidate for inviting the Holy Spirit to
come on a church-sized gathering.

(c) 'We have different gifts, according to the grace given us. If a man's gift is...leadership, let him govern diligently' (Rom 12:6,8)

I believe we are more likely to let God pour out his Holy
Spirit upon us and do whatever he wants in the presence

of a gifted leader rather than a weak one. Daring to pray,
'Come, Holy Spirit,' in church often requires more gifted
leadership qualities than preaching or taking a service.
When *anything* may happen, most of us feel far more
comfortable if the person at the front is firm and confident, creating a relaxed and secure atmosphere in which
the supernatural power of the Holy Spirit can flow more
easily. Initially therefore, it seems right to look for a
born-again person seeking first the kingdom of God,
with good leadership qualities, and then in due course
identify those who are best suited to this ministry. The
most powerful leader is not always the best at waiting in
silence.

2. Does the faith of the leader make a difference?

God is Sovereign Lord of all. When we pray, 'Come,
Holy Spirit,' we invite him to come and do whatever he
wants to do. He is the Lord.

In Acts 9 Luke tells the story of Saul's conversion as
though he is knocked to the ground, hears Jesus, is
blinded and changed from persecutor to preacher totally
as a sovereign act of God. Ananias is involved in helping
him to see and receive the Holy Spirit, but apparently
from a position of obedience rather than faith (Acts 9:11–
17). We cannot easily say that faith must always be present before the Holy Spirit comes.

On the other hand our experience over several years
seems to indicate that greater power is received and felt
when certain people lead the ministry rather than others.
After the disciples prayed in Acts 4:23–31 with indica-
tions of faith present, 'the place where they were meeting
was shaken'.

If God is not in it, faith the size of a mountain will not
move a mustard seed, but when he is, then the faith of the
leader or the congregation in co-operation with God will

often result in greater power being released. Normally, however, I think it is the gift of *encouraging others in their faith* which makes the biggest difference. God seems only too willing to come to those who will welcome him and receive him.

Once lunch with the remaining clergy and their wives was over, everyone returned to their parishes, some of them to await our arrival on a whistle-stop tour. Fortunately the Bishop decreed we should visit the lakeside churches. These are situated in paradise; snow-white sand bordering on clear blue waters, where the occasional fish eagle descends like lightning from the heavens to pick its prey and be gone. I never saw one miss. Not as delicate, but equally as impressive, are the water-horses with all but their nostrils submerged during daylight. Though the snakes bite, the lions prowl and the mighty African elephants crush all in their path, it is the hippopotamus in Malawi which kills most people. The crocs stay in the rivers but the hippos enjoy the reeds of the lake. Beware dusk when these nervous creatures come on to the land, betraying extreme neuroses should anyone come between them and their home; they will not hesitate to attack. Still etched deeply into my memory is the sight of thirteen elephants processing to the water's edge to drink, only to be seen off by six hippos rising like Leviathans from the deep.

Beside the lake was the first church we were to visit and when we arrived, special chairs awaited us. Each place we visited was different yet the procedure was the same. We were seated on thrones and home-made gifts were showered upon us: bed-mats, baskets, hats, pottery tea-sets and beautifully carved ebony. The choir sang with natural harmony and bongos. Tom preached and then I was on.

'Thank you for your gifts. The gift we bring is to pray

for you.[4] We believe God the Father, through Jesus, is going to anoint us afresh with the gift of his Holy Spirit.' I realised many were already Christians bearing the fruit of the same Spirit in their lives, and yet we wanted them to experience more.

'We do not speak. We do not sing. We do not pray. We stand, close our eyes, hold out our hands, and wait.'

Since we were doing everything through an interpreter, there was not much time for anything else, but the response was thrilling. They arose enthusiastically. I prayed, 'Come, Holy Spirit,' and he came every time, but never in the same way. Some wept with repentance and sadness, others beamed with joy. One small group rested in the Spirit and what had been a heavy and oppressive atmosphere lifted, giving way to peace. On one occasion some physical healing was experienced and on another, but only once, some nasty hairy things appeared.[5]

It took place in the church where the Archdeacon was the vicar. After a delightful meal of chambo—the local fish—we slept the night under a picturesque thatched roof. Tom had a 'holier than thou' mosquito net and kept me awake for some time with slapping noises interspersed with cries of, 'Got you, you blighter!' and other such noises which canons of the Church of England make when engaged in warfare.[6] In the morning, we engaged in a different kind of battle.

The church was full. The whole village was present. The choir sang. Tom preached, I did my stuff and the Archdeacon interpreted. Within seconds of standing and welcoming God among us pandemonium broke loose. People began screaming all over the place. Tom and his wife Molly tried to lay hands on as many as they could at one time—and the Archdeacon turned to me for clarification.

'I think these are the demons you spoke about at

Chilema. Yes?' It was obviously a new experience for him.

'Yes,' I said, whereupon he left me alone and went to have a closer look.

It was quite a novel experience for me as well. Standing on my own at the front of an Anglican church in charge of a meeting, unable to speak the language, while about 200 adults simultaneously yelled and screamed at the top of their voices was definitely different. Eventually I realised I would be more use in the mêlée and joined in. I think we ultimately identified just five people who were manifesting demons, which left very easily as Jesus was named in front of them. I realised afterwards that screaming and yelling happens as part of normal worship and celebration in Malawi, and when some started involuntarily, the rest simply joined in to show solidarity with their friends.

It was an interesting tour, but the most thrilling moment was meeting the vicar who had experienced power bringing new life to his legs. I saw him on the Monday after he had spent the Sunday with his own two congregations. 'It worked!' he said. 'I got them all to stand just as you suggested. I asked the Holy Spirit to come, waited, and you'll never guess what: he came— twice.'

It has been heartening to receive letters—and some are still coming now several years later—telling of healings, deliverances and blessings taking place in some of these communities led by a number of the clergy and their wives with whom we spent a week in Chilema—clergy who dared to stand in front of their congregations, pray, 'Come, Holy Spirit,' and wait in silence until he came.

Notes

1. Tom Walker was asked by SOMA (Sharing Of Ministries Abroad) to take this conference and they arranged everything for us.
2. Sister Briege McKenna, *Miracles Do Happen* (Veritas Publications: Dublin, 1987), p 59.
3. Worship Conference, October 1989, Brighton Conference Centre.
4. I was, in fact, also able to give the clergy some excellent Christian literature, courtesy of Sovereign World Trust. Malawi is officially listed as the second poorest country in the world and the church leaders were delighted to receive it.
5. One of the Old Testament words for demon is *sair* (Lev 17:7; 2 Chron 11:15), which means 'hairy one'. See *The Illustrated Bible Dictionary Part One: Aaron-Golan* (Inter-Varsity Press: Leicester, 1980), p 381.
6. Tom Walker has subsequently become the Archdeacon of Nottingham.

2

The God Who Comes

When my wife Carol's parents retired they moved to Spain and settled into the English-speaking community at Javea by the sea. For the price of a three-bedroomed semi-detached house in London they were able to have their own luxury bungalow and swimming pool designed and built in an olive grove on a hill overlooking the golf course. Surrounded by British neighbours and able to attend an Anglican church service led by an English priest once a week, they found themselves deprived only of the cold, damp and smog which fed Anne's asthma when in England. In the late spring Carol and I plus our three girls visited them in their new home.

I sat on the verandah sipping Coke while my daughters splashed excitedly in the pool and the dogs chased butterflies under the olive branches. The contrast with parish work in Birmingham was marked. Here there were no pressures. Ant-like golfers pursued their white spheres on the distant horizon, but I didn't have to contemplate joining them just yet. Now I am middle-aged the anticipation and memory of my golf greatly exceeds the reality. Maybe I would have a go later in the holiday. My main aim was to recover and recharge until the inevitable return date arrived, and yet I missed the folk, the fun and the fellowship in the Spirit at Burney Lane. At least Gavin and Anne were Christians.

'Coming to the Bible study on Wednesday night?'
enquired Gavin.

'What's on?' I replied, stalling for time.

'A Dutch girl who lives in Jerusalem, visiting Spain to
speak in English about prayer,' he replied. It sounded
better than Spanish television or putting the children to
bed, so I went. It wasn't, of course, just down the road,
but the toll we paid to travel on the road to Altea was
worth it.

The motorway is cut into the face of the Sierra de
Bernia where the reddish-grey limestone and sandstone
plateaux terminate by the sea in steep and rugged coastal
cliffs. All around us as we drove could be seen the sculp-
tured terraces, giving the mountainous slopes the
appearance of stairways to heaven. Almond trees and
small vines make full use of the fertile, reddish-brown
soil which these steps provide. As we by-passed Calpe
we caught a glimpse of the Penon de Ifach standing out in
the Mediterranean like the Rock of Gibraltar. Then the
toll road tunnelled through the crumbly stone and on to
Altea. Ahead of us the blood-red sun daubed the sky with
fire before it died just as we reached our destination—a
lounge full of people from several different nations who
all knew each other, a guest speaker and me.

We began with a time of open prayer; person after
person spoke in tongues without an interpretation. I was
puzzled. It all seemed decent and in order, except I
couldn't understand a word of it. Eventually it dawned
on me; they were praying in their own native tongues
and only I, being linguistically thick, was at sea. The talk
was fascinating. Our speaker shared how she and her
friends had followed Ray Borlase's book on intercession
and had subsequently seen some dramatic results in
Jerusalem.[1] Someone talked all the way through it, which
annoyed me a little until I turned round to see a middle-

aged lady translating it all into French for her elderly mother.

Afterwards I was introduced to the gathering. I enthused about God's ministry among us in Birmingham, and was duly invited to be next week's speaker.

I immediately began to regret my enthusiasm. I was there on holiday, and I needed rest and relaxation. But in the darkness going back I realised I simply couldn't help it—and maybe it was no bad thing. 'For we cannot help speaking about what we have seen and heard' (Acts 4:20). Something or Someone kept bubbling up inside and I wanted the whole world to know that. . . . But *what* did I want them to know? What was I trying to communicate?

Critics are always keen to quote to me how Satan tempted Jesus to try and do signs and wonders in the wilderness (Mt 4:1–11), and the 'wicked and adulterous' generation which seeks a sign (Mt 12:39; 16:4). Was I seeking signs and wonders, or the Lord? Was I excited by the healings or the healer?

Like many other Christian adventures, my entry into the signs and wonders ministry was through the door of experience. I saw it, tasted it and enthused about it. I'm not sure it can ever be any other way round. The disciples saw and experienced Jesus, asked questions and then began thinking and teaching about him. On the Day of Pentecost the crowd saw and heard and asked questions, after which Peter stood up and said, 'This is that. . . (Acts 2:16, Authorised Version). Now, I realised, the time had come to do some thinking. I was better at answering the practical questions like, 'How do we do it?' than the deeper theological ones like, 'Why do we do it?' or, 'Is "Come, Holy Spirit" a right activity, biblically based, philosophically acceptable and theologically sound?'

I lay on the beach among a multitude of bronzed bodies. I believed I was going crispy, golden brown myself until I saw a lobster-pink animal looking at me from the mirror in the bathroom. Even so, it was a good activity for pondering. Whenever I visited another church and prayed, 'Come, Holy Spirit,' the more cautious always wanted to know where it was in the Bible, and I was struggling for an answer. This was the first question I tried to sort out on the beach, by the pool and, more especially, in Gavin's well-stocked study.

Is 'Come, Holy Spirit' a biblical way of praying?

Jim Packer writes:

> Is it proper to pray to the Spirit? There is no example of doing this anywhere in Scripture, but since the Spirit is God, it cannot be wrong to invoke and address him if there is good reason to do so. The New Testament shows that though prayer to the Father is the ordinary norm (for that is the way of prayer that Jesus himself practised and taught), prayer to Jesus is proper also (as when Paul prayed three times specifically to Jesus the healer [2 Corinthians 12:8–10]), and prayer to the Spirit will equally be proper when what we seek from him is closer communion with Jesus and fuller Jesuslikeness in our lives.[2]

I particularly like the emphasis on being closer to Jesus. The Holy Spirit comes to make Jesus known to us just as the coming of Jesus made the Father known.

'It cannot be wrong to invoke and address' the Holy Spirit, says Jim Packer, if 'he' is God. Most Christians would, I think, agree with this. Is the Holy Spirit then himself God?[3] It seems an obvious question and yet I remember being caught out by two fervent Jehovah's Witnesses who visited me one bank holiday. They believed the Holy Spirit is a power and not a person—the breath of God but not God himself. I realised it was time to sort this one out for myself.

(a) The Holy Spirit is a person

Jesus said:

> But when he, the Spirit of truth, comes, he will guide you into all truth. He will not speak on his own; he will speak only what he hears, and he will tell you what is yet to come. He will bring glory to me by taking from what is mine and making it known to you (Jn 16:13–14; see also Jn 14:16–17; 16:7–8).

I felt reasonably sure from the New Testament that the Holy Spirit is a 'person' and not just a 'power'; a 'he' rather than an 'it'. He has a mind (Rom 8:27) and a will (1 Cor 12:11); he forbids (Acts 16:6–7); he speaks (Acts 8:29); he loves (Rom 15:30); he grieves (Eph 4:30); and he prays (Rom 8:26).

(b) The Holy Spirit has the divine character of Jesus

James D. G. Dunn writes:

> The Spirit is the Spirit of Jesus—that is, he continues the work of Jesus; indeed we can put it more strongly, he continues the presence of Jesus (Jn 1:32; 6:62f & 7:37ff; 15:26 & 16:27f; 3:16f & 14:16,26; 6:59; 7:14,28; 8:20; 14:26; 14:17 & 16:3; 20:22; 14:15–26; 1 Jn 2:1).... The vitality of Christian experience does not cease because the historical Jesus has faded into the past and the coming of Jesus has faded into the future; it retains its vitality because the Spirit is at work here and now.[4]

Dunn also argues, 'For Paul, the Spirit is the Spirit of Jesus' (Rom 8:9; Gal 4:6; Phil 1:19).

Jesus says he and the Father are one (Jn 10:30) and indicates he and the Holy Spirit are also one: 'All that belongs to the Father is mine. That is why I said the Spirit will take from what is mine and make it known to you' (Jn 16:15). The Holy Spirit has the same character as Jesus and yet he is a different person: 'I will ask the Father, and he will give you another Counsellor to be with you for ever—the Spirit of truth' (Jn 14:16–17).

It seemed right to me to say that the person of the Holy Spirit has the divine character of Jesus.

(c) The Holy Spirit is the third person of the Holy Trinity

I found the following New Testament verses to be significant:

'Then Jesus came to them and said, "... Therefore go and make disciples of all nations, baptising them in the name of the Father and of the Son and of the Holy Spirit" ' (Mt 28:18–19).

'May the grace of the Lord Jesus Christ, and the love of God, and the fellowship of the Holy Spirit be with you all' (2 Cor 13:14).

'There are different kinds of gifts, but the same Spirit. There are different kinds of service, but the same Lord. There are different kinds of working, but the same God works all of them in all men' (1 Cor 12:4–6).

'Peter, an apostle of Jesus Christ, to God's elect... chosen according to the foreknowledge of God the Father, by the sanctifying work of the Spirit, for obedience to Jesus Christ and sprinkling by his blood' (1 Pet 1:1–2).

'... and pray in the Holy Spirit. Keep yourselves in God's love as you wait for the mercy of our Lord Jesus Christ to bring you to eternal life' (Jude 20–21).

Jesus, Paul, Peter and Jude together with John (1 Jn 5:5–9) and the writer to the Hebrews (6:4–6; 10:28–29) speak of God, the Son and the Holy Spirit in the same breath. There are other passages containing this 'triadic pattern' which I also noted.[5] At the very least I concluded that the person of the Holy Spirit with the divine character of Jesus is frequently spoken of in the same breath as God the Father and God the Son in the New Testament.

(d) The Holy Spirit is experienced as God by the early church

In Acts 5:3 Peter says to Ananias, 'You have lied to the Holy Spirit.' In Acts 5:4 Peter says to Ananias, 'You have not lied to men but to God.' Peter's experience of the Holy Spirit at Pentecost (Acts 2), healing the cripple (Acts 3), and before the Sanhedrin (Acts 4) have led him by Acts 5 to conclude that the Holy Spirit is God.

Archbishop Michael Ramsey wrote this:

> In knowing 'the grace of the Lord Jesus Christ and the love of God and the fellowship of the Holy Spirit' (2 Cor 13:14), and in having access through Jesus 'in one Spirit to the Father' (Eph 2:18), the Christians were encountering not only their own relation to God but the relation of God to God. When the Spirit cries in us, 'Abba, Father' and prompts us to say, 'Jesus is Lord,' there is God within responding to God beyond.[6]

It seemed clear to me that the Holy Spirit was experienced as God by the early church, and later found expression in the historical creeds.

(e) Does the Bible say that the Holy Spirit is God?

The creation of the world is linked in Genesis 1:2 with 'the Spirit of God' who was hovering over the waters. Some think this means the Holy Spirit is *omnipotent*.[7]

The psalmist asks God, 'Where can I go from your Spirit? Where can I flee from your presence? (Ps 139:7). He seemed to think the Spirit of God is *omnipresent*.

Paul writes, 'No-one knows the thoughts of God except the Spirit of God' (1 Cor 2:11), indicating the Holy Spirit is *omniscient*.

The writer to the Hebrews refers to the Holy Spirit as 'the *eternal* Spirit' (Heb 9:14, italics mine).

To my way of thinking there was a case for arguing from the Bible that the Holy Spirit is omnipotent, omnipresent, omniscient and eternal.

The Bible speaks of the Holy Spirit as a person with the divine character of Jesus who is spoken of in the same breath as God the Father and God the Son. He is experienced as God by the early church and arguably seen to be omnipotent, omnipresent, omniscient and eternal. Having looked at the scriptural evidence concerning the Holy Spirit, I found myself in agreement with Jim Packer. I believe the Holy Spirit is God and 'it cannot be wrong to invoke and address him'.[8]

The following Wednesday we drove along the same road to Altea, but this time I failed to notice the scenic splendour or the going down of the sun. I was worried. It was one thing believing in the theological acceptability of 'Come, Holy Spirit' and quite another praying it, especially among strangers.

The people of Malawi are some of the poorest in the world. They have mountains which attract winter rainfall and lakes teeming with fish, but they have no minerals to trade and no coastline to provide easy access and economical transport. Despite this need, or maybe because of it, they are a trusting people, open to things of the Spirit. But some members of the Bible study group to which I was now travelling were more in the 'eye of the needle' category (Mt 19:24). One was the son of a country's former president, staying for a while in Spain at one of his homes; several owned swimming pools, and one or two had more than one car. Nobody would be walking or riding a donkey to this meeting.

I taught about the ministry of Jesus, especially proclaiming the kingdom, healing the sick and casting out demons, and shared a few of our own stories. I was given permission to do whatever I thought was right, so I said, 'Let's stand. Relax, close your eyes, think of Jesus. Hold out your hands to welcome him.' Some rose with difficulty from their comfortable chairs and soft settees, but all eventually made it.

I prayed, 'Come, Holy Spirit.'

Hardly were the words out of my mouth before Anne fell backwards into the large sofa. *Not yet, Mother-in-law*, I thought to myself, somewhat concerned it might have seemed a put-up job. *We normally wait a bit first*. But God had come and she had 'gone'. Nobody opened their eyes or took any notice whatsoever; they were already rocking and shaking too much themselves to worry about anyone else.

Within a minute another lady joined Anne on the sofa; others made similarly dramatic ways to the floor; laughter bubbled out of one; tears out of another; hands began shaking from side to side; and Gavin looked as though he were drawing elaborate abstract pictures in the air with his hands. Everybody appeared to be engaged with the Spirit, their beaming faces putting my bright pink countenance in the shade.

I felt as if I were standing in the middle of an electric storm. One or two 'words' were given and claimed, but the general feeling afterwards was of power rather than revelation; a sense of the awesome presence of God not necessarily related to any specific healings or anointings. God is very good and, I believe, loves to be invited to come and do what he wants to do, wherever we may be.

May is definitely the time of year to visit Spain. Everything is open, nothing is full or overcrowded and the sun is warm but not unrelenting. Tennis at the country club, nine holes of golf, lunch, another nine holes and shady walks beneath citrus trees already displaying a few small oranges and lemons can all be enjoyed leisurely without fear of exhaustion or burning. I continued to ponder whenever I could.

I was by now satisfied that the New Testament view of the Holy Spirit gave me permission to ask him to come, but there was a philosophical question people loved throwing at me which I needed to think through. From the mind-blowing problems of the Trinity I turned to the intricate complexities of religious language.

Why do you pray, 'Come, Holy Spirit,' when he is already here?

'God is here; let us ask God to come,' is a sentence which appears to contain a problem. The difficulty arises because we use the same language about God as we do about other people, such as the vicar. Both come to church, but there the similarity ends. If I am in church on Sunday I am nowhere else; I am there in all my fullness; all you can see is all there is. But God is not like that. Our language in talking about God is woefully inadequate. To ask God to come when he is already here sounds nonsensical, but it is the problem of language about God rather than our request. Language, like mathematics, is dependent upon comparison, but to whom do we compare God?[9]

Often we need to use imagery in our struggle to understand this better. In his autobiographical sketch, *On the Boundary*, Paul Tillich wrote: 'The weeks and, later, months that I spent by the sea every year from the time I was eight were even more important for my life and work. The experience of the infinite bordering on the finite.'[10]

I find this image to be helpful in understanding language and concepts about the God who comes. The boy standing on the shore does not experience the whole Atlantic Ocean; he experiences the edge of it coming up the beach. He witnesses the sea's 'dynamic assault on the serene firmness of the land and the ecstasy of its gales and waves'.[11] If he swims in it, is immersed by it and swallows some of it, he may say, 'I have the Atlantic Ocean within me and on me and around me and I feel the enormous power of the waves.' And yet there are sailors and marine life with experience of the Atlantic Ocean of which the boy has never dreamed. Each day as he stands on the beach the mighty ocean comes to him. It seems to have a personality of its own. Yesterday it came, today it comes and tomorrow it will come again.

Our God is much bigger than the Atlantic Ocean and he is a person. Even the ocean is finite, but our God is infinite—and yet he comes. He comes to meet us on the shore of our experience.

Thomas Aquinas, in his *Summa Theologiae*, wrote: 'When Scripture speaks of the "coming" of divine persons it does not refer to a moving from absence into presence, since divine persons are always present, but a moving from one mode of presence into another mode of presence.'[12]

This was the experience of the first disciples. Jesus promised the Comforter's continual presence to them (Jn 14:16). He came in and stayed, and yet before and after Pentecost God, the Holy Spirit, came on them more than once. He was with them always and yet he kept coming upon them.

St Peter was continually experiencing the Holy Spirit coming to him. In Luke 9:1 he was given 'power and authority to drive out all demons and to cure diseases'; a power which is normally associated with the Holy Spirit (*cf* Mt 12:28). Jesus breathed on him in John 20:22 and said, 'Receive the Holy Spirit.' On the Day of Pentecost Peter was 'filled with the Holy Spirit and began to speak in other tongues' (Acts 2:4). Before the Sanhedrin, 'Peter, filled with the Holy Spirit' spoke wisdom beyond his learning (Acts 4:8–13), and in Acts 4:31 he was 'filled with the Holy Spirit and spoke the word of God boldly'. The Holy Spirit therefore came upon Peter at least five times.

Paul, in Ephesians 1:13 writes: 'Having believed, you were marked in him with a seal, the promised Holy Spirit,' but in 5:18 he commands them, 'Be filled with the Spirit.' The Greek, I am told, means 'go on being filled'.[13]

So although the Holy Spirit makes Jesus present with us always, and once we have received him at conversion he remains in us, Scripture indicates that we are to go on being filled day after day.[14] Interestingly, I found there to be no such thing as the 'baptism' in the Holy Spirit in the New Testament. Jesus is seen as the baptiser in the Holy Spirit. The second blessing appears to come between the first and the third.

But if I am to go on being filled, it seemed right to enquire, 'Should I also ask him to come?' Given the inadequacy of language about God, is 'Come, Holy Spirit' the most helpful?

Is 'Come, Holy Spirit' the most appropriate language?

I found four good linguistic reasons which I thought made praying, 'Come, Holy Spirit,' a particularly suitable prayer.

(a) Declaration

Whatever we do publicly in our churches always has the effect of proclamation. Commenting on the Lord's Supper Paul says, 'For whenever you eat this bread and drink this cup, you proclaim the Lord's death until he comes' (1 Cor 11:26). Similarly, whenever we pray, 'Come, Holy Spirit,' we proclaim him as the third person of the Trinity, the Lord, who may be invoked. There are not many people in our church, where we invite him to come regularly, who call the Holy Spirit 'it'. I believe we may pray to the Holy Spirit because he is God, and whenever we do so we declare this truth to all who are present.

(b) Invitation and welcome

Revelation 3:20 says, 'Here I am! I stand at the door and knock. If anyone hears my voice and opens the door, I will go in and eat with him, and he with me.' Verse 21 suggests it is Jesus speaking prophetically, while verse 22 leads us to believe it is the Holy Spirit who brings the message; the one who makes Jesus known; the one who asks to come in; 'He who has an ear, let him hear what the Spirit says to the churches' (Rev 3:22). Despite Holman Hunt's splendid picture of Jesus knocking at the door, lamp in hand, it is presumably not a five-foot-ten-inch man with a beard, long robe and crown of thorns whom we are inviting into our lives, but his Spirit. I decided the appropriate response to someone knocking at the door was, 'Come in.'

(c) Without limit

To ask God to fill us or immerse us implies limitations. 'Fill' suggests power for service like filling a car with petrol. 'And they were all filled with the Holy Spirit and spoke the word of God boldly' (Acts 4:31). Immersion is frequently associated with dipping, washing and cleansing, and Jesus makes this comparison: 'For John baptised with water, but in a few days you will be baptised with the Holy Spirit' (Acts 1:5). 'Come', while being a clear declaration and invitation, is not a narrow or restrictive word which may limit people's expectations. 'Come' may include filling or washing, but it may also include empowering, convicting, healing, comforting, challenging, revealing, releasing and many more without limit; whatever God chooses to come and do at the time. It is an inclusive invitation rather than an exclusive one. For the same reason I decided 'come' seemed more apt than 'come in' which also adds some degree of limitation.

(d) Tradition

For centuries the traditions of the Christian church have permitted and encouraged prayers addressed to the Holy Spirit, as found in its hymnody and liturgy. Peter de Rosa in his book which develops the images of the Spirit expresses well the traditional, liturgical and poetical appropriateness of 'Come, Holy Spirit' in his final chapter:

> I recall as a college student going into chapel on Whitsun-tide evenings and joining in what I still feel to be the Church's finest hymns, *Veni Creator Spiritus* (with which all solemn councils of the Church begin) and *Veni Sancte Spiritus* which for me is unsurpassable. Always it was summer; a warm June evening; roses everywhere, the colour of Pentecostal flame; the simple plain-chant melodies.[15]

At this point I felt reasonably satisfied that praying, 'Come, Holy Spirit,' was linguistically acceptable and appropriate. Asking God to come when he is already here is possible because God is not a person limited by time or space. He is here and he can come, and we experience more of him when he does so. By asking him to come we declare this truth. We invite and welcome him among us to do whatever he wants to do without limit, as Christians throughout the ages have done before us. I knew there was more still to think about, but this would suffice for now.

On the Monday after the meeting at Altea I was invited to speak at an Indonesian restaurant in Calpe. This time the motorway was of no use to us, but if anything the

side road proved to be even more dramatic as we tunnelled in and out of the cliffs with the ever-present blue
Mediterranean far below us. The restaurant was closed
for business, but open to us and the Lord. Some of those
present had attended the meeting in Altea, but some faces
were new to me.

I spoke about healing, or rather some possible spiritual
causes of ill-health, and then prayed, 'Come, Holy
Spirit.'

There were signs of God's presence as before. A
'word' was given for a heart complaint and claimed by a
lady who was suffering some discomfort at the time. At
the laying-on of hands more power and heat were experienced and the discomfort went. Several days later the
lady testified to still feeling fine.

The restaurant was more spacious than the lounge
where we had met previously so it was easier after the
initial wave of God's Spirit, accompanied with shaking,
glistening, holy joy and tears, to ask people who wanted
specific prayer to identify themselves. I was keen to
encourage them to have a go on each other so they could
continue the ministry once I returned to England.

I specifically remember noticing the president's son
and the Indonesian manager receiving prayer. Within a
short while both fell over on the floor where they stayed
for some time, side by side. It was obvious to the
onlooker by the expressions on their faces, perspiration
on their brows and changed breathing patterns that God
was sovereignly doing something special with both.
Some time later when they were helped to their feet the
manager exclaimed, 'Wow! I haven't felt like that since I
was involved in the revival of Indonesia in the sixties.'[16]

I came home to Burney Lane and enthused about what
had taken place. No one in our congregation owns several homes, cars or swimming pools. Some of them come
on the bus or walk to church as the only option available.

But there was a warm joy that God could and would do it there as well as here, like the Jerusalem Church's response to the conversion of Cornelius: 'So then, God has even granted the Gentiles repentance unto life' (Acts 11:18).

We continued to worship God, preach Christ crucified, and ask the Holy Spirit to come among us. Surely we were getting it right, and yet opposition crouched at the door. I still found I believed what we were doing was right, but in debate I was defensive.

Yes, it was a way of letting God come among us and do what he wanted to do. Even though the prayer, 'Come, Holy Spirit,' was not found in Scripture, it did seem right to pray to God the Holy Spirit as well as continuing with our petitionary prayers to God the Father through Jesus. There could be little doubt in our minds of the biblical results which flowed from the ministry; people were saved, healed and delivered. Linguistically it felt appropriate to ask God to come, while not seeking to limit his coming or our response. But I still sensed there was something missing; I was looking for a deeper theological reason which could turn my defensive arguments into more positive proclamations.

One day I spotted a possible answer as I sat meditating in my study with my eyes open. A retired clergyman who used to live in our parish had died and left me some of his books. The title of one of them, as yet unopened, lit up in my mind.

The God Who Comes

Carlo Carretto writes:

> God has always been coming. He came in the creation of light, and He came yet more in Adam. He came in Abraham but was to come more fully in Moses. He came in Elijah, but was to come even more fully in Jesus. The God who comes takes part in the procession of time.

With history He localises Himself in the geography of the cosmos, in the consciousness of man, and in the Person of Christ. He has come and has yet to come.[17]

That was it. Our God is a God who comes.

Whenever we pray, 'Come, Holy Spirit,' we declare to the world that our God is a God who comes; we exercise our faith in the God who comes; and when he answers our prayer we meet for ourselves the God who comes. He is not an unknown God because he has come; he is not an unknowable God because he comes; he is not a God who leaves us bereft of hope in a sin-sodden world because he will come again.

The psalmist declares it: 'Our God comes and will not be silent' (Ps 50:3).

The God who comes in the Bible

I could not only find the concept of God coming in the Bible, but the actual word 'come', when applied to God, litters its pages. The concept and the language are biblical: 'Then the Lord came down in a pillar of cloud; he stood at the entrance to the Tent and summoned Aaron and Miriam' (Num 12:5).

This was the same Lord who 'came down to see the city and the tower that the men were building' (Gen 11:5); who 'came to Abimelech in a dream one night' (Gen 20:3); who 'came to Balaam' and spoke to him (Num 22:20).

Just before Moses died he reflected on God's activities and said: 'The Lord came from Sinai and dawned over them from Seir; he shone forth from Mount Paran. He came with myriads of holy ones from the south, from his mountain slopes' (Deut 33:1–2). Moses was in no doubt that God had come to him and his people.

I discovered how the Old Testament frequently speaks of God's Spirit coming. The Spirit of the Lord came in power upon Gideon (Judg 6:34), Samson (Judg 14:6,19; 15:14), Saul (1 Sam 10:10) and David (1 Sam 16:13). He came with prophecy upon Amasai (1 Chron 12:18), Jahaziel (2 Chron 20:14) and Zechariah (2 Chron 24:20).

Many of the prophets looked to the coming of the Lord for salvation. Isaiah repeatedly says, 'See, the Lord is coming' (Is 26:21; 40:10; 66:15) while Ezekiel almost prays, 'Come, Holy Spirit.' 'Come from the four winds, O breath, and breathe into these slain, that they may live' (Ezek 37:9). God answers his obedient cry, 'I will put my Spirit in you and you will live' (Ezek 37:14). Daniel (7:22), Hosea (6:3), Micah (1:3), Habakkuk (3:3) and Zechariah (14:5) all speak of the coming of God as bringing deliverance and salvation to his people, while Malachi sums up the awesome nature of this moment: 'But who can endure the day of his coming?' (3:2).

The God of the Old Testament, the God whom the people of Israel believed was with them all the time, is the God who comes.

As I read the New Testament the story of God's coming continued even more powerfully. Angel Gabriel said to Mary, 'The Holy Spirit will come upon you' (Lk 1:35). John said, 'The true light that gives light to every man was coming into the world' (Jn 1:9). Jesus taught his disciples to pray, 'Your kingdom come' (Mt 6:10; Lk 11:2) and then said, 'If I drive out demons by the Spirit of God, then the kingdom of God has come upon you' (Mt 12:28).

Not only has the Father come in Jesus, who is empowered by the Holy Spirit, but Jesus promised the Father and Son would come to those who love and obey him: 'Jesus replied, "If anyone loves me, he will obey my teaching. My Father will love him, and we will come to him and make our home with him" ' (Jn 14:23). He also promised the Holy Spirit would come: 'When the Counsellor comes... he will testify about me' (Jn 15:26). 'When he comes, he will convict the world' (Jn 16:8).

The early church experienced this coming of the Holy Spirit: 'When Paul placed his hands on them, the Holy Spirit came on them, and they spoke in tongues' (Acts 19:6). Despite this coming of the Spirit which made Jesus known, they still awaited Jesus' second coming. Paul said, 'Wait till the Lord comes' (1 Cor 4:5); 'Proclaim the Lord's death until he comes' (1 Cor 11:26).

When the Spirit came on John, God spoke: 'I am the Alpha and the Omega, the First and the Last, the Beginning and the End' (Rev 22:13)...'who was, and is, and is to come' (4:8). From beginning to end I found the New Testament reveals to us the God who comes. 'Amen. Come, Lord Jesus' (Rev 22:20).

Our God is one who rolls up his sleeves and comes to us with water and towel to wash our feet and get his hands dirty; he comes to bare his arms, to carry the Roman gibbet and shed his blood for our sakes; he strips himself of all his glory and comes into the world naked, in a stable among dirt and smells, poverty and persecution—even as a little baby. This is our God—the Servant King—the one who comes to meet us where we are and take us to where he is. He becomes what we are—flesh—that we might become what he is—children of God (Jn 1:10–18). He comes on us and in us and through us by his Spirit to make us more like him. He is the God who comes.

The God who comes in history

Every testimony of transformed lives, answered prayer and signs and wonders in the name of Jesus is a testimony to the God who comes in history. As well as the scriptural records the history of the church is littered with stories of people who have been changed by God breaking into their lives. I know three of them personally.

I was invited to consider becoming Vicar at Burney Lane by Bishop Hugh Montefiore. When he was a pupil at Rugby School he maintained the Jewish beliefs of his family until one day Jesus came to him. He was convinced Jesus came and spoke to him in a vision and ever since then he has been a practising Christian.[18]

Earlier this year I was privileged to have Cynthia as a member of my ministry team at a conference in Brighton. To see her clambering over seats and laying hands on other people was a great joy. Only a few years ago Cynthia was confined to a wheelchair and given a year to live, until one night she experienced a vision of Jesus coming into the room and healing her.[19]

In 1989 I met a man who was raised from the dead over forty years ago. Edmund came to preach in our church and stayed overnight in the vicarage. He still has his death certificate which was issued at the time. He told me how he left his body, saw the silver cord being cut (Eccles 12:6), and had the amazing experience of talking with Jesus in heaven. Suddenly the voice of his landlady broke into the peace and joy of heaven. 'Don't let him die. Lord, don't let him die,' she prayed.

Jesus told him he would have to go back, turned him round and gave him a gentle push. Edmund returned to his body some three hours after he died, and needed to minister to the mortician when he came round. His landlady had been praying these words at the time he was restored—not in the mortuary, nor even in the hospital but some distance away at his digs.[20]

I have read about Augustine of Hippo, St Francis of Assisi, George Fox and the first Quakers, but I have met and known Bishop Hugh, Cynthia and Edmund. I believe our God is a God who comes in history.

The Deists in the seventeenth and eighteenth centuries, who in many ways were the forerunners of the modernists and the liberal theologians, believed God made the world and set it in motion, like winding a clock and leaving it alone. They claimed he does not interfere. But the Christian God is not one who remains impartially aloof, but one who comes, who gets involved, who meets us where we are, who came and died for us, who comes and lives in us and with us, and yet is still to come, for there is always more of God.

Whenever we stand together in church and pray, 'Come, Holy Spirit,' we affirm that our God is the God who comes; we lift our faith and wait expectantly for him to come. We invite him and welcome him to come and do whatever he wants to do; he is the Lord, there is no other.

This is the encounter which excites my soul, touches my body and gives life to my spirit. It's not what he does—people in love simply want to be together—it is that he comes. He is the God who comes, who chooses to come and promises to come. Though our language is inadequate, it is still appropriate, for when we pray, 'Come, Holy Spirit,' our experience of God is of one who comes.

Discovering great truths about God always tests my faith in the here and now. It is always much easier to believe in the God who came and will come again, than the God who comes. I returned to Spain in 1989 and this time was asked if I would take the Communion service in church on the Sunday, as the vicar was away.

Many of the English-speaking people in Javea attend the Anglican service on Sundays. The homily is short; the notices announcing coffee mornings, pool-side parties and barbecues are long; the fellowship in the bar outside the church afterwards seems endless.

The service is held in a Roman Catholic village church. Tucked underneath the elephantine mountain of Montgo, the white stone walls and chunky tiled roof present a picturesque postcard view to the visitor on arrival. Every Sunday when the Anglicans borrow it for weekly services the bell swings gently in a recess carved out of the apex of the roof over the doorway, inviting people to come in. Once inside, the wooden-beamed ceiling, sparse furnishings and smell of incense-flavoured mustiness surround the participant with a religious atmosphere of formality. The president of the service is invited to sing the traditional Merbecke setting of the Eucharist. Time is limited. On the occasion when I visited, the monthly Catholic Mass was due to be celebrated immediately afterwards and the building needed to be cleared promptly. Sermons should be no longer than ten minutes.

There was no time to pray, 'Come, Holy Spirit.' They were not ready for it anyway. Not even the God who comes could squeeze in here, except perhaps in the Eucharist.

'No time, Lord; I'm on holiday. I'll upset the apple cart,' I mumbled apologetically.

'I am the God who comes,' he said. 'I want to come.'

Every week on Tuesday mornings a Bible study, partly organised by Gavin and Anne, was held in the crypt of another Roman Catholic church. About five or six came regularly. 'Invite them to that,' God seemed to be saying.

There were ten minutes in which to sell a Bible study to the expatriates. I did what I thought God was telling me to do; one Bible story on healing; two stories of retired people being healed in our church; and an invitation to a time of Bible teaching and prayer for healing in the crypt, which Carol's parents were very happy for me to offer.

It was very simple, but it had one enormous advantage. It scratched where people itched. What retired people want most, whether they own several homes, cars and swimming pools or not, is good health. One other God-given idea also popped out during the sermon: 'Has anyone ever visited the doctor while suffering from pain, and been told, "What do you expect at your age?" I believe it's a curse. God does not say, "Once you are sixty-five you have to suffer." The curse needs to be broken.' And though they were traditional Anglicans, you could almost hear a silent 'Amen' vibrating in the air.

The crypt was packed out. More chairs had to be brought in. Several stood for over an hour at the back. I taught some biblical principles of healing, asked God to come on a few volunteers while everyone else watched, and God's power and love could be seen on some of the faces and bodies. There were tears, shining faces, and some rocking backwards and forwards. We divided up into threes, and all who wanted had a go. Quite dramatically one man's arms started pumping up and down like pistons. There was plenty to see, though there were no instant miracles or healings.

What did happen was that people queued to see me afterwards, wanting to know more about Jesus, to discuss personal problems and to confess private sins. One young person came round for individual ministry at the house and I was asked to visit and pray with a number of seriously ill people. Each time the conversation was about Jesus. Prayer and the laying-on of hands was welcomed. The crypt was packed again the following week when their vicar was present, and God came again in like manner.

Two years later Bill told me his life had been changed as God spoke to him through the brief sermon in the little Spanish church. He said, 'I always thought I was a good, traditional, church-going Christian until then. Your sermon made me realise there was something more.' He sought out Gavin and Anne afterwards about how to ask Jesus into his life, which he then did.

George said he was born again at the second meeting in the crypt. He received Jesus into his life and the experience was like a bucket of water being slowly poured over him, filling him with new life, love and power. He went from there to lay hands on a friend of his who was suffering from cancer but refused to accept there was life after death. Power and heat flowed through George's hands and his friend made a short-term recovery of a remarkable nature. He told George of his new-found faith in Jesus before he died.

God came to the people of Malawi and met them where they were. While I was in Spain I met the family of a famous writer, the son of a former state president and owners and directors of various companies. God came to them also. His love is unconditional. He comes to all who will welcome him; all who will respond to his coming in like manner.

'The Spirit and the bride say, "Come!" And let him who hears say, "Come!" Whoever is thirsty, let him come; and whoever wishes, let him take the free gift of the water of life' (Rev 22:17).

Notes

1. Ray Borlase, *The Trumpet Call to Prayer* (Marshall Morgan & Scott Publications Ltd: Basingstoke, 1986).
2. J. I. Packer, *Keep in Step with the Spirit* (Inter-Varsity Press: Leicester, 1984), p 261.
3. Although through history Christians have prayed to the Spirit, especially in times of revival, and there is adequate evidence of this in many hymns and liturgies, theologically it has become more of a problem with the onset of the charismatic movement, as Christians from every denomination have begun to experience him among them.

   In 1962 Arthur Wainwright wrote, 'The main issues at stake in the doctrine of the Trinity are the unity of God and the deity of Christ. Few of the controversies of the Church have been provoked by disputes about the person of the Spirit.'

Perhaps it is this lack of historical discussion on the Holy Spirit which creates so many problems when churches move towards renewal. It feels as though we are entering unfamiliar territory. See Arthur W. Wainwright, *The Trinity in the New Testament* (SPCK: London, 1962), p 249.

4. James D. G. Dunn, *Jesus and the Spirit* (SCM Press Ltd: London, 1975), pp 18, 350.

5. Acts 20:28; Rom 14:17–18; 15:16,30; 2 Cor 1:21–22; 3:3; Gal 3:11–14; 4:6; Eph 2:18,20–22; 3:14–16; 4:4–6; Phil 3:3; Col 1:6–8; 2 Thess 2:13–14; Tit 3:4–6; 1 Pet 4:14.

6. Michael Ramsey, *Holy Spirit* (SPCK: London, 1977), p 119.

7. Dr H. L. Wilmington comes to this conclusion in his book *Wilmington's Guide to the Bible* (Tyndale House Publishers Inc: Wheaton, Illinois, 1981), p 642.

8. Whenever I visit an unfamiliar church, there is not normally time to justify praying, 'Come, Holy Spirit,' and some people are initially unhappy with it because it is not obviously a 'biblical prayer'. In Africa people are often used to talking about 'good' and 'bad' spirits. In such circumstances I often pray, 'Father God, I ask you through Jesus Christ to send your Holy Spirit upon us.' It is biblical, it is trinitarian and it is unambiguous. I find exactly the same things happen as when I pray, 'Come, Holy Spirit.'

9. The conservative evangelical Colin Brown reminds us of the importance of understanding religious language. He writes, 'Because Christianity involves communication, the philosophy of religion will pay special attention to the structure and function of language and the part it plays in religious experience'

(Colin Brown, *Philosophy and the Christian Faith* [Inter-Varsity Press: London, 1969], p 289).

Those critical of the idea of asking God to come when he is already here need perhaps to be aware of the limitations of language and concepts about God whose 'coming' among us is totally unlike any other person's coming. Any who wish to explore the subject further would probably find C. S. Lewis' chapter on 'Horrid Red Things' (pp 83ff) in his book *Miracles* most enlightening (The Centenary Press: London, 1947). They would also be advised to take note of, at least, the works of Wittgenstein, I. T. Ramsey and Martin Buber, often discussed in general books on the philosophy of religion.

10. Paul Tillich, *The Boundaries of Our Being* (William Collins Sons & Co Ltd: Glasgow, 1973), p 300.

11. *ibid*.

12. I came across this quote of Thomas Aquinas in Francis A. Sullivan's book, *Charisms and Charismatic Renewal* (Gill & Macmillan: London, 1982), pp 70–75.

13. James D. G. Dunn is worth reading on the subject. He says, 'According to Luke and Paul baptism in the Spirit was not...something which happened only once or twice in apostolic days' (James D. G. Dunn, *Baptism in the Holy Spirit* [SCM Press Ltd: London, 1970], p 226).

14. John Wimber says, 'God frequently and sovereignly fills his servants with the Spirit, as he did in Acts 7:55 when Stephen saw Jesus in heaven' (John Wimber with Kevin Springer, *The Dynamics of Spiritual Growth* [Hodder & Stoughton: Sevenoaks, 1990], p 141).

15. Peter de Rosa, *Come Holy Spirit* (William Collins Sons & Co Ltd: Glasgow, 1975), p 120.
    Veni Creator Spiritus: Come, Creator Spirit.

Veni Sancte Spiritus: Come, Holy Spirit.

16. An interesting and reasonably objective account of the Indonesian revival has been provided by Kurt Koch ThD, *The Revival in Indonesia* (Kregel Publications: Grand Rapids, Michigan, 1971).

17. Carlo Carretto, *The God Who Comes* (Darton, Longman & Todd Ltd: London, 1974).

18. An account of Bishop Hugh's conversion to Christianity can be found in the book *Bishop Hugh Montefiore* written by John S. Peart-Binns (Quartet Books Ltd: London, 1990), pp 22ff.

19. Cynthia and I were members of the ministry teams at 'The Battle Belongs to the Lord' conference in the Brighton centre, 10-13 June 1991. A longer account of her healing is recorded in *The Hot Line* by Peter H. Lawrence (Kingsway Publications: Eastbourne, 1990), pp 189–190.

20. Edmund records his own story in *Life after Death*, an experience of death and coping with bereavement (Captain R. E. Wilbourne [Church Army insight paper: New Series No 2, London]).

3

Doing What We See the Father Doing

In the summer of 1990 I was sent to Coventry. As I drove into the city with several ministry team members from our own church I saw the famous three spires. Like stone fingers these church towers have dominated the skyline for centuries, standing through war and peace, pointing heavenwards as symbols of the real source of life. During the 1940/41 air raids Hitler's bombs devastated most of Coventry, but miraculously, and maybe defiantly, the three spires survived. St Michael's Cathedral and the Church of Grey Friars were ruined in the war except for their towers, but Holy Trinity Church was saved by those who shovelled fire bombs from the roof. This mediaeval building was our destination.

Visiting any city centre church inevitably presents a parking problem. Those who used the multi-storey facilities and walked past the department stores on their way to the day conference came across Coventry's most famous historical figure. On the edge of the shopping precinct stands a statue of Lady Godiva clothed in her chastity and seated on a horse. I suspect most shoppers hurrying past are unaware of her connections with Holy Trinity which stands only a few yards away and until 1775 included her in the stained-glass window over the south door. It was founded soon after the year 1043 when Earl Leofric and Lady Godiva endowed the new

Benedictine Priory, and was built by the monks for the lay tenants of the monastic lands.

I stood in front of the picturesque and historic place of worship with my briefcase in hand and paused. It is a frightening prospect being asked to teach and minister in a building so high and lifted up. The dominating spire, the historical atmosphere accentuated by the adjacent timber-framed buildings of Priory Row, and the fifteenth-century-style windows made it more imposing and cathedral-like than the more famous St Michael's next door. Nervously I made my way inside.

My anxiety intensified as I entered the hallowed place. Outside the spire had dwarfed the rest of the building, but now I could see why its architectural style is described as perpendicular. The interior soars upwards towards a heavenly dusty-blue roof ablaze with golden stars. I felt 'humbled, fat and small', especially when standing at the crossing under the tower's painted wood vault.[1] Some 236 feet below the spire's summit was a small stage with microphones and this was my appointed place for the day. I was pleased about that; the pulpit was at least twelve feet above contradiction and I have no head for heights.

As conference delegates were taking their places in the polished pews, the sound of footsteps on stone floors echoed around the walls. Maybe it is good from time to time to worship God in less comfortable and more elevated surroundings, but at this moment I longed for our carpeted lounge, my silent slippers and a cosy armchair tucked away in the corner. I was used to asking God to come in an informal setting without the austere eyes of the past looking down. I couldn't help wondering what the serious stained-glass Matthew, Mark, Luke and John would say.

The more friendly faces of flesh and blood looking at me from the nave were a great help. It was God they had come to worship, hear from and welcome, and it was him they expected to experience. This is always a tremendous comfort. To have only five loaves and two small fish to offer this great God in such a place feels totally inadequate, but when he comes it is always enough.

Those present had come to learn how to minister in the power of the Holy Spirit so, not knowing any of them, I started by teaching from the beginning. I like to teach beginners four things *they* should be doing when ministering to someone else in the power of the Holy Spirit as a prerequisite to seeing what *God* is doing. I find self-awareness and self-discipline are vital in learning to co-operate with God's activity. This is what I taught:

1. Laying-on hands

We lay hands on other people gently.

Linda suffers from multiple sclerosis. When such a disease comes to someone in the prime of life it is not only the physical discomfort, pain and loss of mobility which can cause simple living to become an uphill struggle. The depression and the removal of hope and dignity also require great strength of character to bear with a smile and grateful heart. Linda battled on while Christian friends joined in the warfare through prayer.

On one occasion an enthusiastic prayer group felt God telling them to visit Linda, lay on hands and pray for healing. In due course they arrived, while Linda did her best to receive them with faith and encouragement. They all laid on hands and said their best prayers with boldness and confidence, but as time wore on it became obvious to Linda that not much was happening. As frustration began to set in and enthusiasm began to depart, the team tried harder. They prayed harder, encouraged harder and, probably without realising, pushed harder. After an hour

they and Linda were exhausted and the session was grate-
fully concluded on both sides. Before the group had
arrived Linda was feeling quite well within herself, but
after they had gone her neck was in so much pain she had
to wear a surgical collar.

It's very easy to mistake enthusiasm for faith and allow
our own desires and frustrations to take over when seeking to help other people. When we are beginning to pray
for healing in the power of the Holy spirit we learn how
to lay on hands—gently. If the hands are laid on the head
I believe the pressure should be just enough to rest on the
hair and not on the head. Comfort will be communicated
through this and sufficient contact will be made for God's
power to flow from one to another.

Keeping our hands outstretched in one position can,
however, as Moses found out, become quite uncomfortable after a while (Ex 17:12). The person receiving ministry may be healed, while the one praying goes home with
a painful arm. Sometimes heat flows powerfully through
the one hand which is making contact and a person feels
unwilling to move the hand for fear of a power loss. It is
our experience that if the right hand is replaced with the
left, the power or heat flows again through the left just
the same. If the person standing is taller, it may be
necessary to lay a hand on his shoulder or even stand on a
stool, but as it is frequently helpful to maintain contact
and stay with a person for some time, experimentation in
this area is important.[2]

With physical healing we have found it helpful to lay
hands whenever possible on the sick part—usually
women with women and men with men. Even then, if
private parts are involved, dignity is best maintained by
asking the people receiving prayer to lay their own hands
over the affected area, laying ours on top of theirs.

Some people find that whenever they ask God to come
their own hands begin to shake. One Sunday an Anglican

vicar in Birmingham invited us to take his morning service. After I had preached the congregation stood and I prayed, 'Come, Holy Spirit.' Within a very short time six people went over in the power of the Holy Spirit and one or two began shaking.

As the ministry progressed one lady found her right hand flapping up and down as though she were bouncing a ball a thousand times a minute. Another lady said she was suffering from a headache. I remembered hearing how power in the hands could sometimes be a sign of God's anointing, equipping a person to minister to someone else. So I took the lady's flapping hand and placed it upon the other lady's headache. I assumed that as I did so her hand would stop bouncing, and God's power would flow from one to the other.

I was wrong. Before I could intervene the headache-lady received a pounding on her crown from a hammering hand. But surprisingly when I stopped the action and asked her how she was feeling, preparing myself to apologise profusely, she replied, 'Much more peaceful. The pain's virtually gone.' I am still convinced I made a mistake, but in his mercy God used it for his purposes.

A shaking hand is fine as a sign or when receiving prayer, but if I am standing, eyes closed, receiving the Holy Spirit, and someone approaches me to place a hand whirring like a helicopter blade on or near my head, I do not normally find it very helpful. I suspect that shaking hands when praying for someone else is often a sign of a problem rather than an anointing. If it cannot be helped I always allow the person to participate, but with caution as I do not feel such hands should come too near people's faces when ministry is taking place. A demonstrative style will nearly always detract from what God is doing and focus attention on the person ministering, which is not helpful.

We lay on hands gently and as unobtrusively as possible.

2. We keep our eyes open

During one of our teaching days at Christ Church words from God were given, people claimed them and those nearby were encouraged to minister. A vicar and his curate took one lady into another area, stood her up and prayed for God to heal her. The curate kept his eyes open and noticed the lady fall over in the Spirit. He caught her, lowered her gently to the ground and adjusted his own position accordingly. The vicar, however, carried on praying, hands held out, eyes firmly closed, totally unaware of the new situation until the curate kindly informed him and suggested a lower profile. When someone falls over under the power of the Holy Spirit we encourage those who are helping to catch them, lay them down gently and decently, and then continue the ministry at ground level.

It's difficult to see what the Father is doing when our eyes are closed, but many mature Christians are ill at ease praying with their eyes open. During training sessions I often go round poking my finger gently into closed eyes—sometimes the same ones several times. The best way of learning to pray with our eyes open is to practise praying while driving the car. It normally solves the problem one way or the other.

We lay on hands gently and unobtrusively and keep our eyes open.

3. We shut up

Many evangelicals, when praying for someone to be healed, pray something like this: 'O Lord, we do just lift up Sister Ellen's left leg to you, just as we lifted up her right leg to you last week. We do just thank you, Lord, that Ellen has been arranging the flowers in our church so beautifully for thirty-five years and has never missed a jumble sale. And, Lord, we do thank you that as I preached last week with a good introduction, three clear points and a conclusion, you always listen to us and do whatever we tell you. And so, Lord, before this congregation and before the host of heaven and before the football scores come on television, I ask you to come in power and might and heal this leg. Amen.'

Whenever I say things like this people often laugh, but I've heard it again and again. I heard one person begin praying for someone else with the laying-on of hands who became very emotional in the middle and ended up praying for himself. My true-to-life prayer parody is probably not praying at all. The length indicates a nervous lack of faith and the content is more akin to preaching than praying, mixed with a desire to tell Ellen the nice things I should have said to her face long ago but never quite did.

Jesus said, 'And when you pray, do not keep on babbling like pagans, for they think they will be heard because of their many words. Do not be like them, for your Father knows what you need before you ask him' (Mt 6:7–8).

I would have thought that if someone was going to pray for a four-day-old corpse to be raised from the dead it would need a special prayer—at least one written by the liturgical commission; subjected to three revisions; authorised by the General Synod; and in constant use for five years. 'Lazarus, come out!' (Jn 11:43) hardly seems to do justice to the occasion. It is worth taking a good hard look at the few words Jesus normally used when ministering in the power of the Holy Spirit.

At Acts '86 my mother-in-law was privileged to watch someone pray for a leg to be lengthened.[3] It was quite a colourful scene as the short leg belonged to a nun in a black habit while the young man leading the ministry was resplendent in bright yellow shirt, purple braces and emerald green trousers. He prayed, 'Come, Holy Spirit,' and was then silent. Before quite a crowd the leg was seen to grow to its appropriate length. Then someone said the leg looked twisted and this was confirmed by the patient. A hand was consequently put on the knee accompanied by the words, 'In the name of Jesus, leg be straightened!' Again they all saw it, and heard it click into place. The nun stood and walked about on two perfectly straight, matching legs. 'Yes, that'll do,' she said. 'That'll do nicely.' Watching someone with experience and faith praying for healing never requires a notebook. So little is said, there is nothing to write down except any previous prayer habits which may have to be unlearned.

The ability to pray, 'Come, Holy Spirit,' and then shut up is one of the hardest things asked of Christians and church people. It does not come easily or naturally. We so often bring our own baggage and garbage with us into ministry situations. Sadly there are some Christians who dearly love the Lord who simply cannot shut up. I like to encourage them towards intercession and prayer meetings and away from laying hands on others, at least for the time being.

We lay on hands gently and unobtrusively, keep our eyes open, pray, 'Come, Holy Spirit,' and then shut up.

4. We let God do it

Sometimes when God's Spirit comes on a person tears come to the surface and need to be expressed. In such circumstances it is natural for some to stroke or hug the person, but often this will intrude on what the Spirit is doing. Someone who has not received much love may welcome this human affection, but it will invariably move the spotlight from what the Lord is doing to what the person is doing. It may also have the effect of suppressing what the Holy Spirit is wanting to help the person express. It is difficult in this area to make rules, but anyone who needs to hug and stroke the person receiving prayer whenever tears or sadness are apparent may also be blocking with his or her own agenda what the Spirit is doing.[4]

There are times when an experienced counsellor may discern the need for physical contact; an adult who was not bonded to his mother soon after birth may scream very loudly when the Spirit comes and need to be embraced; someone who was abused physically as a child may at an appropriate moment benefit from being encouraged to allow the loving touch of others; and a few years ago during a time of prayer I burst into tears and was so grateful for the Vineyard pastor who gave me a firm, secure hug.[5] The experienced or spiritually discerning person will often know when to hug and when to leave alone, but I normally encourage beginners to learn the discipline of not stroking until extreme emotions are being expressed—there is quite a significant difference between a few tears and someone sobbing his heart out. What is important at the start is not allowing would-be ministers to paw or hug people in order to deal with their own needs or embarrassment.

I believe most beginners can follow these four simple rules:

1. We lay on hands gently.
2. We keep our eyes open.
3. We pray, 'Come, Holy Spirit,' and then shut up.
4. We avoid hugging and stroking initially.

The majority of Christians can manage it and be trained to do it. The basic truth being taught is: 'Don't get in God's way.' We cannot heal anybody, save them, cast out demons in our own strength, or put lives right;

this is the work of God. I see our role primarily as that of a midwife. We are there to encourage somebody else to give birth to new life; we cannot do it for them. Our aim is to help someone to receive God and let him do what he wants to do. When it comes to looking for those capable of praying for others in the power of the Holy Spirit I am always seeking to identify those with a sensitive spirit capable of letting God be God. Those who get in God's way and block what he is doing may need to be excluded from laying hands on others until sufficiently souled and healed.

The day at Coventry had been advertised as a workshop so it was now time to give everyone an opportunity to put this simple teaching into practice. Each building has its limitations, but fixed pews present one of the hardest problems. We quickly numbered the rows; I encouraged everyone to stand, and then suggested that those in the odd-numbered rows turned around. This brought face-to-face contact in most cases.

'Even-numbered rows close your eyes,' I announced. 'Heads up, hands held out and relax. Odd-numbered rows keep your eyes open, lay a hand gently on the shoulder or forehead in front of you, pray, "Come, Holy Spirit," and then shut up.'

I am sure there are more gracious ways of saying it, but having been a schoolteacher this is how it came out— with a smile, of course. It seemed to work. There were visible signs of beaming, eyelids fluttering, shaking, falling and tears. Over coffee I encouraged people to share with their partners what was happening and what was helpful, and many came back with testimonies of God's love and the experience of power. After the break everyone changed over and the process was repeated with similar results.

Despite all the amusing stories about vicars with their eyes shut, and practising while driving the car, I still found three people praying with their eyes closed. I also felt it necessary to put a finger to my lips and say 'shh!' to one or two who had a tendency to fill the silence with a little too much verbiage. Generally, however, it was lovely to see what the Lord was doing and to hear stories being shared over lunch.

People often ask if there are dangers in every-member-ministry, and of course there are. Satanists may try to register for such a workshop and come aiming to put curses on unprotected people. People like Simon Magus (Acts 8:9–24) who want power for power's sake may turn up at every course possible. Insensitive and unloving people with little self-awareness but a desperate desire to be needed may cause others harm rather than give help.

I think therefore it is right at such workshops to ask for the minister's signature of consent to be on an application form. I also normally have trained members with me who wander around during ministry times to supervise and advise whenever necessary. Several of our team members came with me to Coventry, but this is also why I believe all meetings should be covered with as much prayer and intercession as possible, and always include times of worship.[6] Having said all this, we don't stop driving cars because we see an accident—we learn to drive them better.

' "Teacher," said John, "we saw a man driving out demons in your name and we told him to stop, because he was not one of us." "Do not stop him," Jesus said' (Mk 9:38–39).

At lunch time I stayed inside to eat my sandwiches beside the 1215 North Porch which had probably been the Prior's entrance into the Parish Church, and then took the opportunity of wandering around. I visited the High Altar, situated beneath the East Window depicting Jesus on the cross, fronted by beautiful carvings of his birth, death and resurrection. The approach to the altar was a little curious. Painted on the sides were Michael, Gabriel, Raphael, Uriel and George. The first four I could understand. Michael and Gabriel are biblical, Raphael comes in the deuterocanonical Tobit, Uriel in 2 Esdras, and all four angels are mentioned in the pseudepigraphical book of Enoch. Maybe this was a reminder that Holy Trinity began life as a Roman Catholic church, which gives canonical status to some books of the Apocrypha. But who was George? I made my way to the other end of the building.

While I had been teaching from under the spire with the High Altar and East Window behind me I had been looking at the great West Window. I now went to have a closer look at it. Christ was the central and dominant figure seated in majesty on a rainbow with his feet resting on the world. Shafts of light came from him in all directions. Around him were groups of 'famous Christians': saints, scholars and leaders of monastic movements. I had no idea so many had been watching me. Angels and Gospel writers behind me, the famous Christians of history in front of me, and George.

After lunch I tried to take people further on. One or two problems had arisen which now needed to be addressed. Once we have learned how to help people co-operate with God's activity we can turn our attention to seeing what he is doing.

Blessing or distress?

When the Holy Spirit comes on a person it is normally easy to spot natural phenomena occurring. The face may shine, the hands tremble or shake, the breathing pattern alters, the person begins to sway, and so on. Once we have learned to observe such signs and permission has been given to minister, we then ask ourselves, 'Am I seeing blessing or distress?' The face is the key area to watch; a sense of peace, a beam or a smile is usually a sign of blessing, whereas a frown, tension or more obvious displays of discomfort indicate distress. In our experience blessings came first and more abundantly until we had learned a little more about coping with problems.

1. Blessing

Bill, an experienced clergyman, attended one of our training sessions, though I was the only one who knew his identity. As I asked the Holy Spirit to come upon us his face began to beam and warm up considerably. Very shy, very inexperienced teenage Donna approached him cautiously and very gently laid a hand upon his head. After the break I asked for any comments and Bill spoke up: 'I was ministered to perfectly by Donna,' he said, 'She laid a hand gently on my head, stayed with me right to the end and did not say a word.'

Most people find when God is blessing them that a helpful, sensitive hand on the head or shoulder is a comfort and a help. Sometimes merely to know someone is there, just in case, helps us to relax more and receive more; sometimes the hand adds a little more spiritual power; sometimes it is good to have someone with whom we can talk things through when God is finished. It can, however, be very boring and tiring for the one ministering, so sacrificial love and determination are as necessary in would-be team members as sensitivity. Occasionally a person prefers to be left alone and we need to be aware of this, but most people find it helpful to have unobtrusive and sensitive support when God is blessing them.

What is not helpful is a heavy hand, a loud voice or a powerful personality interrupting what God is doing. Although we do need to be confident in God and full of faith, the shy Christian is sometimes of more value than the extrovert when God is blessing someone. Here are some suggested ways of proceeding:

(a) We sensitively lay our hands on the person whom God is blessing, hopefully discerning whether this is welcome.

(b) We keep our eyes open at all times and watch what God is doing.

(c) Occasional words of encouragement are often helpful, for instance: 'Thank you, Jesus', 'Bless you, Lord', 'Jesus loves you', and so on.

(d) Prophecies and dramatic words are not normally required for people whom God is already blessing. Our main role here is simply to bless what the Father is doing. If a word does come it may be better to give it later rather than sooner.

(e) We may need to help the person to go on receiving if interruptions occur. Keeping my eyes open and mind alert has occasionally helped me to stop someone else falling into us. If someone nearby starts shrieking, I normally say: 'It's all right; someone's with them. Keep letting God come on you.'

(f) After a while it may be helpful to encourage the person to go on receiving but to share what God is doing. It is normally quite acceptable to ask what is happening providing we do not interrupt or bring God's blessing to an abrupt end. I once thought God was blessing someone who had in fact fallen asleep, and I blessed what the Father was not doing for about an hour.

(g) We talk afterwards and follow up as necessary. Some know what God has been doing and some don't. Now may be a good time to share anything we received earlier or just to give reassurance—people do not always know immediately what God has been doing. Frequently people doubt their experience or begin to feel silly. 'I saw God on you, just like I have on others before,' can be very comforting.

2. Distress

During a time of ministry in our church a lady began to show signs of great distress and discomfort. Pain, tension and fear registered on her face. An inexperienced male stood at a safe distance saying things like, 'Bless you, Father. Thank you for what you're doing. Keep doing it, Lord.' Eventually the lady could cope with it no longer. She stopped everything, thanked the person for trying, and walked out to the car with mixed emotions of fear, panic and anger. She was not at all keen to return for any more such sessions at Christ Church. Fortunately a more experienced person saw what was happening and intercepted the lady in the car park.

It transpired that the lady had been sexually abused as a child. Being very open to God that night, she was able to let the Holy Spirit come on the suppressed emotions and demons connected with her earlier trauma and bring them to the surface. When Jesus comes, 'He will bring to light what is hidden in darkness' (1 Cor 4:5). This meant the lady began to feel again for the first time in years all the pain and hurt of being raped, while a man was saying calmly at a distance, 'Bless you, Lord, for what you're doing.' It's small wonder she could stand it for only so long.

This is why I consider it to be vital for everyone who takes part to learn quickly the difference between blessing and distress. In simple terms we let blessing continue uninterrupted, but we do not leave distress unchecked for too long. We bless God for his blessing; we ask the Holy Spirit to reveal the source of distress. If the ministry team is not large enough to cope with all God is doing then we try to ensure every case of visible distress receives attention first. If there are not enough experienced people available to cope, then it may be better to encourage individuals who are in difficulties to stop what is happening until an experienced person is available or an appointment can be made.

This is how I might approach someone who is showing signs of distress:

(a) 'Tom, do you know what is happening?'
    'No idea, I just feel awful.'
    'Holy Spirit, help us to see what the problem is.'

Then if Tom does not see or understand the problem and no one receives a word from God which Tom confirms as likely to be right, we stop and talk. It becomes a *counselling* situation.

(b) 'Tom, do you know what is happening?'
    'Yes, I can see myself trapped against a wall. A man—I think it's my father—is beating me.'
    'Can you see Jesus?'
    'No, just my father beating me.'
    'Holy Spirit, help Tom to see Jesus.'

If Tom then sees Jesus coming and resolving the situation, we stay with what is happening until distress gives way to peace and blessing. This continues to be a *ministry* situation. If he does not, we stop and talk about it.

It's important when praying in such circumstances that we do not quickly say, 'Tom, picture Jesus doing this or that.' If the ministry becomes stuck as in (a) and we think God is giving us a picture to share, we do so, but if it seems appropriate to wait and see, then we continue to make room for what the Spirit is doing in the person: 'Tom, let Jesus come and do what he wants to do. Father God, send more of your Spirit, that Tom might see Jesus,' and so on. The work of the Holy Spirit is often to point to Jesus (Jn 14,15) and our role as midwife is to help Tom receive whatever the Holy Spirit is doing.

As with the problem of knowing when to hug, it is not easy knowing when to share our ideas or those we feel

God may have given to us. Even correct words from God may be better given later than sooner. If in doubt I know I need to keep telling myself to wait and be patient.

I remember on one occasion a lady was weeping and her friend called me over to help in the ministry. She explained to me, 'Her brother has just died.' Immediately she laid a hand on the lady's head and said, 'Picture Charlie going to Jesus and let him go. You must let him go.'

I stopped her gently with: 'Don't tell her what to do. Holy Spirit, come and help her to see what you want her to see.' This time she simply saw the coffin as at the funeral, where she had been unable to cry, and for some while she cried and cried. We thought it was time to let Charlie go and to rejoice at his salvation, but God knew it was a time to weep. Praying in the power of the Spirit is not feeding in our own good ideas or counselling: it is helping a person to receive more of God and whatever he wants to do.

(c) 'Tom, do you know what is happening?'
'No, I feel awful. Everything is very dark. I need help.'
'Holy Spirit, increase your power on Tom and come on the root of the problem.'

Then if Tom hisses, shouts, screams, blasphemes or slithers on the floor like a snake it may be right to command a demon to leave in the name of Jesus, either in church or preferably in a private room. This becomes a *deliverance* situation.

Whenever possible I like to obtain the person's permission before addressing what I believe to be a demon. If I believe an evil spirit is manifesting in a person I normally command it to tell me its name and then to leave in the name of Jesus. People are usually aware themselves when something has left. I continue to ask

God to come, repeating the process if another one sur-
faces, or speaking words of God's peace if blessing
appears. Such ministry will always need to be carefully
followed up with sound biblical teaching, further help
when necessary, and fellowship.

If nothing leaves in a short space of time it is normally
better to stop what is happening, make sure we are talking to Tom and not to demons, and begin looking at the
root causes, rather than go on struggling indefinitely.
Depending on the time available, an appointment may
need to be made.

It is very common for a person to start by showing
signs of blessing, which then turn into symptoms of
distress. Often God assures people of his love and power
before gently taking them to the root of a problem, like a
loving father approaching a child with a splinter in his
finger. This is why we need to keep our eyes open,
concentrate and stay with a person throughout the
experience if possible.

Physical healing

Anyone who has never seen the visible signs which
sometimes accompany physical healing can easily be
deceived. I have seen God healing a cripple whose body
shook and gyrated from head to foot for a considerable
time. I have seen a man's arms pumping up and down
like violent pistons as his defective hearing was healed. I
have seen a person shake all over for half an hour while
being healed of infertility. I have seen trapped nerves
released and healed as the legs kicked about and twitched
in spasm-like movements. In each case I was extremely
concerned and wondered if I should interfere, but I was
pleased eventually that I simply blessed what the Father
was doing.

The key in all these cases was the face. Despite the

extreme physical movements, the facial features appeared each time to remain neutral. The body was shaking, but the face was not exhibiting pain, anxiety or distress, and on some of the occasions I was able to question the person concerned while the healing was taking place. If in doubt we can always ask the person what is happening. Physical healing is normally felt physically in the body whereas emotional hurts and demons tend to cause stress in the mind. People usually know themselves if we feel able to ask them.

With a modicum of common sense and our eyes open, it is quite possible to see naturally what the Father is doing supernaturally and then work alongside him.

In the afternoon I stood beneath the crumbling spire among the angels and archangels, the glorious company of the apostles, the goodly fellowship of the prophets, the noble army of martyrs, and George. I prayed, 'Father God, I ask you through Jesus to send your Holy Spirit upon us. Come, Holy Spirit.' In a strange kind of way whenever I looked at the Venerable Bede, Archbishop Cranmer or Ignatius Loyola I felt uncomfortable—but whenever I looked at the face of Christ on the West Window in front of me all seemed to be well. God graciously enabled us to experience some examples of blessing, relieved distress, deliverance and physical healing during the final session.

One lady who came to the training day was in charge of another church while they were awaiting the appointment of a new minister. Blessing appeared all over her face as we welcomed the Holy Spirit, and shortly after team members laid hands on her she appeared to go out like a light. Graham Turner caught her, lowered her to the floor and then remained with her for some time as God continued to bless her.

When the lady eventually came round she shared a

vision of how Jesus had come to her and called and anointed her for the task of evangelism. This was thrilling to experience and hear. God was invited to come, God came and God did it. What a privilege it is simply to be present when God comes to call and bless his children.

Bill, a member of our ministry team, did not intend to be with us at Holy Trinity on that Saturday, having other ideas and plans. But in the middle of Friday night he awoke, prayed and sensed God telling him to come. During one session he encountered a lady exhibiting signs of deep distress and, being in some ways prepared and warned the night before, he approached her sensitively. He stopped and talked with her for a while, making sure a lady from the team was in attendance, and found himself doing very little other than listening. There were long-standing worries and relationship problems.

After a while Bill prayed, 'Come, Holy Spirit,' over her once more, and waited. Great power in the form of heat came on all three and the lady sobbed and sobbed. When the tears ended, distress gave way to peace and the lady confessed to feeling much better and greatly loved by God.

Sister Christine observed an elderly couple who were welcoming the Holy Spirit, but the lady appeared to be in some difficulty. When Christine approached her cautiously the lady asked if they might go over to the side to share some problems. Apparently her husband had suffered recently from a stroke and since then she'd lost the joy she received when first experiencing the power of the Holy Spirit.

Christine listened and then prayed with her about the husband's illness, requesting healing for him and patience and wisdom for her. After this Christine prayed, 'Come, Holy Spirit.' The Spirit came on her powerfully but gently, and after a while she opened her eyes and thanked Christine, who moved on to someone else.

Six months later a lady approached Christine at Christ Church during a follow-up day for a conference in Brighton. 'Hello, do you remember me?' she asked brightly, looking absolutely radiant.

'No,' Christine admitted, 'I don't.'

'I was the one you prayed with at Coventry, and since that day I haven't looked back. The joy of the Lord has been with me constantly.'

We don't often hear later what the Lord has been doing in people's lives, but it is sometimes thrilling when we do, especially when we can see it confirmed on the face.

Jane, a regular member of our ministry team, was drawn to another lady who was crying and as she laid gentle hands upon her the lady bent forward as if under a great weight. The Holy Spirit seemed to be highlighting an emotional problem with a physical and clearly visible demonstration somewhat reminiscent of occasional Old Testament prophetic activity. Jane did not deem it necessary this time to stop and counsel as she felt the Holy Spirit was almost acting out in front of her the problem and what needed to be done.

Jane said, 'In the name of Jesus I take this yoke from off your back.' Slowly, the lady straightened up and shared how it felt as if her burden had now gone completely.

Margaret was called over to help with a lady who was sprawled across a pew and in great distress. Her breath was only coming in weak gasps and occasionally she spoke through the gasps in a small voice which did not seem to be her own.

In the name of Jesus, Margaret challenged the demon which claimed to be a family spirit. It left quickly, though not too quietly, once it had been exposed. After a few minutes of relaxation another demon manifested and this time the lady herself had a name running through her mind accompanied by a feeling of intense sorrow. The name was a family name which someone in each generation was given. When commanded to leave in the name of Jesus it also went quite quickly.

The lady recovered in a very short time as the Holy Spirit blessed and restored her. In conversation afterwards she marvelled at how God had answered so many questions through his expulsion of the two family spirits. All of her life she had been puzzled about strange urges to run, and gasping dreams, all of which she now understood. She definitely felt the evil spirits had gone.

A church warden who was suffering from knee problems was present for the day. As Mandy and Jane prayed for him the Spirit of God could be seen and felt. After praying for the knee they also sensed it was right to command the hip and ankle to return to their correct position in the name of Jesus. He waggled all the affected parts a little. They did it again and after a while he began to walk more freely. He claimed at the time to be feeling better. Four months later he bumped into Jane and testified to having no more problems.

None of our team members would profess to be anything other than very ordinary Christians, with very ordinary jobs, worshipping in a very ordinary urban priority area—but serving a very extraordinary God. When God comes the initiative, the power and the praise all belong to him.

Not everything we did at Coventry was as effective as we would have liked it to be. Learning to cope with apparent failure is an important part of learning to minister in the power of the Holy Spirit. After the meeting in Holy Trinity Church we took our best and most experienced team members to try and help a lady who was bound by evil spirits. We had three experienced vicars, a nurse and several team members used to casting demons out of all kinds of people.

We prayed, worshipped, claimed protection by the blood of Jesus and then confronted. Everyone was spat upon and Graham Turner's face was badly scratched, but no amount of praying, singing, commanding or anything else we had seen work with others was of any use. As is so often the case, the manifesting symptom which was causing so much pain and distress was a demon, but the problem was something else. This was a deep inter-cessory and counselling situation which we could not solve in an afternoon.

We left, offering plenty of advice but with heavy hearts, despite all God had done earlier in the day.

I still become very nervous whenever I am invited to speak and minister in other churches. Even at those with a less imposing structure than Holy Trinity. The day of the meeting drags by very slowly as I sweat profusely in prayer or try desperately to direct my attention to other matters. Like every other Christian activity which causes apprehension, once it begins the nerves give way to con-centration and, at times, the peace and power found in the presence of the Holy Spirit. Then there are two frequent happenings which always make the nervous preparation time worthwhile.

The first is the special moment towards the end of a session when I look out on the body of Christ and see them all engaged in twos and threes in God's work. There are occasions when it seems everyone is either receiving prayer or praying for someone else. Christians lovingly laying-on hands, listening, caring, weeping, ministering to one another—so much more helpful and real than the formal services I used to attend where all we did was look at the back of someone's head for an hour and then go home, sometimes without even speaking.

The second concerns the comments which come my

way afterwards. In the days when I used to preach without having a ministry time I received very few comments and passed my time in rest and quietness. Those which were uttered belonged mostly to the category of 'Good sermon, Vicar.' Complete silence was taken to mean the opposite. Very rarely did I hear people speaking about God irrespective of the subject matter I chose, but these days opinions are not slow in coming forward. If the ministry goes 'badly' or people do not like it I receive all the blame; if it goes 'well' and people respond positively God is given all the glory. I'm happy with that. It's always thrilling to hear people sharing afterwards what God has done for them.

Notes

1. I think it was Spike Milligan whom I first heard use this phrase.
2. Occasionally people object to us advocating such frequent laying on of hands during ministry times, quoting 1 Timothy 5:22. 'Do not be hasty in the laying on of hands.' The commentators on this verse maintain the context refers either to ordination or the reconciliation of a penitent offender. I have not yet found a biblical scholar who thinks the context of 1 Timothy 5:22 suggests a reference to ministry.
3. Acts '86 was a European Christian conference held at the National Exhibition Centre, Birmingham in the summer of 1986.
4. Mary Pytches, in her book *A Healing Fellowship* (Hodder & Stoughton: London, 1988), has a helpful chapter entitled 'To touch or not to touch' which deals more fully with this subject.
5. It was in fact Martyn Smith, pastor of the Manchester Vineyard.
6. I have not said very much in this book about prayer

meetings and private intercessions because I assume most churches encourage this. At present this is what we do:

(a) Hold a weekly prayer meeting on Friday evenings.

(b) Ministry team members pray with the leaders before every Sunday service.

(c) We have a prayer chain listing people on the phone who will, when contacted, pray for any need.

(d) Morning Prayer and extemporary prayer is said every Tuesday morning.

(e) Holy Communion is celebrated with intercessions on Thursday mornings.

(f) The Anglican Community of St John the Divine hold daily offices and prayers in our parish.

(g) Prayer needs are published in our weekly notices.

(h) From time to time we walk around our parish on a Friday night and pray on the streets.

(i) The local ministers meet once a month and pray for each other.

(j) We have bi-monthly prayer meetings with all the local Christian churches and organisations, when we pray for one another and the area.

We do believe in prayer and try to give it a high priority.

4

Ministering in Response to Request

The attractive blue-tinted glass of the Johannesburg Sun Hotel makes the sky-scraper recognisable from almost anywhere in the city; a great help to a visitor with a poor sense of direction. In 1988 this was my home for a week. Team members from America and England came to help with a signs and wonders conference, and I was privileged to be one of them.[1]

My friend William Mather and I were given a room on the thirty-seventh floor, from where we could take in the panoramic view of the golden city. Like any big metropolis there were high-rise buildings, green parks and sports fields, and the inevitable post office tower with its communication dishes. But in the distance, dotted around the perimeter, were unsightly earthen mounds which looked like overgrown mole hills or mini-volcanoes.

'What on earth...?' I began, but William interrupted. 'Dere's gold in dem der hills,' he explained. Of course. Unlike most other large cities of the world, Jo'burg is not built in a valley beside a river but 5,760 feet up on the Ridge of White Waters, the world's richest known source of gold. These hills were mine dumps left over from previous excavations and not removed lest further intensified sifting should produce more nuggets.

Our conference was not due to start for a couple of

days so we wandered slowly through the nearby park enjoying its display of autumnal glory. It seemed strange in the month of April to be gazing at trees in the early stages of shedding their brilliant red leaves.

Beyond the park in the middle of the open market by the station my artistic companion William took out his sketch book and water colours and began painting the vivid scene. A large crowd gathered and we all began chatting with much fun and hilarity, especially when one man swapped an apple for a pencil-portrait of himself. Despite being the only white people around we felt welcomed and affirmed. One young man asked me how many languages I spoke. I had failed French at school so I said, 'One.' He spoke eight, fluently, and he and his friends couldn't help smiling at their intellectual superiority.

I said to him, 'There are many Christians in the West praying for you to gain your freedom.' He was visibly shaken; the surface humour vanished instantly. He asked me to repeat it while he sought to regain his self-composure. He had no idea that Christians of all colours cared about him and his people's plight.

All too soon our two days of sight-seeing came to an end and after a hearty breakfast on the third morning we left for the exhibition centre praying that God would enable us to cope with whatever and whomever he sent to us. Jesus always met requests for help with time, counselling and frequently ministry, and we were there to attempt the same. Learning to meet people's specific requests is very different from simply wandering around in general sessions blessing what the Father is doing. In our experience team members are most often required to: lead someone to Christ, encourage others to deal with sin, pray for healing of various kinds, and help people receive God's good gifts.

Becoming a Christian

After the Holy spirit was seen and heard to come in power on the Day of Pentecost, Peter stood up and preached about Jesus. 'When the people heard this, they were cut to the heart and said to Peter and the other apostles, "Brothers, what shall we do?" ' (Acts 2:37). Peter then outlined the way of salvation: 'Repent and be baptised, every one of you, in the name of Jesus Christ so that your sins may be forgiven. And you will receive the gift of the Holy Spirit' (Acts 2:38). As a result, 3,000 were added to their number. This was followed by the healing of one crippled man, after which the number rose to 5,000 (Acts 4:4). On each of the occasions when Peter spoke he related the signs to the word of God and shared the good news about Jesus Christ. Peter knew the importance of being able to do this at all times. In his first epistle he wrote: 'Always be prepared to give an answer to everyone who asks you to give the reason for the hope that you have. But do this with gentleness and respect' (1 Pet 3:15–16).

In churches where the Holy Spirit is frequently invoked it is easy to lose sight of the importance of salvation and the need for being prepared at all times to share the gospel. And yet as Acts 2, 3 and 4 demonstrate, when the Spirit comes in power the opportunities for introducing people to Jesus are often far greater than at other times.

After a few sessions when different speakers asked God to come, the mixed South African congregation began to see, hear and experience phenomena which were unfamiliar to some of them. A lady with a large, visible goitre passed close to us on her way forward to claim a word for healing. She returned to her seat ecstatic, leaping about and pointing to the evidence of her neck. The goitre had completely gone.

In such an atmosphere a female member of our team

and I began a conversation with a local lady who, by her own confession, was not yet a Christian. Friends had begun taking her to church and had brought her to the meeting, but it was soon obvious to us that she equated being a Christian with being good rather than being saved. I tackled this problem head-on.

According to Jesus in the Gospels, and to Paul in Romans, either being good or being saved will lead to eternal life:

(a) Receiving eternal life by being good

'Now a man came up to Jesus and asked, "Teacher, what good thing must I do to get eternal life?"...Jesus replied "...If you want to enter life, obey the commandments" ' (Mt 19:16–17).

Paul says, 'To those who by persistence in doing good seek glory, honour and immortality, he will give eternal life...it is those who obey the law who will be declared righteous' (Rom 2:7,13).

(b) Receiving eternal life by believing and trusting in Jesus

Alternatively, we can believe and trust in Jesus.

Jesus said, 'Just as Moses lifted up the snake in the desert, so the Son of Man must be lifted up, that everyone who believes in him may have eternal life' (Jn 3:14–15).

Paul says, 'But now a righteousness from God, apart from law, has been made known...This righteousness from God comes through faith in Jesus Christ...to bring eternal life' (Rom 3:21–22; 5:21).

The choice is simple. We can trust in ourselves or in Jesus: in our good works or his; what we have done, are doing and will do or what Jesus has already done for us on the cross. If we can keep God's laws and live a perfect life in God's sight then we shall be granted eternal life.

On the other hand if we believe and trust in Jesus and accept the sacrifice he gave for us we receive eternal life now (Jn 6:54).

'Whoever believes in the Son has eternal life' (Jn 3:36).

'But now that you have been set free from sin... the result is eternal life. For the wages of sin is death, but the gift of God is eternal life in Christ Jesus our Lord' (Rom 6:22–23).

Jesus said to a rich young man enquiring about eternal life, 'No-one is good—except God alone' (Mk 10:18). He told the parable of the Good Samaritan to the expert in the law who thought he could 'inherit eternal life' by being good, thereby demonstrating to him his own failure (Lk 10:25–37). Paul was equally dogmatic: 'There is no-one righteous, not even one... all have sinned and fall short of the glory of God' (Rom 3:10,23).

For the person who believes he can ascend to heaven by being good this teaching is vital. 'Good' in God's sight equals perfection and if we trust in ourselves one small sin disqualifies us from entering his presence. Jesus and Paul teach us about our failure to be good in God's sight in order to demonstrate the need of being saved. Once people can see the folly of striving in their own strength to gain eternal life, salvation is but a prayer away.[2]

The unconverted lady followed our arguments and seemed to grasp the theory fairly well. Most people seeking eternal life, when given the choice of trusting in self or Jesus, can see the sense in trusting Jesus. It does not, however, mean they will.

To illustrate further the way of salvation by faith I turned to Luke 23:39–43 as it provides a concrete story rather than an abstract concept. The penitent thief admitted his sin, believed in Jesus, asked to be saved and Jesus himself promised him a place in paradise. It is an account with a marvellous message for those who believe they are not good enough to be Christians; God's mercy shines through even in the darkness of crucifixion. This was something I felt our friend needed to hear, and she agreed with us.

At this point we took the lady back to her Christian friends, as she said she was now ready to become a Christian. This seemed right, as they would be nurturing her in the faith and I knew that, as Baptists, they would take the importance of an appropriate initiation ceremony seriously.

At the end of the week we drove to Soweto to hold an open-air meeting in the football stadium. Although it sounds like a Bantu word, Soweto actually means "SOuth WEst TOwnship'. It is the largest and most famous of all the black townships in South Africa.

I stood on a mound outside the arena and looked over the vast area of small chalet-type bungalows huddled together in close proximity. Officially and legally they house over a million people, but in reality it is probably more than twice that number. Graham Leach, a BBC Southern Africa Radio Correspondent, who has visited Soweto by night and talked to many of the police there describes it as 'possibly the most violent city in the world'.[3]

It seemed right to observe a few moments' silence before moving on. These were the people for whom so many Christians had been praying. This was the black political centre for the continuing struggle against apartheid; the place where the riots of 1976 began, leaving hundreds dead in different parts of the country. I did not foresee then the ideological watershed of 2nd February 1990 when President F. W. de Klerk turned his back on the apartheid philosophy.

I entered the stadium and sat on the grass facing the platform and the burning sun. It was as strange seeing it move across the sky from right to left as it had been seeing the moon upside down when we came out of the exhibition centre. Physically and politically this was a totally new world to me, and yet spiritually the same gospel was just as applicable, with the same power to save.

I had the privilege of counselling a man from Soweto who came forward in response to the preached message, eager to receive Jesus as his Saviour. I went through the steps outlined in Scripture for becoming a Christian, as summarised in the response of Peter's hearers at Pentecost, who:

(a) Believed in Jesus
(b) Repented of their sins
(c) Were baptised
(d) Received the Holy Spirit.

I asked the man through an interpreter if he believed in Jesus and was willing to repent of his sins. Once he responded in the affirmative I suggested he prayed his own prayer incorporating those two factors of belief and repentance, which he did.

I always find this to be more satisfactory than reading someone else's prayer from a booklet. It shows me if a person really understands what he is doing and it encourages him to do business directly with God through Jesus. If I am helping literate children or teenagers, I often send them away to write their own prayer before bringing it to me when they are ready. By finding pen and paper and writing a prayer, a young person frequently shows me he means what he says and knows what he is doing. It also helps him to pray directly to God in his own words.

I found a local pastor from Soweto who assured me he would look after the man who came forward and nurture him in the faith. Then, together, we laid hands on his head and prayed, 'Come, Holy Spirit.' In due course his face began to beam and he shared with us the feeling he received of sins forgiven. We encouraged him to believe that the Holy Spirit was now resident in his life and to give thanks for his salvation.

It is also possible to lead a person to Christ when he comes to us asking for healing, anointing or equipping. Jesus told his disciples to heal the sick in the context of proclaiming the kingdom (Lk 9:2). Healing, being filled with the Holy Spirit and receiving spiritual gifts are never offered in the New Testament apart from the gospel.

In my opinion it is right to affirm our faith in Jesus Christ, repent of our sins and be filled with the Holy Spirit every day of our lives. I therefore suggest to anyone whom I do not know who asks for help in Jesus' name that we take these steps first before seeking to meet any other request. For those who are not sure of their salvation in Christ it is, of course, particularly appropriate, providing they understand what is being asked of them and are able to concur. Once I am reasonably sure the Holy Spirit is in residence in a person then I am more confident about tackling emotional hurts, physical sickness, demonic infestation, receiving spiritual gifts, or even praying for sick friends and relatives (Mt 7:11; Jn 14:12–14; 15:16).

Approaching the subject, however, is not always easy. It is seldom helpful to ask a church member if he has been saved, and yet when someone comes forward to ask for prayer there is frequently an opportunity to share something of the gospel.

If I am ministering to a stranger I invariably ask what he is seeking and when he became a Christian, listening particularly to the second answer. Asking 'when' rather than 'if' will often reveal the necessary information without causing offence. Sometimes a person says he has been a Christian all his life and then I ask if he remembers when he made the decision himself to go on being a Christian. Many people brought up to go to church lose the habit as teenagers, so in contrast to this any adult who has continued in the faith must have made a decision for himself at some stage. If a person believes he is definitely a Christian I ask him how it happened and what he has experienced of the Holy Spirit since then.

The answers to these questions will often indicate to me when a person knows he is saved and has received the Holy Spirit. With those who are not sure I see the seal of the Holy Spirit (2 Cor 1:22; Eph 1:13–14) as the most helpful biblical way of bringing assurance. So often people are unsure because there was no laying-on of hands at conversion, no asking the Holy Spirit to come and dwell in the new convert, no expectation of his coming, and no teaching that God's presence in our lives should bring new experiences and discernible changes. In the New Testament there always appears to be visible or audible confirmation when people received the Holy Spirit (Acts 2:1–12; 8:18; 9:17–18; 10:44–47; 19:6). Canon John Collins writes, 'I don't see how one can be filled with the mighty, glorious, Third Person of the Holy Trinity imperceptibly.'[4] Many evangelical Christians are sure of salvation but not of the indwelling presence of the Holy Spirit. This, I believe, is the moment to stop talking, exercise faith and ask God to come.

During my time in South Africa I was privileged to lay hands on a number of people who until then were not very confident in their faith or familiar with things of the Holy Spirit. Four of them fell to the ground where they appeared to be bathed in the sunshine of God's love. Two others found their hands shaking and were thrilled with the sense of God's power and anointing. A further three experienced such internal warmth and acceptance that tears began to roll down their cheeks. In my opinion these were perceptible signs of people being filled with the Holy Spirit. All of them continued to express joy afterwards in the God who comes.

Any team member who prays with his eyes open will

be able to recognise such signs and encourage the one who is receiving when he senses the presence of the Holy Spirit. When I discern God's presence on someone it is then, at a suitable moment, that I ask God to grant the person's initial request. Afterwards I ask about church connections, suggest some suitable literature if the person is literate, and make a note of his name and address so that I can contact a suitable minister to provide follow-up. He can then make arrangements to deal with Simon Peter's point about baptism according to denominational requirements as appropriate.[5]

Whenever a person asks for help in Jesus' name we have an opportunity to help someone know the Healer as well as the healing.

Sin

Jesus said that when the Holy Spirit comes 'he will convict the world of guilt in regard to sin and righteousness and judgment' (Jn 16:8). When Jesus himself 'returned to Galilee in the power of the Spirit' (Lk 4:14), and helped Simon Peter catch a few fish, Peter's response was, 'Go away from me, Lord; I am a sinful man!' (Lk 5:8). The coming of the Holy Spirit may sometimes convict people of sin and we need to be ready to deal with it.

Henri, an Argentinian, approached me at the exhibition centre in Johannesburg saying he was virtually deaf and would like to be healed. He had very large hearing aids fixed to the back of both ears. I agreed to have a go. As far as I could tell from our conversation he appeared to be a committed Christian, so after a short time of declaring our faith in Jesus and repenting of our sins I prayed, 'Come, Holy Spirit.'

I waited and watched. I discerned very little but encouraged Henri to relax and receive all he could during the sessions. He returned the next day and sought me out. His ears were no better, but he had felt more at peace after I had prayed with him. Would I have another go?

I repeated the process and again there was nothing to see or feel other than a sense of God's peace with us both. I think I was more disappointed than he was.

The following day was the last of the conference and Henri only managed to get at me as the final session was beginning. Could I have one last try? I was not sure: there were no small rooms and ministry in the main hall would distract others. Also, the air was by now very cold. During the day we wore shirt sleeves, but in the evening we donned coats and wrapped ourselves in blankets. Autumn in the mountains without heating when the sun went down was a challenge even for the British. Anyway, I agreed.

Sharon from Birmingham came with us and eventually we found a large broom cupboard and piled in. I'd already had two goes, so Sharon prayed, 'Come, Holy Spirit,' with an instant reaction. There are times when ministering in the power of the Holy Spirit seems to be all about finding the right partner.

Heat came upon Henri, for which we were all grateful. Our stretched-out hands were soon warmed by his fire. He became weak and wobbly, and eventually tears began to flow. It went on for some time—maybe as long as half an hour. Finally Henri opened his eyes, gave them yet another wipe, and then said he had no idea how much unconfessed sin had remained in him for the last thirty years. It was very moving and very humbling simply to be present. God came in power, convicted him sovereignly of many sins from which, in the silence of his own mind, he repented and for which he received forgiveness. We all quietly returned to the meeting.

The following day at Soweto we were surprised to see Henri there with his wife. 'Good news and bad news,' he said as I commented on the absence of his hearing aids. 'I can hear every word from the platform without my hearing aids, but I can also hear every word from the wife.' She gave him a friendly pat and we thanked God together. Sometimes when the Holy Spirit comes we are convicted of sin and only God knows what the consequences may be.

Sharon and I sensed it was right to allow Henri to sort out his sins with God personally and privately, but the letter of James suggests there will be other times when it will be more helpful to confess our sins to another Christian. 'Therefore confess your sins to each other and pray for each other so that you may be healed' (Jas 5:16).

In such circumstances helping someone to become clean can sometimes be delicate and difficult and we need to recognise that some will only be happy doing it with a priest. In these cases our role may simply be to encourage him to do so, but if it seems right under the authority of the leader to do it ourselves, there are at least five steps worth considering:

1. Confession

A person who has been convicted of sin often wants and needs to confess it to another Christian but may be too ashamed to do so. Unless the person wants a priest, this is probably best done with someone of the same sex. If he responds to the question, 'What is happening, Fred?' with something like, 'I think God is convicting me of sin,' it is probably right to suggest going somewhere private.

If a person is hesitant about telling me his sins, I try to avoid any form of persuasion, while seeking to make it easier for him. I assure him of strict confidentiality, and say that I have heard it all before. Then, if it seems appropriate, I ask the Holy Spirit to come and show him what to do. It needs to be his decision.

If a person then feels it right to confess to me, I try to avoid two approaches:

(a) '*No! Surely not...I can't believe it...You haven't...You can't have...Not you!*' It can be very unhelpful to display any sign of shock, and yet how would we have reacted if Moses had confessed murder to us; King David, adultery; and Peter, denial of Jesus? We need to be prepared.

But equally damaging is the other extreme:

(b) '*Oh! Is that all? Did it three times myself last week. No problem.*' It can be just as unhelpful to tell someone I've committed the same sin as he has, even if it is so. A person should not be given the impression that sin is acceptable: he wants to confess it to be forgiven, not to be excused.

Once someone has confessed, however, I believe he is to be praised for what he has done. Someone who confesses a secret and maybe serious sin to another Christian, needs acceptance, love and encouragement. The sin is an evil thing in God's sight, but the confession leads angels in heaven to rejoice (Lk 15:7). It is the confession we are witnessing, not the sin, and I believe our response should be like that of the angels.

2. Absolution (Jn 20:23)

When a person confesses his sin I declare God's forgiveness—his willingness to forgive whenever we confess—and I usually add my own forgiveness: 'Fred, I declare to you the forgiveness of God the Father, Son and Holy Spirit, and I forgive you myself.' Depending on time, it may be appropriate to read a passage of Scripture here to assure the person of God's mercy and forgiveness. He can turn to it later himself. I personally find it helpful to read and study Luke 15, but one or two verses may be more appropriate as time allows (eg Ps 51:17; Dan 9:9; Joel 2:13; 1 Tim 1:15; 1 Jn 1:8–10; 2:1).

3. Receiving forgiveness

Facts are facts. If someone repents of his sin, confesses it and believes Jesus has dealt with it on the cross, he is forgiven, however he may feel. But if a person does not feel forgiven he will probably not live a forgiven life. Non-Christians will see guilt and false guilt being lived out before them whatever the person says, as the change in a person's legal standing before God may not always lead to victory in experience.

Once I have pronounced forgiveness (points 1 and 2 can be dealt with in a quarter of an hour) I try to encourage a person to sit back in a chair while I ask the Holy Spirit to enable him to receive forgiveness and feel forgiven. This may take an hour or more, but is well worth the time. To see a person's face change, sometimes accompanied by tears as the Holy Spirit comes on him taking forgiveness from the head to the heart, can be one of the most thrilling moments for any minister. It can also be, as with Henri, the gateway to healing and wholeness.

4. Restitution

Wherever possible, any wrongs or bad relationships should be put right (Mt 18:15–17,21–35).

With bad relationships an encounter or a letter may be necessary if the other party is aware of the sin and the problem. If a relationship is already damaged or broken then I believe it is always our responsibility to do what is right from our side of the fence to repair it (Mt 5:23–24). Sometimes if we confess our sin, repent and apologise to the person concerned, he may not be willing to forgive us. We may continue to pray for him, but basically it then becomes his problem.

It is not normally helpful to ask a person's forgiveness for sins done against him of which he knows nothing.

The exceptions are serious sins which may require for-giveness or restitution before the former relationship can be continued.

If something has been stolen from someone he has the right to prosecute or be recompensed. The sufferer can-not avail himself of his rights unless he knows what has happened. He may choose to forgive, but in such cases I believe it is right for the repentant sinner to give him that freedom of choice. I know of several people making financial payments weekly to make good past crimes. This can be the price of daring to pray, 'Come, Holy Spirit.' Forgiveness of sin does not always deal with the consequences of sin, which still have to be faced.

Similarly, when a couple marry, each partner promises to remain faithful to the other for life. This is part of the contract. If one of them commits adultery then the church (Mt 19:9) and the state recognise the right of the other to ask for a divorce. The innocent party is denied biblical and legal rights if the guilty one does not confess the sin. Hopefully confession will lead to forgiveness. That is a difficult and sensitive problem, and timing may be important.

One person I know committed adultery, but after prayer with others felt it right not to tell her husband immediately. This was done with the knowledge and support of those counselling her. A year later she felt it right to tell him and did so, and they both coped remark-ably well, but he agreed he could not have coped a year before; he was in fact experiencing great troubles himself at the time and I believe the decision was a correct one. This was a difficult situation, but the principle and inten-tion, even in this case, was to confess it to the injured party at the appropriate moment, and I think normally this is right.[6]

When we have sinned, our duty is to repent and con-fess. When we have been sinned against we are commanded to forgive. Anything less will leave impaired relationships with God, one another and ourselves.

5. Changed lifestyle

Go, and sin no more (Jn 5:14; 8:11).

Rejoicing at the forgiveness God offers never absolves us from the responsibility of trying harder next time, and sometimes the one ministering may have to offer practical help: 'Have the pay cheque sent to me; ask Social Security to pay your bills first; avoid walking home past the pub or the betting shop; sell the video,' and so on. This is why confessing sins to another can be so helpful. The minister can then help not only to forgive the past and restore in the present, but to overcome in the future. To avoid repeating certain sins our lifestyle may have to be changed.

The day after we visited Soweto the English members of the party led by John Mumford flew to East London.[7] This major port has been developed around the natural harbour formed by the Buffalo River as it flows into the Indian Ocean. It is a town with a perfect climate. The berg winds blow warm air down from the plateau to the coast, guaranteeing a temperature between 20°C and 30°C all the year round. My hosts lived in a large house and drove a Mercedes car, but they had no heating in their home and no overcoats in the wardrobe.

Walking across the deserted sandy shore into the Indian Ocean was like entering a warm bath. The beautiful beaches and heated sea provided a haven for sunbathers, swimmers, surfers and sharks. I limited myself to paddling at the edge.

On the Sunday our group was divided into three and sent to different churches where various members of our party preached and led times of ministry. The following evening we began a three-night course on 'healing' which was held in the Dutch Reformed Church for all local Christians.

Healing

There were occasions when Jesus went to people bringing God's healing touch uninvited, but according to the Gospels this was the exception rather than the rule. Far more frequently, 'people brought to him all who were ill' (Mt 4:24). At times they *begged* (Mk 1:40; 6:55–56; 7:26,32; 8:22), *shouted* (Mk 10:47), *asked* (Lk 4:38), *followed* (Mt 9:27), *pleaded* (Lk 8:41), and *called out* at a distance to be healed (Lk 17:13). The vast majority of healings in the Gospels came in response to an expression of need.[8]

Towards the end of one of the sessions in East London John gave instructions for the ministry teams to offer supervision, while the local Christians had a go at praying for the sick—some for the first time.

I attached myself to a group praying for an elderly lady who was suffering from deafness, sinus trouble and pain in the arm. Hands were duly placed in appropriate places, someone prayed, 'Come, Holy Spirit,' and then they all waited—most of them with eyes closed. For several minutes I went around the group touching eyelids with a gentle finger until everyone was in a position to see what the Father was doing—which was apparently nothing. I suggested pausing for discussion.

The lady had been standing with her head bowed, looking slightly embarrassed, indicating a feeling of unworthiness. I suspected she was yet another victim of the physicians' curse on old age. I attempted an interpretation of the signs: 'I'm not seriously ill. Why bother with me? I've got to expect some sickness and discomfort at my age.' Through question and answer we established all these as facts—and also discovered that she was the mother of the church's minister.

Despite John's words, I sensed the need to do a little bit of ministry myself: 'Close your eyes. Lift your head up high. In the name of Jesus I break the curse that says you have to be ill at your age. I renounce the lie that Jesus does not want to be bothered with you, and I declare you to be a daughter of the King, a princess of heaven.' After this I encouraged her to open herself to the Holy Spirit as a child of God.

The locals then laid on hands again, invited God to come and the lady's face beamed beautifully. She was indeed a child of God. At appropriate moments they commanded the sinuses to be unblocked, the ears to open and the pain to be gone. Power was felt by all through the hands, tension eased, and according to her own testimony the lady's nose cleared, the hearing improved and the pain disappeared.

It is not too difficult to say a simple prayer for physical healing with someone at the end of a meeting, or to pray with them for a sick relative. If it seems appropriate to pray for physical healing on the spot, I pray, 'Come, Holy Spirit,' as already outlined, and see what happens. If power begins to flow, especially in the affected area, I then command that part of the body to be healed in Jesus' name. There may be times, however, when it seems the physical problem is but a symptom of a deeper problem, and then we probably need to make an appointment to see the person when more time is available.

My own experience of people with deep emotional needs or demonic problems is that they are unlikely to have their lives put right with a five-minute prayer at the end of a meeting. Such situations need sensitivity. If the Holy Spirit brings up an emotional problem or a demon in the course of a meeting I will normally 'have a go'. During the day in Soweto a lady manifested demons which appeared to leave through foaming at the mouth, with the minimum of fuss, when commanded to do so in

Jesus' name. This was worth doing there and then and the lady felt much better afterwards.

If progress is made with an end in sight it may just be right to stay after a meeting, see what the Lord is doing and co-operate with him. Sometimes there is more power present in a large gathering, and a person's move towards wholeness and maturity can be greatly speeded up by short sessions of ministry at the end. But if I'm tired and it's late, the more sensible approach may be to reach for the diary or ask someone from our healing team to see the one in need during the week.

Perhaps the trickiest person to deal with is the one who comes forward seeking prayer for a sick relative or friend, often the commonest category. It is never wrong to pray with someone for another person and there are times when this will seem to be the most appropriate action, but this was rarely the approach of Jesus. With the four friends (Mk 2:3–12), the Roman Centurion (Mt 8:5–13), the Canaanite woman (Mt 15:21–28), and the father of the demonised boy (Mk 9:14–29), Jesus either praised them for their faith or pushed them towards responding in greater faith before their friends or relatives were healed. With this in mind I often ask such a person if he is worried about his friend or relative, and suggest we minister into the worry first before praying more specifically for the person who is ill. In the course of this discussion I also ask at an appropriate moment when he became a Christian and began experiencing things of the Spirit.

Hopefully this way in will have the same effect as with the others. Once a person feels the power of God, faith may also come for believing in healing, and that is the moment when I pray for the friend or relative.

I prayed for one lady in East London whose close relative had lung cancer. Considerable power and heat came upon her. It was well worth doing for the encouragement and blessing she received for herself, even if her relative was not healed. Unfortunately I was not able to obtain any feedback about her relative, though it is worth saying we have seen some healings in Birmingham as a result of praying in this way.[9]

During the day we were free to investigate East London and many of us took whatever opportunities presented themselves. Historical pain and tribal tension were all around us. In 1971 the Black Homelands Constitution Act was passed. Ten regions were set aside within South Africa where black people of the same tribe were obliged to live, only being allowed into towns and white areas to work. This scheme cost billions and probably created more white fear and black hatred than any other act. The homelands were the most tangible expression of the National Party's apartheid ideology involving the forced removal of three-and-a-half million people, many from their ancestral homes.

Four of the homelands were supposed to be self-governing, although no other country ever recognised their independence. Two of these 'independent' homelands, Ciskei and Transkei, intended for members of the Xhosa tribes were situated either side of East London. In Ciskei the President-for-life Chief Lennox Sebe struggled with unrest and attempted coups from the very start. In Transkei General Bantu Holomisa overthrew Pretoria's man in 1987 and declared his allegiance to the territory's most famous son, Nelson Mandela. The white Christians I met in East London in 1988 who were praying for racial equality knew that if it came through bloodshed the whites sandwiched between these two independent homelands would probably be the first targets. 'But,' said one white bishop's wife to me with courageous determination, 'what is right is right.'

We visited Mdantsane in the Ciskei, the second largest black township in South Africa, which provides much of the labour for East London. The housing was very similar to that in Soweto but seemed to be spread over a larger area. We drove around the Ciskei and Transkei areas past vast numbers of citrus and deciduous fruit trees, occasional ostrich farms and visible signs of the National Party's ideology. I wonder what will now happen to the capital cities, parliament buildings, cabinets, flags, anthems, presidential palaces, police forces, armies and giant independence stadiums? I suspect they will become the abandoned relics of a discredited dream. Dr Stoffel van der Merwe, general secretary of the National Party, recently confirmed the formal end of the homelands policy. We continue to pray for equality without bloodshed.[10]

Human ideologies and dreams, sometimes surely inspired by Satan, come and go, but God's promises are eternal. We aim in the power of the Holy Spirit to pull down Satan's kingdoms and bring in the kingdom of God. I believe the united prayers of Christians worldwide have helped to break the demonic strangleholds over the government of South Africa. Receiving God's spiritual gifts will help Christians wherever they live to advance God's kingdom on earth until the King returns.

Spiritual gifts

Paul encourages us to desire spiritual gifts eagerly (1 Cor 12:31; 14:39) and to ensure no one is ignorant about them (1 Cor 12:1).

Helen came to East London seeking the gift of speaking in tongues. I didn't notice she was heavy with child when I laid a hand on her forehead and prayed, 'Come, Holy Spirit,' so I was not too perturbed when she crashed over on the floor. As she lay there power continued to flow, her face became radiant and a new language poured out of her. When she rose to her feet rejoicing and praising God it was obvious no harm had been done.

Some with particularly open personalities, like Helen, or those who at certain moments in their lives become open may begin speaking in tongues very easily. For others it isn't always so straightforward, and it was certainly a struggle in my own case.

God's gifts often come through our personality rather than bypassing it and this is where so many have difficulty in receiving spiritual gifts from God. They think such gifts will arrive as large dollops of something extra, like a pair of wings, but the God who is in us frequently works through our normal senses.

This is especially true of speaking in tongues. We do not receive the gift and then use it; we receive the gift as we begin. When we desire to speak in tongues we have to start speaking, trusting that God will provide the words. It is this trusting which I found so difficult for so long when I first started. When I pray in tongues my spirit prays; when I pray in English my mind prays (1 Cor 14:15). When learning to speak in tongues we need to recognise that it is not a 'mind' activity: we do not form the words in our minds first before speaking them. It is an intuitive spirit activity.

When Christians want to receive this gift I find the best way is to help them relax, lay on hands, ask God to come and give the gift, and speak in tongues myself, encouraging them to join in when they can. Some worry about demonic tongues or fleshly tongues and this is why, when anyone seeks gifts, it is important to make sure they are born again first. If this is assured there is not normally any problem. Extremely reserved British castles with moats around them probably need to be sent home with a copy of *The Holy Spirit and You*, and encouraged to practise on their own.[11] The Bible is not explicit that speaking in tongues is for all Christians, but in practice the majority who search for the gift seem to receive it.[12]

Most of the other spiritual gifts listed in 1 Corinthians 12 cannot be exercised alone. I need someone else who is sick before I can receive and use healing; I require some spirits to discern and someone else's tongues to interpret before I can use these particular gifts. This is why I regularly have sessions in small groups. Having asked our heavenly Father to give us good gifts, we often go round a small group encouraging everyone to have a go at prophesying, giving a word of knowledge or wisdom, speaking in tongues, interpreting and laying hands on the sick. We need to provide an escape route—'pass' is allowed—but it is surprising how many, given an opportunity, encouragement and permission to fail, are often amazed at how well they do. What begins as a clinic often ends in real blessings to many.[13]

Even so, when an individual asks for anointing or is seeking a spiritual gift, team members need to know how to follow Paul's example of imparting spiritual gifts to others (1 Tim 4:14; 2 Tim 1:6). As with all other requests, after the initial interview I lay hands gently on the forehead and ask God to come. Once the Spirit comes on a person I then ask the Lord for the specific gift and maybe a sign that he is giving it.

A lady in East London came to me seeking the gift of evangelism and as the Holy Spirit came upon her tears began to flow freely. She interpreted this as Christ sharing with her his compassion for the unsaved.

Sometimes those asking for power gifts such as healing find their hands warm up or tingle. I often try to find someone present at the time for those with whom we have prayed to lay on hands, or else I encourage them to have a go under the authority of their own church leader as soon as possible when they have returned home.

One lady in Johannesburg told me she was seeking the

gift of healing and I prayed over her in the usual way. Power could be seen and felt flowing on her, especially in the hands which shook and became very hot. Before I could stop her she opened her eyes and went to a sick person who was waiting for prayer. I don't know any details, but in a few moments she returned giving thanks to God and shared with us all how the person on whom she laid hands had been healed. The clearest sign from God to someone seeking an anointing for the gift of healing is to be used by him in bringing his healing to another.

Those wanting discernment and prophetic gifts sometimes see a message in their minds. I prayed with two men in South Africa for such giftings who during the conference claimed subsequently to be given a word and a picture which proved to be helpful and upbuilding to others. One was a minister seeking vision for his church, who said he now knew what God wanted him to do.

If there is anything more thrilling than receiving spiritual gifts, it is encouraging and enabling others to do so. We always seem to receive more, the more we seek to give away.

Having learned to lay on hands gently, keep our eyes open, pray, 'Come, Holy Spirit,' and shut up, we have learned something which can be useful for almost any situation. Preparation is invariably necessary, but whether it concerns being filled with the Holy Spirit, the assurance of sins forgiven, the healing of various hurts or receiving spiritual gifts, the same model and principle can be applied. This often gives the beginner security and the confidence to have a go. At the very least it appears to be a good place to start.

There was some time left at the end of our visit for us to enjoy a display of Xhosa tribal dancing and an evening barbecue. This was followed the next day by lunch at the vicarage. Ordinary plates were unnecessary. Our food was served in scooped-out local pineapples and eaten from our laps in the garden. We ate the plates for dessert. William also found time to tackle ostrich riding and surfing in the giant rollers of the Indian Ocean before we flew home. I would have had a go myself but someone was needed to look after the bags. I still prefer staying healthy to seeking healing.

Notes

1. Signs & Wonders and Church Growth Conference, 26–29 April 1988, Johannesburg, South Africa.
2. One of the best teachers I have heard on God's grace is Terry Virgo. Those who struggle in this area might find it very helpful to work through his book *Enjoying God's Grace* (Word [UK] Ltd: Milton Keynes, 1989).
3. Graham Leach, *South Africa* (Routledge & Kegan Paul plc: London, 1986), p 9.
4. From a lecture given by the Revd Canon John Collins on *The Changing Church* course at Queen's College, Birmingham, August 1986.
5. People often come to me following their recent conversion saying their previous baptism or confirmation service did not mean much to them and they would like to be 'done again' with total immersion. As an Anglican priest this presents me with a few problems, as rebaptism is not permitted. The *Alternative Service Book* offers a service for 'The Renewal of Baptismal Vows on Various Occasions'. I see no reason why this cannot be done accompanied with a total immersion cleansing ceremony, especially suitable for those who have undergone deliverance.

    Alternatively, it may be good to encourage such people to see the Lord's Supper as the ongoing sacrament, which when received with repentance and trust, brings a fresh sense of acceptance and forgiveness to confirm their growing faith. I think it is important with initiation to stay within the boundaries of the denomination in which the convert will be nurtured.

6. John L. Sandford has some wise words to share on this subject. Particularly important is this sentence: 'The one principle we would suggest is that the decisions about which actions might be appropriate never be left to only one man or woman' (John L. Sandford, *Why Some Christians Commit Adultery* [Victory House, Inc: Tulsa OK, 1989], p 27).

7. John Mumford is the pastor of the South West London Vineyard.

8. In much of this book I am sharing how we learned to minister one to another, Christians to Christians. Sometimes this is severely criticised by those who feel healing should always go together with evangelism and not be practised on fellow believers. To my mind the New Testament does not teach either or, but both. Many times sick people who came to Jesus were praised for their faith: they were believers in Jesus. James also in his letter to Christians encourages us to 'pray for each other' that we may be healed (Jas 5:16).

9. A clergyman friend attended some of our teaching sessions at home and decided to put some of our ideas into practice himself. A lady in his church asked for prayer for a friend with cancer so he laid hands on her with others, and prayed, 'Come, Holy Spirit.' For something like fifteen minutes she experienced great power and heat in her throat before it all faded. When she returned home her friend who had throat cancer said he felt much better and a subsequent visit to the hospital confirmed the cancer had now gone.

My interpretation of such healing is not that healing is coming through the friend; healing comes
through Jesus. Rather, the manifestations in her own
body were a word of encouragement from God
which lifted faith to believe God for healing.

10. One of the most helpful and interesting books I have
    come across on the subject of South Africa is *The
    Passing Summer* a South African pilgrimage in the
    politics of love by Michael Cassidy (Hodder &
    Stoughton: London, 1989).

11. Dennis and Rita Bennett, *The Holy Spirit and You*
    (Kingsway Publications: Eastbourne, 1971), p 25.

    I came into the gift of speaking in tongues by
    reading this book and doing what it suggested at
    home by myself for several weeks.

12. I have discussed the apparent problem caused by
    1 Corinthians 12:27–30 to the idea that all Christians
    can receive the gift of speaking in tongues, in *The
    Hot Line* (Kingsway Publications: Eastbourne, 1990),
    pp 187ff.

13. I first saw this done at a Bill Subritzky conference
    with very helpful and encouraging results. (The Bat-
    tle Belongs to the Lord, January 1990, Brighton.)

5

Why Does Nothing Ever Happen to Me?

I once shared a house with four other theological students in the city of Nottingham. In former days it was joined to other houses in a terrace, but when we moved in it stood alone as the sole survivor on our side of the street of the council's slum clearance policy. We were living in the parish of St Ann's under the watchful eye of Roy, the vicar, who was later rewarded with a mitre for his efforts in training us to be clergy.[1]

One day we found a mouse. It was not altogether surprising given the circumstances in which we lived, but its presence produced an interesting and somewhat revealing set of responses.

'We'll buy a cage and keep it as a pet,' suggested soft-hearted Taffy.

'Don't be silly,' responded the ever-sensible and practical John. 'It's a health hazard. We'll have to drown it.'

'Let's put it in David's bed,' was my thought for the moment which failed to win any votes.

Harold proposed, 'We need to call a meeting to discuss the matter.' He went on to become a lecturer in a theological college.

David was not with us when the discovery was made so I informed him of the news on the phone. David did not believe there was a mouse.

I think the actual words he used were something like,

'Lawrence, I know you and your tricks. I don't trust you. I don't believe there is a mouse.' But whatever words were used unbelief was definitely expressed.

Soon after I had moved to Christ Church, Burney Lane, David became Team Vicar of a nearby parish and in due course I was invited to speak and minister in his church.[2] David was always sympathetic to the charismatic movement, but liked to take his time, observing and thinking things through from a distance before jumping in himself. Neither my belief in the mouse nor in things of the Spirit could automatically persuade David. He had to experience them for himself. He did eventually see the mouse and believe.

After my visit to his church David went to a seminar for clergy on ministering in the power of the Holy Spirit, where he was a little perturbed at what he saw. As the leader asked for words of knowledge a lady came forward in a very bold and self-assertive manner, declaring there was someone present with a headache. David found himself a little annoyed at her manner and not greatly impressed by the 'word' and its lack of detail. He responded to her in the same way as he had initially to the mouse.

Some time later David attended another much larger three-day conference and found himself at odds with what was happening.[3] He enjoyed the worship and found the preaching helpful, taking quite full notes, but the ministry time was ruined for him by seeing the same lady who had given the 'word' in action again—this time very close to where he was sitting.

As she held her hands slightly away from a person for whom she was praying one hand began to shake quite strongly with a rocking action. Feelings of annoyance buzzed around inside David. *Silly woman! What are you wobbling your hand like that for?* he asked in his own mind.

The second day was no better. Not only did nothing

happen to him, but he found himself doubting what was happening to others. David keeps a spiritual diary and this is what he wrote:

The whole meeting went into prayer and ministry around the arena and I felt more and more withdrawn from what was going on. I left at the end feeling the same as I had the day before, even though others with whom I had come did not share my problem. I thought hard about it. I used my analytical mind and asked, 'Which part of me doesn't believe?'

'Is it my mind/intellect?' I was quite happy with the teaching. Having studied the Scriptures and read books on healing myself, I know that I have no problem in believing in the power of Christ with my intellect.

'Is it in the will?' It can't be! I regularly and often preach and teach about healing. What's more, I pray for others to be healed. I am very willing to do this.

'Is it in my emotions?' Is it to do more with what I *feel* about what's going on rather than think about it? Is it what we call 'a gut reaction'? I came to the conclusion it was just that.

I pondered it semi-prayerfully and felt there were two things I should do. One was practical: sit nearer the front. The other was this: I believed the Lord wanted me to confess and repent of the sin of unbelief, scepticism and criticism. I also sensed he was saying it wasn't good enough to do this in a quiet corner on my own, but with someone else.

So on the Saturday afternoon, just before session three began, I prayed with my friend Ian and his wife a prayer of humble repentance, admitting there was unbelief in me, and asked the Lord to deliver me from it. I felt good afterwards: humble, fresh, clean.

When the leader prayed for the Holy Spirit to come on the third day David opened his hands to welcome God afresh into his life. A little later those who wanted to receive a ministry of healing and power were invited to raise their hands, and David responded immediately. The leader asked the Lord to anoint them and confirm it with a definite sign; a clear indication to those who were receiving the Lord's gift.

David experienced power and after a while opened his eyes. As he did so he smiled. He smiled at the Lord's sense of humour. His own right hand was shaking with a rocking action just like the hand of the lady who had annoyed him.

There really was a mouse and there really is a God who loves to come and give good gifts to his children. If nothing ever happens to me it seems unlikely the problem is on God's side of the fence.

When many things of the Spirit happen to others but not to me over a long period of time, then it is normally because my spirit is not open to the Holy Spirit or something in my emotions, mind, will or body are affecting my spirit and may need some attention. In learning how to welcome the Holy Spirit I found it very helpful when I began to understand myself better.

Tom Marshall puts it like this:

> Man is a thinking, feeling, willing being. That is to say, his basic nature consists of cognition (mind), affections (emotions) and volitions (will). Together these constitute man, a living soul. Man also has a body, relating him to the external world; and he has a spirit, through which he can relate to the spiritual realm and to God. Man is thus a tripartite being—spirit, soul and body (1 Thessalonians 5:23).[4]

I have found this analysis to be extremely useful, although Archbishop George Carey in his book *I Believe in Man* sounds a cautionary note also worth heeding: 'This description of man as *soul* and man as *spirit* must not, of course, be misconstrued as implying that man is composed of different and self-contained compartments.

It is clear that the biblical authors wrote and spoke on the firm assumption of man's psychosomatic unity.'[5]

Seeing myself as spirit, soul and body has helped me to see the biblical story of redemption in a new way, and many have found this understanding to be helpful in learning to be open to God the Holy Spirit.

In the beginning God created man and woman in his own image (Gen 1:27) by breathing his Spirit into them (Gen 2:7). They were at peace with themselves and with one another. They were in harmony with the world, and in perfect communion with God. The Holy Spirit controlled their spirits, which controlled their souls (minds, emotions and wills), which in turn controlled their bodies and bodily appetites.[6] Our spirits, emotions, minds, wills and bodies are created by God and all are very good.

When Adam and Eve sinned they were driven from the Garden and from God's nearer presence. Their spirits now lost the control of the Holy Spirit through disobedience to him. Immediately, the image of God in their spirits was distorted. They ran away, became afraid and were alienated from him. From then on the soul and the flesh of mankind took over and began to dominate the spirit.

Cain felt angry and murdered his brother (Gen 4:5–8).

When God chose to send a flood on the earth, 'every inclination of the thoughts...was only evil all the time' (Gen 6:5).

The people tried by their own will power to build the tower of Babel to reach into the heavens (Gen 11:4).

Fleshly appetites ruled the city of Sodom and Gomorrah (Gen 19:1–29).

In the days of the Judges everyone did what was right in their own eyes (Judg 17:6), but God did not leave his people without hope. Prophets emerged who began prophesying of a day to come. The Lord said through Joel, 'I will pour out my Spirit on all people' (Joel 2:28).

In the fullness of time God responded to mankind's need for salvation by sending a Saviour. The remedy for alienation was atonement. The Son of God came 'to give his life as a ransom for many' (Mk 10:45), the new Adam redeemed mankind (1 Cor 15:22), and it was now possible for his followers to be put right with God (Rom 3:21–24). The new beginning enabled mankind to become 'a new creation' (2 Cor 5:17) as God once more breathed his Spirit into them: 'On the evening of that first day of the week, when the disciples were together, with the doors locked for fear of the Jews, Jesus came and stood among them and said, "Peace be with you!"... he breathed on them and said, "Receive the Holy Spirit" ' (Jn 20:19,22).

Earlier in conversation with Nicodemus Jesus had explained, 'Flesh gives birth to flesh, but the Spirit gives birth to spirit. You should not be surprised at my saying, "You must be born again" ' (Jn 3:6–7).

When we believe in Jesus and his death on the cross, repent of our sins and welcome him into our lives, then he breathes his Spirit into our spirits making healing, restoration and communion with God possible again. Through Jesus we can now allow the Holy Spirit to control our spirits, which can then control our souls (minds, emotions, wills), which in turn can control our bodies and bodily passions. This is wholeness, healing and peace with God. The New Testament indicates this should be the aim of every Christian.

Paul teaches in Romans 8 that once we 'are in Christ Jesus' (v 1), which means having the 'Spirit of Christ' within us (v 9), it is possible to live 'according to the Spirit' (v 4) and be 'controlled... by the Spirit' (v 9). This will restore the right balance. Our spirit comes alive (v 10), our bodies come alive (v 11), our mind is at peace (v 6), and the right image of Father God is restored to us (vv 15–17).

To some degree this is what I think happened to my

friend David. His reaction to the lady with the wobbly hand could be summarised as follows:

> I *felt* uneasy;
> I *thought*, 'You silly woman!';
> I decided, 'I *will* not commit myself to this ministry.'

David reacted in his soul. His attention focused on the woman, not upon the Lord, and he used his rational, emotional and volitional faculties to weigh up the situation. His soul dominated his spirit. He allowed the external and visible problems to blind his spiritual discernment and, rather than responding in faith, he found himself grappling with unbelief.

Instead of allowing the knowledge of God contained in his spirit to control his soulish reactions, David's feelings dictated unease to his thoughts, and on the basis of this he made his decision. The image of God was then affected in his spirit. 'I do not believe what is happening is of God. God would not be a party to it.' This is a common process and a common problem: projecting our own diseased feelings on to God.

The answer came not in emotional healing. David did not have to pray through all the women in his life who had upset him. The answer came by tackling the spiritual problem and reversing the process. He confessed his sin against God, turned from it and received forgiveness for his sin through the atonement of Jesus. As he did this the true image of God in his spirit was restored, which then controlled his emotions, mind and will. He now expressed himself positively in his soul:

> I *felt* favourably towards the ministry;
> I *thought*, 'I'll go for it';
> I decided, 'I *will* give him all my heart and let him do anything.'

Consequently David went nearer the front, and stood up immediately when invited to do so. Underlying this new response was an acceptance of what God was doing and saying. Interestingly, when the Holy Spirit then came on his spirit his body was also affected as it began to shake.

It is my belief that the Holy Spirit, who 'gives birth to spirit' (Jn 3:6), normally comes on or through our spirit when we invite him to come.

At a joint celebration meeting in our church David MacInnes preached, after which we invited the Holy Spirit to begin moving among us.[7] David wandered around, laying hands on a few people, and eventually we closed the meeting. I am a little short-sighted when not using my spectacles, but I noticed, as I walked down the aisle with David, a lady who was sprawled all over a man on the back row. 'I hope that's the Spirit!' I began joking to David, when suddenly I realised who it was. 'It had better be the Spirit,' I said. 'That's my wife!' David then laid hands on Carol and confirmed it was indeed the work of the Holy Spirit. Nothing like it had ever happened to her before.

'What was it like?' I asked afterwards. 'What was happening?'

'It was very strange,' Carol began, 'not at all how I expected it to be. I always thought when the Holy Spirit came I would feel or see something—some joy or sadness or new revelation. But I felt and saw nothing.'

'So what was it like?' I asked again.

'An awesome sense of power, which I never wanted to end.'

A few days later I asked Carol a further question. 'What difference has this experience of the Holy Spirit made in your life?' I enquired.

She began to go red. My wife looks particularly

beautiful when shyness turns her crimson. 'I'm too embarrassed to say,' she responded.

'Go on,' I said. 'I won't tell.'

'I'm getting on better with your mother,' Carol eventually confessed, and it has continued to this day.[8]

Carol's experience of 'an awesome sense of power' has come the way of countless people in our church and meetings ever since: those lying on the floor, sprawled out over chairs, shaking or rocking, even bouncing; those with shining peace registering on their faces who so often testify: 'I felt nothing in my emotions and saw nothing in my mind, but I never wanted it to end.' Holy Spirit meets human spirit and often it is a life-changing encounter.

In 1 Corinthians 6:17 Paul writes, 'He who unites himself with the Lord is one with him in spirit.' In contrast, the one who is not united to the Lord 'does not accept the things that come from the Spirit of God, for they are foolishness to him, and he cannot understand them, because they are spiritually discerned' (1 Cor 2:14).

Frequently, the one who is not united to the Lord is translated as being 'unspiritual' (RSV, J B PHILLIPS, NEB), but the word in Greek is *psuchikos* which comes from the word *psuche* meaning 'soul'. Derek Prince translates this word as 'soulish' and summarises Paul's teaching as follows: 'The "soulish" person seeks to apprehend spiritual truth in the realm of his soul, but is unable to do so. The "spiritual" person is united with God through his spirit and is thus able to receive spiritual revelation directly from God.'[9]

Just as Paul argues the way to the Holy Spirit is not through the soul, so Jesus indicates it is not through the flesh either: 'Flesh gives birth to flesh, but the Spirit gives birth to spirit' (Jn 3:6).

It therefore seems to me that if we are to learn to open

ourselves more and more to the Holy Spirit we need to work on four areas:

1. Becoming strong in spirit
2. Being cleansed in spirit
3. Preventing our emotions, minds and wills from controlling our spirits
4. Preventing bodily problems from distracting our spirits.

Paul writes, 'Live by the Spirit, and you will not gratify the desires of the sinful nature' (Gal 5:16). When we learn to 'live by the Spirit', giving top priority to spiritual activities, then I believe we are better placed for welcoming the Holy Spirit upon us.

1. Becoming strong in spirit

Luke says of John the Baptist, 'And the child grew and became strong in spirit; and he lived in the desert until he appeared publicly to Israel' (Lk 1:80). We are also told he was 'filled with the Holy Spirit even from birth' (Lk 1:15). It is our experience that those who have been filled with the Holy Spirit at new birth and are working on becoming 'strong in spirit' are those who are best equipped to receive whatever the Lord is doing when the leader prays, 'Come, Holy Spirit.' I believe we become 'strong in spirit' by concentrating on spiritual activities.

Worship

'God is spirit, and his worshippers must worship in spirit and in truth' (Jn 4:24).

Worship is intended to be an activity of the spirit. Worship differentiates humans from all other animals. It is believed that an animal does not have a spirit.[10] Animals do not worship. Humans, on the other hand, from the earliest cave-dwellers have always been worshippers. Whether it is different gods, pop idols, famous sports personalities or rich movie stars, worship seems to be an inborn desire in all human beings. It is a desire of the spirit.

Unfortunately, not all churches are full of people worshipping God in spirit and in truth. It is possible for Christians to sing songs rather than to worship. It can be a bodily activity—making pleasant sounds to the ear like birds in the trees. It can be a mind activity—appreciating the poetry, analysing the theology, or using it as a polemic against other Christians of different persuasions. It can be an emotional activity: there are those who call themselves 'charismatic' who love to dance, sing, clap and wave their arms in the air because they love to dance, sing, clap and wave their arms in the air. It can be an activity of the will: I'll stand when everyone else stands, open my mouth and make the same sounds as they do because I have chosen to come to this church and to conform. All of this can be just singing songs and not necessarily worship.

But when we forget about ourselves, concentrate on him and give him all the praise that is due his name, then our spirits, inspired by the Holy Spirit, begin to fly and the visible world pales into insignificance. Then, if our arms are raised, our feet move and our bodies sway it is more likely to be an outward expression of our spirits in harmony with his Spirit dancing within us. It is the internal encounter with God which makes worship 'charismatic' rather than the external movement of our bodies.

So often what begins with praise may deepen into worship. When we desire to praise God with all our being, then our spirit begins to worship. Giving worship a high priority will help us to become strong in spirit.

The word of God

'The word of God is living and active. Sharper than any double-edged sword, it penetrates even to dividing soul and spirit, joints and marrow; it judges the thoughts and attitudes of the heart' (Heb 4:12).

When did we last do something we had not planned to do as a result of what we read in the Bible?

Just as singing songs need not be a spiritual activity, so reading the Bible need not involve our spirit. An academic may study it carefully in Hebrew and Greek to gain a PhD. A preacher may read it to find something to support his sermon. A Christian may dip into it like a pack of tarot cards for guidance because he knows reading horoscopes is wrong.

It is when we place ourselves under the 'word of God' and allow it to form our views and dictate our behaviour that we shall be penetrated even between soul and spirit and become more like Jesus.

Spiritual gifts

'Follow the way of love and eagerly desire spiritual gifts' (1 Cor 14:1). 'If I pray in a tongue, my spirit prays' (1 Cor 14:14).

The somewhat funny little gift of speaking in tongues, or singing in tongues, has puzzled many of us even to the point of dissension. But of one thing we can be certain: speaking in tongues and singing in tongues are activities of the spirit—Scripture says so (1 Cor 14:14–15). This means that in our attempt to grow 'strong in spirit' we should not only desire and seek this gift but use it regularly.

Some people see it to be a 'trigger' gift. If I am about to worship, read the Bible or seek the Lord for other spiritual gifts in a ministry situation, then praying quietly in tongues first will guarantee that my spirit is engaged and functioning. Many find this often leads into further and deeper spiritual activity.

The intuitive knowing of God, the discerning of spiritual reality and the receiving of words, pictures, prophecies and wisdom from God seem to occur when the Holy Spirit comes on our spirit.

'The spiritual man makes judgments about all things... we have the mind of Christ' (1 Cor 2:15–16).

Receiving and using spiritual gifts is a subject all of its own, but those who eagerly desire them, seek them through prayer and are willing to 'risk it' under the supervision of wise and biblical leadership will inevitably find themselves growing in spiritual knowledge and wisdom.[11]

Conscience

'I speak the truth in Christ—I am not lying, my conscience confirms it in the Holy Spirit' (Rom 9:1).

Nowhere does the Bible specifically say the conscience is housed in the human spirit, but one of the tasks of the Holy Spirit is to 'convict the world of guilt in regard to sin' (Jn 16:8). Paul writes about how the conscience helps us to know right from wrong (Rom 2:15), so it seems appropriate to suggest that when the Holy Spirit comes on the human spirit in a Christian, the conscience is activated to convict of sin. It is my belief that the conscience is to be found in the human spirit.

The content of the conscience can be affected by environment, culture and sin. This is borne out by Paul who says, 'Such teachings come through hypocritical liars, whose consciences have been seared as with a hot iron' (1 Tim 4:2), and, 'To those who are corrupted and do not believe, nothing is pure. In fact, both their minds and consciences are corrupted' (Tit 1:15).

The Holy Spirit comes to cleanse the conscience, as well as to activate it. Without the work of Jesus on the cross our consciences can make us feel accused and condemned (Rom 2:15), but through the blood of Jesus that guilt can be taken away: 'Therefore, brothers, since we have confidence to enter the Most Holy Place by the blood of Jesus...let us draw near to God with a sincere heart in full assurance of faith, having our hearts sprinkled to cleanse us from a guilty conscience' (Heb 10:19,22).

There is now no condemnation. When God convicts someone it is normally because he wants them to be cleansed of sin and guilt, restored to wholeness and given a fresh start. The conscience on its own condemns (Rom 2:15); the Holy Spirit comes to make the cross of Christ effective in our lives and take our guilt away. The conscience approaches a child who has fallen over in the mud with punishment; the Holy Spirit, like Jesus, approaches him with a sponge and towel (Jn 13:5). But when the two work in harmony within our spirit we are helped to repent of our sin, to live righteous lives, and the guilt and condemnation are washed away.

This means that whenever we listen to our conscience under the control of the Holy Spirit and become more righteous, we are engaging in an activity of the spirit. John the Baptist, filled with the Holy Spirit, overcame many temptations to sin, not least of all by living in the desert, and every time he resisted temptation by listening to his conscience he 'grew in spirit'. Pursuing holiness and righteousness will help us to become more spiritual and less dominated by soul and body.

Concentrating on worship, studying and obeying Scripture, seeking spiritual gifts through prayer, using them and learning to follow our God-given consciences are some of the positive steps we can take in becoming more open to the Holy Spirit. There are, however, negative things which also need to be addressed.[12]

2. Problems in the spirit

Men and women are made in the image of God (Gen 1:27) and God is spirit (Jn 4:24). It seems right to suggest that the image of God is to be found in our spirits.

For various reasons, many people grow up believing wrong things about God. John and Paula Sandford write, 'Because our hearts are not pure, we impute to God motives and ways which are not His. We do not see God, but only our projection of Him.'[13] This projection will often prevent us from receiving all God wants to do and be in and through us. Many are in no position to allow God to come upon them in power or to believe he will, because of the wrong image of him resident in their spirits.

I have met many devoted Christians who put everything into living for Christ and dying to self—not realising they have a wrong image of God in their spirit which automatically leads to a wrong image of self as well. They are living for the wrong Christ and putting to death the wrong self, often wondering why the abundant life and joy which they were promised is missing.

A very faithful member of our church and a totally devoted follower of Jesus Christ once gave me a collection of her Christian poems, inviting me to comment upon them. This was a sign of how far she had come since receiving ministry. Brought up in a very strict home full of the fear of God while receiving very little affirmation, it was a mark of God's true grace that she dared to trust me with her manuscripts.

I read the verses through carefully, writing words of encouragement and praise wherever I thought they were deserved, saving my negative comments for just one poem. This is what I wrote: 'What you have written here reveals your relationship with God as you see it. You are not living under the New Covenant; you are not even living under the Old Covenant. You are still trying to appease the gods.'

This was an enormous risk. It could have ruined a lot of progress which had already been made, and yet it was the truth. A few months later the lady moved to another part of the country and wrote a long letter to me containing this honest comment: 'Writing what you did on one of my poems was the most helpful thing you did for me in the years I worshipped at Christ Church. I hated you for it at first, but you were right. Coming to terms with this truth and repenting of it has transformed my life.' She had been a Christian for about thirty-five years when she wrote this.

If we have been born again and regularly spend quality time concentrating on spiritual activities, yet still nothing ever seems to happen to us, it is often our soiled spirit, which may have perverted the image of God within us, which first needs attention.

Because of our experience or the teaching we have received, many of us have wrong ideas about God, and only the Bible can give us a right, objective view of God. We need to know the right image of God before we can repent of believing the wrong one and restore our spirit to the way God originally intended it to be. My friend David analysed his thoughts and reactions from a good biblical knowledge of God and this helped him to realise his need for repentance.

The Bible reveals God the Father to us as 'Merciful Lord'; Jesus as 'Saviour' and 'Judge'; and the Holy Spirit as 'dove' and 'fire'.[14] In the world such combinations do not go together. The one who rises high in business and becomes the boss, the lord, will not stay there very long if he forgives all his company's debtors. The judge in a court of law sentences the guilty and has no right to pardon. In literature the dragon breathes fire and the dove brings peace. Because sin distorts the image of God within us, and our fallen world offers few models of power and mercy coupled together, many people approach the coming of God with inadequate vision. And yet this combination is what we all desire in a father.

On the one hand we want a close relationship with someone who is merciful, kind, generous and sensitive, who will love us, affirm us, listen to us and help us to be a 'somebody' in his presence. On the other hand we want him to be strong and to protect us from all evil. If we walk with him in the park where menacing villains come towards us intent on mischief, most of us would willingly swap all his gentle, loving sensitivity for power, might and strength at that moment. We want a father who is loving *and* powerful.

The Bible assures us our God is both. The message of Easter speaks of crucifixion love and resurrection power. The One who lets the little children come to him even when he is tired is also the One who turns over the tables and drives the money-lenders from the temple with a whip (Mt 19:14; Jn 2:15).[15]

People who have difficulty in letting God come to them and on them normally see God as powerful or merciful, but not both. They can often be put into two categories: (a) those who are afraid he will come; and (b) those who are afraid he won't come.

(a) the ones who are afraid he will come may see a person crashing to the floor (Acts 9:4), hear someone shrieking (Acts 8:7), or notice a whole lot of shaking going on (Acts 4:31). They do not want it to happen to them. Basically, they reject the lordship of God in their spirit by arguing with their minds against it, often claiming it cannot be of God. When falling, shrieking and shaking are shown to be biblical, they will sometimes repent, sometimes remain as observers or sometimes leave. The power of God and his lordship need to be acknowledged if we are to let him do what he wants to do.

(b) Many say, 'I don't believe he'll come on me. I believe he'll come on Tom, Dick and Harry's cat, but not on me.' The unworthy position fails to recognise the worthiness of Jesus who died for us, and is saying, 'God does not love me as much as others.' It is as much a stubborn and rebellious position as not wanting him to come. It is denying that the God of mercy, who has no favourites, is the God who comes.

It is sin which cuts us off from God; a spiritual problem which requires a spiritual remedy. We turn from sin and turn to Christ; this is repentance. When we repent of holding on to a wrong image of God in our spirit and turn to him afresh, we often begin to experience for ourselves the God who comes.

Sandra had two good friends who seemed very open to the Spirit. Their lives were quite dramatically changed and healed as the Holy Spirit was seen to come on them again and again. They hardly ever attended a meeting when someone prayed, 'Come, Holy Spirit,' without shaking, beaming, weeping or falling. But nothing ever happened to Sandra.

The longer it went on, the harder it became for all of them. Sandra's friends suggested she did this, tried that, or attended such and such a meeting. They prayed, counselled, encouraged, preached, despaired, but never gave up. Eventually it all became counter-productive and felt to Sandra like Job's comforters. The struggle within her was caused by her love for God, her love for her friends and the deep, genuine needs and hurts of which she was aware in her life. Bless her, she did not give up either, but came to see me. This in itself was an act of courage, faith and repentance. By coming she turned from the view that God did not love her as much as he loved her friends, and admitted her need of help in removing the barrier she had now created.

'They seem to think,' she began with some feeling, 'that if I don't shake, fall over or burst into tears when the Holy Spirit comes, I'm not a proper Christian.'

I nodded sympathetically. 'You can forget all about

your friends this afternoon,' I said. 'They're not here and I don't care if you shake, rattle or roll, swing from the chandelier, or do nothing. We've got three hours, so let's just relax and ask him to come.'

'Promise if anything happens you won't tell them,' she said.

'Promise,' I answered her. Sandra stood, closed her eyes, held out her hands and I prayed, 'Come, Holy Spirit.' Within thirty seconds her hands were shaking. After a minute she crashed spectacularly backwards into the armchair, and before five minutes had gone by tears were flowing down her cheeks.

Sandra did all that was necessary by coming to the door. It was very hard for her, but such a positive step contained everything which was in the Prodigal Son's first step home.

3. Problems in the soul

Having been born again, become frequently engaged in spiritual activities and repented of a wrong image of God in our spirits, it is then often helpful to ensure reactions in our souls are not dictating to our spirits. Whenever we stand to welcome the Holy Spirit but find ourselves preoccupied with things of the soul, it is unlikely we will experience the Holy Spirit in our spirits.

In *The Household of God*, Bishop Lesslie Newbigin emphasises the strengths of the Protestant, Catholic and Pentecostal traditions, but he also alludes briefly to some of their weaknesses.[16] He picks out a common over-emphasis in all of the three major denominational strands of Christianity and each one corresponds to a different part of the soul.

Mind

'Protestant history,' says Bishop Newbigin, 'has led to an over-intellectualising of the content of the word "faith".'[17] It is often the 'Protestants' who are in most danger of allowing the mind to dominate the spirit.

When somebody prays, 'Come, Holy Spirit,' those for whom Christianity has always been predominantly a cerebral activity may have difficulty allowing the Holy Spirit to come upon them. They automatically engage their minds, decide very firmly what they are and are not prepared to let God do, then think all the time about what is going on. Apparently, our minds can only think of one thing at a time, so I normally encourage people with such a problem to think of Jesus.

Praying, 'Come, Holy Spirit,' is not a mindless activity, but if my mind dominates and controls my spirit rather than serving it, I may receive very little from the Holy Spirit. I cannot think my way to spiritual blessing.

Will

Lesslie Newbigin maintains, 'The Catholic is right in insisting that the continuity of the church is God's will. He is wrong when he suggests that the doing of that will is the condition of our standing in his grace.'[18] Those with a 'Catholic' upbringing may need to guard against the will power of 'works' taking the upper hand and burying the spirit beneath a pile of good deeds. When James writes, 'Faith without deeds is dead' (Jas 2:26), the implication is that faith which does not lead to works is not faith; our good deeds are intended to be the evidence of our faith. If the cart comes before the horse and we find ourselves trying to attain faith through works, or to reach God in our own strength, then we are back to the Tower of Babel.

There is no way we can get from God what we want through our own determination. This is what some believe about faith, because of the way some preachers shout about our lack of it. But faith is a spiritual gift. It is our response to God's initiative. It comes when we engage more and more in spiritual activity. Faith is not will power. It is not lodged in the soul. Faith is trusting in God and not in ourselves.

The Christian who thinks he is doing well in his own strength may be the one who has most difficulty with yielding his will to God. 'How blest are those who know their need of God' (Mt 5:3, New English Bible). I cannot 'will' my way to a spiritual blessing.

Emotions

The Pentecostal tendency towards distortion 'may be described...as the setting of ardour against order', comments Bishop Newbigin, borrowing a phrase from Dr John Mackay.[19] Those with a 'Pentecostal' approach to Christianity may be tempted on occasions to allow emotions, especially enthusiasm, to dominate the spirit.

The over-emotional person often confuses enthusiasm with faith and tries, sometimes subconsciously, to work up from the inside a 'spiritual' reaction. We do not have to 'feel' something before the Holy Spirit can come on our spirit. Learning to wait quietly for God to come to us in an unemotional environment will often help us to differentiate the spiritual from the emotional.

We cannot feel our way to spiritual blessing.

I suspect there is something of the 'Protestant', 'Catholic' and 'Pentecostal' weaknesses in all of us, but my mind, my will power and my feelings need to be subject to my Holy Spirit-filled spirit if I am to serve God rather than oppose him.

4. Body

Sometimes bodily problems need to be put right before we feel comfortable enough for the Spirit to engage our spirits.

I once tried to do a three-hour teaching session in the middle of winter in an old church with a heating system better designed for keeping ice-cream cold than bodies warm. At the end when I prayed, 'Come, Holy Spirit,' not a lot appeared to happen. When many are cold and a few are frozen, it may not be too surprising if our spirits do not come to life.

Conversely on another occasion I asked the Holy Spirit to come in an overheated room without ventilation, and everyone fell asleep.

There have been times after a long sermon when some have needed a 'loo break' before welcoming the Spirit.

Some of our ladies kick off their shoes when they stand for a time of ministry.

Very often people come to our meetings with physical sickness, and when I invoke the Holy Spirit they immediately concentrate on their physical ailments. This is understandable, but welcoming the Healer rather than seeking the healing is the way to be engaged by the Holy Spirit.

In welcoming God it is often helpful to make sure bodily problems do not dominate the activity of waiting for the Holy Spirit to come upon us.

'Letting go and letting God' is a catch-phrase derided by some but nevertheless applicable to those whose problems with body and soul prevent the Holy Spirit from coming on their spirits. So many try to get to God through mind, emotions or will rather than letting God come to them through their spirits. When nothing ever seems to happen to me I probably need to give my soul and body to Jesus and let him breathe on my spirit.

'During the fourth watch of the night' Jesus came to

the disciples walking on the water (Mt 14:25–33), and impetuous Peter wanted to have a go. Whenever Jesus appeared on the scene Peter did not seem to worry too much about his mates, but I wonder what they thought about it? Having read about the ordinariness of the other disciples in the Gospels I wouldn't be surprised if their reactions were something like ours might have been.

There may have been a jealous one with his eyes on Peter: 'Look at him! Look at Peter! Always pushing himself forward. Jesus' favourite. Why is it always him and never me?'

There may have been a cynical one with his eyes on his mate: 'Hey, Jude, look at this! This is going to be great. Nudge, nudge; wink, wink; say no more. Know what I mean? Bet he sinks! There he goes. Splash! Told you so, told you so!'

But I suspect the majority would have been the fearful ones. Their eyes would not have been on Peter or each other or anyone. Their eyes would have been on the floor of the boat or out to sea—just in case Jesus should catch their eye and ask them to come.

Peter's enthusiasm became spirit-controlled as he turned his eyes upon Jesus: ' "Lord, if it's you," Peter replied, "tell me to come to you on the water." "Come," he said.'

Peter made sure it was Jesus, obeyed his word, left behind his friends and his security, concentrated on Jesus and moved in the supernatural. Once he looked at the wind and the waves, however, the emotion of fear took over and he sank. Even then, because it was Jesus he was seeking to obey, he was safe.

Concentrating on God-given spiritual activities, repenting of our sins against God, resisting the temptation to allow our emotions, minds and wills to control our spirits, and being prepared to attend to bodily problems when necessary, will help us to be more open to the

Holy Spirit. Then, if we seek the biblical Jesus and obey his voice, maybe we will learn to walk on water as well. Unfortunately, the mouse didn't quite manage it.

Notes

1. The Rt Revd Roy Williamson, Bishop of Bradford.
2. St Thomas' Church, Aldridge, referred to in Chapter 2 of Peter H. Lawrence, *The Hot Line* (Kingsway Publications: Eastbourne, 1990), pp 50ff.
3. Acts '86, National Exhibition Centre, Birmingham.
4. Tom Marshall, *Free Indeed* (Sovereign World: Chichester, 1983), first page of the introduction.
5. George Carey, *I Believe in Man* (Hodder & Stoughton: London, 1977), p 29.
6. The classification of soul as emotions, mind and will is somewhat arbitrary. Mind, emotions and will seem to many people not to belong to the spirit or the body and are therefore commonly classified as belonging to the soul. I personally find speaking about spirit; mind, emotions and will; and body helpful because most people can differentiate between them, define their problems more clearly and understand better how to proceed in seeking healing and restoration.
7. At that time Canon David MacInnes was Diocesan Missioner in Birmingham, before moving to become Vicar of St Aldate's, Oxford.
8. A shorter account of this incident is recorded in *The Hot Line*, Lawrence, *op cit*.
9. Derek Prince, *Blessing or Curse* (Word Publishing: Milton Keynes, 1990), p 132.
10. George Carey writes:

> . . . the spiritual nature of man is found in the breathtaking notion that man is made in God's

image. This, according to Genesis, is the difference between man and other creatures. In the command 'Let us make man in our image, after our likeness' (Gen 1:26), we have described the beginning of a new creative act and a wholly different relationship between creator and creature. Man alone is made in God's image (Carey, *op cit*, p 30).

11. In *The Dynamics of Spiritual Growth* John Wimber has two very useful chapters on 'Releasing Gifts in Us' and 'Releasing Gifts in the Church'. John Wimber, *The Dynamics of Spiritual Growth* (Hodder & Stoughton: London, 1990), pp 151ff, 156ff.

12. John and Paula Sandford's book *Healing the Wounded Spirit* offers some excellent analyses on the problems Christians can have in their spirits. The chapters on 'The Slumbering Spirit' and 'Spiritual Imprisonment' are well worth reading. John and Paula Sandford, *Healing the Wounded Spirit* (Victory House, Inc: Tulsa OK, 1982), pp 103ff, 145ff.

13. John and Paula Sandford, *The Transformation of the Inner Man* (Victory House, Inc: Tulsa OK, 1982), p 28.

14. Merciful Lord (Ps 103:8,13; Lk 15:11–32; Job 38–41; Ex 15:1–18); Saviour and Judge (Jn 3:16–17; Jn 5:22; Mt 25:31–46; Acts 10:42); dove and fire (Mt 3:11,16; Acts 2:3; 1 Thess 5:19).

15. David A. Seamands writes very interestingly and quite amusingly about wrong ideas of God. He refers to 'The Legal God, The Gotcha God, The Sitting Bull God, The Philosopher's God and the Pharaoh God' (*Healing of Memories* [Scripture Press Foundation: Amersham-on-the-Hill, 1986], pp 104–105).

On the other hand, Floyd McClung has written one of the most helpful books on the biblical nature of God that I have read (*The Father Heart of God* [Kingsway Publications: Eastbourne, 1985]).

16. Lesslie Newbigin, *The Household of God* (SCM Press Ltd: London, 1953).

17. *ibid*, p 52.

18. *ibid*, p 86.

19. *ibid*, p 103.

6

Emotional Healing

I made an appointment to see a doctor. There was nothing wrong with me, but there was with him. He had suffered from serious depression for fourteen years and no one was able to cure him. By the time he approached me for help he was permanently taking anti-depressant tablets which just about kept his suicidal tendencies at bay. He is a good Christian doctor, and as he had tried everyone and everything else, I agreed to see him.

The thought of my seeing a doctor to try to help *him* was enough to give *me* depression! What would he think? I have no counselling qualifications. I am simply a vicar. I flipped through my books and files. I was sure Dr Frank Lake had said something about depression when I was studying at Nottingham.[1] I prepared myself as well as I could and prayed earnestly as the time of the appointment approached. I saw him on my own in my study and encouraged him to share his story.

I asked about his parents, his siblings, friends and important relationships. I slipped in phrases like 'endogenous' and 'reactive depression'. I questioned him about 'tactile deprivation' and the possibility of 'performance orientation'. Generally, I felt that I had approached the subject as professionally as I could for an amateur. He sat placidly in the chair, co-operated fully with everything I

139

asked and related his problems as though he were treading a well-worn path.

We prayed for a few moments at the end of the interview and agreed to meet on two more occasions with my friend Graham Turner present. He thanked me and left. After he had gone, questioning thoughts raced around in my head. How did I do? What did he think? Would he be back?

The following week Graham and the doctor were there on time and I continued with more questions. He continued with more answers. This went on for a good quarter of an hour until the penny suddenly dropped. I stopped, paused and asked a different question: 'Doctor, what did you think about last time?'

'Oh! Very good,' he stuttered.

'Were you impressed?' I asked rather forthrightly.

'Yes, as a matter of fact, I was,' he said more positively. 'I didn't think you knew all that stuff.'

'Did you find it helpful?' I almost demanded.

'Well,' he replied hesitantly, 'if I'm totally honest, I've heard it all before.'

How naïve and foolish I had been! He hadn't come to see me as an unqualified counsellor or amateur doctor in order to be impressed. He had come seeking God's help when physical and psychiatric remedies had failed. 'I thought so,' I said somewhat apologetically. 'No more talking. I suggest you stand, close your eyes, hold your hands out, and we'll ask God to come.'

The doctor stood, almost with relief, and did as he was told. Graham stood on his left while I stood on his right as we prayed, 'Come, Holy Spirit.' We both laid hands on him gently, kept our eyes open and said nothing else.

Almost immediately his right hand began to shake and move involuntarily from side to side. We blessed what the Father was doing and encouraged him to go on receiving all God wanted to give him. Eventually the movement ceased and he opened his eyes. This time he confessed to feeling a little better. After he had gone I smiled at Graham. 'Did you notice how he shook on my side but not on yours?' I commented, tongue in cheek.

We all met again the following week and repeated the process. This time Graham insisted on being positioned on the right-hand side. Once more the doctor's right hand shook, and once more he felt a little better.

Graham saw the doctor again on numerous occasions. Eventually, deep problems surfaced and were dealt with gradually by God as the doctor attended general sessions in Graham's church. As the Holy Spirit was welcomed, problem after problem began to surface and leave, and after a while the doctor was able to stop all his anti-depressants. 'I feel two hundred per cent better,' he said on one occasion to Graham.

The best thing a Christian can offer people with problems is to pray, 'Come, Holy Spirit,' with them. It may take time to prepare a person, but ordinary Christians are not meant to be amateur psychiatrists, and not all are able to be well-read counsellors. Our highest aim is to be ministers of God's grace.

I attended a week's conference in 1990 led by Leanne Payne and sat most of the week next to a friend of mine who is a psychiatrist.[2] He, like many other well-qualified professionals who attended the course, was impressed by her in-depth knowledge and understanding of major psychiatric and relationship disorders and yet, when all the lecturing and talking about analysing the problems was over, Leanne repeatedly offered one major solution: she prayed, 'Come, Holy Spirit.' Power came upon many with serious difficulties and began to bring release and healing.

In her book *The Healing Presence*, Leanne Payne suggests four possible reasons why some Christian counsellors spend more time talking than praying:

1. 'Many of us are simply guilty of spiritual sloth.' A lack of discipline.

2. Some 'feel it is easier and less "risky" to rely on prevailing educational and psychological theories'; theories which 'help them maintain a "professional distance" in contrast to the personal involvement prayer entails'.

3. With others the problem 'amounts to a "psychologizing" of the gospel message, a serious reductionism of the faith'.

4. 'The gravest problem underlying our prayerlessness is that we are idolatrous—we want to bring healing or help to people through our own cleverness, apart from dependence upon God.'[3]

It is not easy to train non-book people to be skilled counsellors or Christian psychotherapists, but it is possible to train sensitive, born-again believers to pray, 'Come, Holy Spirit.' This is not an all-embracing technique which always provides instant success, but we have found it to be a way of letting God put us in touch with him, ourselves and our real difficulties. This can be an important step along the way to wholeness.

Once we move from general and public sessions in church to specific and private ministry with individuals in our homes, I have found it necessary to give more teaching to our teams.

Preparing the counsellor

(a) We minister in pairs with someone of the same sex as the counsellee always present

In church we try to send men to minister to men and women to women, but it is not always practically possible. Our team leaders keep a careful lookout for ladies who were hurt by men and who may recoil if a male member of the team comes too close, but in a large gathering our teams are given freedom to minister as seems appropriate at the time. Jesus himself laid hands on ladies in public (Lk 4:40; 13:13). In private, however, greater caution is always advised. Ideally a male and female pair will cover all eventualities.

In my opinion everyone who seeks to help individuals in private should be encouraged to read or be taught the helpful truths found in John Sandford's book *Why Some Christians Commit Adultery*.[4] Those who are absolutely certain they have no problems in this area are those whom I encourage most to read it. The danger is not just physical adultery, though there seems to be a lot of it about, but spiritual adultery as well.

(b) We make a verbal contract before meeting

Some of those with emotional problems may also have dependency difficulties. If I see a man in this category every week for a month, six months or a year without preparing him for the time when I will not see him again, he may be devastated when I break the news to him. Everything which has been done is likely to be undone by yet another major rejection, as he sees it, in his life. Whenever I agree to see someone I always try to make it clear beforehand how many times I will see him and for how long. I think such a verbal contract is vital for everyone, even if I know the person and don't suspect a dependency trait. Satan can bleed a church dry in no time at all by sending dependent people to all its team members.

When these agreed sessions are over it is progress, not perfection, that I then look for in his life. A baby in nappies is dependent for a while, but with love and encouragement will move at the right pace towards independence. There are times when it may be right under God's guidance for churches to support dependent people, but hopefully and prayerfully not for ever. If he makes progress or is seen to make a real effort along the lines we have agreed, I may then enter into another verbal contract to see him again at a later date.

(c) We understand the dangers of needing to be needed

I heard recently how approximately eighty per cent of clergy and doctors in the USA are the eldest children in their families. When baby brother or sister came along they were given the new role and identity of helping Mother with the baby. This is how they received attention and affirmation. Consequently, they grew up needing to be needed, and chose a profession which met that need. Though I am the younger child in my family I still recognise this dangerous trait in me. There have been times when I have ministered beyond God's anointing, allowed a needy person to make unnecessary demands upon me and suffered spiritually, mentally, emotionally and physically as a result. When a counsellor is motivated by the need to be needed and the counsellee is driven by the need to be dependent, then it may not be the kingdom of God which is advanced.

(d) We understand the danger of domination, manipulation and control

Domination, manipulation and control are the weapons of Satan and the goals of the kingdom of darkness. Freedom and maturity in Christ are the purposes of God and the aims of a Christian counsellor. Oughts, musts, gottos, need-tos and shoulds are not appropriate terms when we are seeking to share the truth which sets us free. Sometimes our team members whisper, 'DMC!' to other team members when they spot inappropriate language being used.

(e) We learn to observe strict confidentiality

Most Christians are not intentional gossipers, but it is very easy to share needs for prayer, or stories to instruct others, without realising we are betraying confidences. It is vitally important that we agree in any interview whether it is 'strict confidentiality', 'our spouses only may be told', or 'anyone may know if it is upbuilding and edifying'. Sometimes confidences are betrayed because they have not been agreed and people have different expectations.

(f) We aim to pray, 'Come, Holy Spirit,' as soon as possible

Our agreed aim in any counselling situation is to prepare a person for God's coming and not to delay the moment unnecessarily. Whenever I see team members after a session which they have been given permission to share with others I invariably ask them, 'What happened when you invited God to come?' We always try to encourage one another to focus on what God is doing.

Preparing the counsellee

In church there is usually a time of worship and the preaching of God's word before the leader invites God to come. Engaging in such spiritual and often Spirit-filled activities will then prepare a person for receiving more of whatever God wants to do. Starting from cold in my study is sometimes a much harder task. I notice the difference between a person who has never experienced a session of ministry in our church and one who worships regularly with us. The total stranger may well need longer in preparation before we pray. Here are five things I frequently aim to do:[5]

(a) Put a person at ease

In my study, which looks on to a car park, I try to help those seeking help to relax by drawing the curtains, unplugging the phone, serving coffee, introducing the colleague who is partnering me for the session and exchanging small talk. If someone is nervous about seeing me, all these things can be helpful, providing they do not take over-long. Waiting at the dentist's in comfortable surroundings will never remove all the apprehension, and putting off the moment indefinitely will not ease the pain.

(b) Listen to the person's problem

If someone has come with a major crisis or difficulty in his life, for me to say, 'Come in. Sit down. Shut up. Come, Holy Spirit,' may not be very helpful. A person who comes for help wants and often needs to be heard. On the other hand, God may not see a person's problem in the same way as the person, and my role as a Christian is to put him and his problem in touch with God. In a two-hour session I would normally want to pray, 'Come, Holy Spirit,' with at least an hour remaining of our time together.

(c) Deal with spiritual problems

Sin is what cuts us off from God. I like to be sure someone has been born again before I invite the Holy Spirit to come on that person. Once that has been established, a short time of confession and absolution, depending on what has been shared, may be helpful before we start.

(d) Deal with physical problems

Once we have decided it is time to ask God to come I normally encourage a person to start by standing, but suggest they sit as soon as their legs become tired or wobbly. Adopting a position right in front of a comfortable armchair gives far more physical security than we can offer in our church. The ones in my study also have wings on them where I can rest my elbow for long periods of time while laying may hand on a person's forehead.

(e) Deal with soulish problems

After listening to a person and explaining what I would like to do, I often say something like, 'If the Holy Spirit engages you deeply, you can stay in my study as long as it takes.' I have occasionally written letters and sermons while a person has been out in the Spirit. 'Take your time—there's no panic. If nothing happens that's fine. If your mind wanders or worries, picture Jesus. Try to lay aside your anxieties, hopes and fears. Be like a person having major surgery in an operating theatre: don't tell the surgeon what to do. Don't tell him what not to do or where it hurts—trust him. Jesus said to his Father, "Into your hands I commit my spirit," and died (Lk 23:46). Try to do the same.'

In the private session no one uninvited is watching and if we can remove all restrictions, including time worries, and encourage a person to wait upon God, then distracting thoughts in the mind, fears in the emotions and striving in the will may more easily be released into God's hands than when in church.

Then I pray, 'Come, Holy Spirit.'

There have been many times when this is all I have needed to do in any one session. The Holy Spirit comes, engages the person's spirit and does what he wants to do while I simply watch and wait.

This is what happened to Michael, aged about twenty. He was diagnosed slightly schizophrenic by a doctor, though it is doubtful if he could have said the word, let alone spelled it. As soon as God's Spirit came upon him he started calling out with great excitement everything he was experiencing. This is what the lady who was helping me managed to write down afterwards with Michael's approval:

At the very beginning all I could see was a very bright light, and then after some time I was looking at myself lying down on what seemed to be a bed. I was split open right down my body, and Jesus was drawing out from me many things (like strands) but I couldn't put names to them. Jesus then put his hands together over my stomach and all was closed without any sign of a wound or scar being left. My head felt very dizzy, like a spinning top.

A deep black hole then appeared and all the things that had come out from me went into and down the hole. I followed on down the hole to about half way, but the rubbish carried on down. The bottom of the hole became very bright with shining lights. I heard the word 'Shalom', and then seemed to 'float' down to the bottom. I was kneeling down and I could see Jesus. Jesus said to me, 'Michael—Michael—you—are—free—in—you.' There were 'two' of me and then they came together and joined into one. I realised others were with me—round me. I knew them and yet I didn't know them. All the people with me were joining into one.

I was alone with Jesus, very close to him, so very close, in what appeared to be a room, and yet I was outside in something like clouds or wisps of mist. I could see Jesus in detail—as if every detail was magnified. I could see the nail marks in his hands, but I couldn't see the crown of thorns, as his face was glowing light. I could see through and beyond Jesus. Jesus began to go, to fade and I began to cry. Jesus said to me, 'Don't cry. Reach out your hand and I'll be there.'

I went back up the hole and could then see beautiful colours like a rainbow.

The word 'Shalom' was new to Michael and he asked what it meant. The experience was a very real one. He shed real tears when he thought Jesus was leaving him, and positively beamed when it was all over. It did not bring complete healing or take all his problems away, but it was a significant step for Michael in receiving more of God's love, which was sufficient for the day.

Enabling and encouraging a person to be filled again and again with the Holy Spirit is for many the first step in emotional healing. It is a living encounter with the God who loves and affirms in a way an emotionally hurt or damaged person may not have met before. It is replacing the negative experience of life with a positive experience of God. A sense of power often accompanies this feeling of love as it did when we prayed with the doctor, and this frequently increases hope in the recipient and may lead to faith. So often emotionally damaged people feel powerless and therefore hopeless. The experience of God's power nearly always brings hope with it. Our God is a God of mercy and power.

When the Holy Spirit comes upon our spirits it is possible that many emotional problems and difficulties will be healed. For those with deep problems, however, this may simply be the beginning. I do not believe we should always anticipate long drawn-out ministries with everyone we see, but it would be naïve to think God will sovereignly and instantly solve all our problems for us. Because God has given us freedom and responsibility, his healing frequently requires our response. God's coming to us sometimes fills us with his awesome presence, power and love, and sometimes reveals to us things we have to do. For those with major difficulties his revelations are often the next step.

Identifying the problem

Graham Powell writes, 'It is very difficult to identify and deal with a feeling until I am feeling it.'[6] When the Holy Spirit begins to deal with a negative feeling inside us he often brings it to the surface and causes us to feel it. This helps us to identify the feeling, while the distress motivates us to deal with it. This is why when we pray, 'Come, Holy Spirit,' and people are willing to let him do what he wants to do, the orderly, peaceful church gathering may sometimes be turned into turmoil and mess.

The advantage of letting the Holy Spirit reveal the problem to us rather than identifying it ourselves is fourfold:

(a) Overcoming lack of self-awareness

'I've heard about people like me but I've never made the connection,' sings Don Maclean.[7] Am I the person my friends think I am? With practice I can fool all of the people some of the time. Am I the person I think I am? 'The heart is deceitful above all things' (Jer 17:9). Alone in his cell Dietrich Bonhoeffer asked these questions of himself and wrote the poem, 'Who am I?' In it he asks, 'Am I then really that which other men tell of? Or am I only what I myself know of myself?' He comes to this conclusion: 'Who am I? They mock me, these lonely questions of mine. Whoever I am, Thou knowest, O God, I am thine!'[8] I am the person *God* says I am. My real problems are the ones which God identifies.

(b) Finding the root of the problem

The symptoms and the root of a problem are sometimes very different from each other.

I had a picture once of a building held up by six pillars, one of which was always cracking and needing to be repaired. 'The real problem,' God seemed to say, 'is not the pillar that keeps cracking but the other five, which are not bearing their full weight.' Sometimes one major problem in our lives becomes so obsessive, we fail to recognise the other problems which are major contributing factors if not the cause itself.

When we pray, 'Come, Holy Spirit,' it is often the root of a problem which God highlights and identifies rather than the presenting symptoms.

(c)Discovering the hidden agenda

Sometimes the root of a problem is hidden in our unconscious mind.

Many of us know people who have been involved in bad car accidents and, though they made full recoveries, cannot now remember anything which occurred. The details of major traumas we suffered are often still within us—not in the conscious or sub-conscious mind, but in the unconscious one. Bad things may well have happened to us which we cannot recall and therefore know nothing about. Unfortunately, such incidents may still be affecting our feelings and behaviour in adult life.

When the Holy Spirit comes, what is hidden in our unconscious mind may be disclosed.

(d) Overcoming denial

Many people with serious problems and relationship difficulties frequently deny there is anything wrong.

Sometimes those who were badly abused as children were taught or conditioned to be loyal to the family, or are too ashamed to admit the truth.

Sometimes those from 'good, middle-class Christian homes' are unaware of the problems and difficulties which parents, teachers, relatives, friends or church leaders may have caused them. It is all they have known.

Sometimes people feel guilty about making a fuss, especially if their parents still worship in the same church. Compared to the suffering in the Third World, or those brought up in homes where they are battered, they feel very fortunate and basically all right. Anyway, 'Christians should not have problems'.

The coming of the Holy Spirit can help us to see ourselves, our families and our hurts as God sees them. God hates sin. He hates the harm and damage done to us or anyone else through others' sin. To deny sin and thereby to approve of it when it is done to us by our parents is not what God means when he tells us to honour our fathers and mothers. God calls us to respect those in authority over us; to bless them for all that is good and holy, but to forgive them for all which is unholy and sinful. To do this we must identify what was sin and what was not sin when it was done to us.

If we were not affirmed, loved, given worth, freedom and discipline by our parents as God would have wanted it to be, then we were brought up in a dysfunctional home and will bear the scars. Only when we allow the Holy Spirit to reveal these scars to us are we taking the first steps towards wholeness. When we begin to see ourselves and our hurts as God sees them, then we are on the way to being what he wants us to be.

On one occasion I saw a lady who is a mature Christian, accompanied by a female counsellor. She felt her womanhood had come under attack during the previous eighteen months. She suffered major problems with her female parts: closed fallopian tubes, fibroids and a lump in the breast which needed to be removed surgically. This, together with her father's death, had caused emotional stress and she wanted to be right with God. Her family was known to be a good Christian one. We prayed, 'Come, Holy Spirit.'

She was engaged by the Spirit slowly. Time and time again my colleague and I had to stop ourselves from sharing what we thought as the Spirit began to go deeper. In the end we simply waited. Distress gave way to cries and muted screams: 'No, no, I can't believe it!' It was important for her to see and feel for herself what had happened in childhood. There was great power upon her and what she saw and felt was very vivid.

The lady herself had no idea that the root of her problems was sexual abuse hidden deep in her unconscious mind. If the Holy Spirit had not revealed it to her personally in such a vivid and powerful way, she would certainly have denied it. The changes now taking place in her life suggest she was not deceived.

When the Holy Spirit comes powerfully upon us, he may choose to reveal a major problem to us. Then there is more work to be done.

Forgiveness

If I fail to receive the Holy Spirit the problem is normally *my sin*. When I am emotionally damaged or hurt the problem is normally *sin done to me* by someone else. The Bible teaches us that we receive healing from the sin done to us by forgiving the sinner: 'For if you forgive men when they sin against you, your heavenly Father will also forgive you. But if you do not forgive men their sins, your Father will not forgive your sins' (Mt 6:14-15).

The pain we ourselves receive when we are unforgiving is highlighted by Jesus in the parable of the unmerciful servant: 'In anger his master turned him over to the jailers until he should pay back all he owed. This is how my heavenly Father will treat each of you unless you forgive your brother from your heart' (Mt 18:34-35).

It is bad enough suffering the hurt and damage caused when someone sins against us, but if we fail to forgive them we may go on suffering from this hurt and damage all our lives.

Jesus himself was the positive example of his own teaching: 'When they came to the place called The Skull, there they crucified him, along with the criminals—one on his right, the other on his left. Jesus said, "Father, forgive them, for they do not know what they are doing" ' (Lk 23:33-34).

If it is possible for Jesus to forgive those who have mocked, scourged and crucified the Lord of all glory, then it is possible for us to forgive those who have sinned against us. For those who have been deeply hurt, however, it is not an easy road. Once we have identified the cause of an emotional pain and the need to forgive I usually put three questions to those I am seeking to help.

1. How does God feel about what happened to you?

Many of those who have suffered greatly feel God is really the one to blame. We cannot continue to offer God as the solution to a person's problem if he feels God is the one who caused it in the first place. Such a negative feeling about God most frequently comes from one of two main sources:

(a) Unanswered prayer. Night after night the little child prayed, 'Lord Jesus, please don't let Daddy do that to me again,' and night after night he did.

(b) Natural disaster. When family or friends have suffered tragedy because of disease, famine, flood or earthquake it may be God who is blamed.

Mature Christians, or those whose problems are not too deep, may find their negative feelings about God healed when the Holy Spirit comes upon them. The person sees and feels the incident or tragedy again, and this time Jesus comes into the picture. He weeps with those who weep. He is seen to deal powerfully and effectively with the abusers. He cradles the suffering child in his arms and carries him to safety.

Such an experience in the Spirit changes his image of God; he now feels God loves him, cares for him and really does have the power to heal him. Hope rises. It seems to the sufferer that God is now on his side and, 'If God is for us, who can be against us?' (Rom 8:31). This is why when a person relives a traumatic incident in the power of the Holy Spirit I always ask if he can see Jesus. An encounter with Jesus may remove the feelings of blaming God, and thus open the person to the channels of God's healing power and love.

There will be times, unfortunately, when it is not that easy. The sufferer does not see Jesus or feel forgiving, and then we need to talk. Unbelief in the God of love and power is frequently the problem. When someone has been deeply in the grip of Satan it is not easy for them to believe that God is on their side or that Jesus is Lord. I am told that when Satanists abuse children they also teach them, 'This proves Satan is Lord. Jesus has no power to stop us, otherwise he would.'

When such victims come to us for help, it is the love of God experienced in the body of Christ which is most urgently needed. We have to out-love the world in the power of the Holy Spirit before hurting people will be ready to share our beliefs. When someone who has been badly damaged experiences the love of Christians in a real way the time will probably come when they want to question us about the lordship of Jesus. How can we claim Jesus is Lord in a world so full of pain?

(a) Defending God. Philosophical arguments about evil and the God of love can never replace trust—there will always need to be a step of faith. But before hurting victims can take this step they may need to hear the reasons for our faith and to think them through for themselves. The philosophical problem of pain is normally expressed in the question: 'How can God be all-loving and all-powerful when there is evil in the world?'

The simple answer commonly given is that God limits his power in order to give us free will.[9] God hates sin and abuse of every kind, but he does not remove domination by dominating the person who is causing it. The victim suffers because others sin against God—not because God chooses it or wants it. Until Jesus is revealed to all at the end of time, his lordship is seen only by those who choose him by faith. Fathers are given responsibility by God to love their children, but they are free to abuse that responsibility until the Day of Judgement. Love is a choice. Whenever a father chooses sin or abuse, God hates it and feels for the victim, but he allows it to happen for a season.

The same free-will argument may also help those who have suffered from a natural disaster or sickness. This time it is Satan and his fallen angels who are the abusers. They are the ones who misuse their power and responsibility to cause pain and suffering. The first and second chapters of Job suggest there are times when Satan has the power to use nature to cause suffering (see also Romans 8:22), and in Acts 10:37–38 Peter describes those whom Jesus healed as being 'under the power of the devil'. It is God who is for us and Satan who is against us.

(b) Proclaiming God. As a Christian I never like to allow others to put God in the dock for too long. There are many things about God and life that philosophy will never answer and which I shall never know before I die, but there are many things about God revealed to us in the Scriptures which I want to proclaim. I believe it is vital in helping anyone with emotional problems to ensure they regularly hear the good news of Jesus Christ. I think those who feel God is not on their side need to hear the following:

(i) God gave up his glory to come to earth as a baby born in a stable. ' "The virgin will be with child and will give birth to a son, and they will call him Immanuel"— which means, "God with us" ' (Mt 1:23).

(ii) He came 'to preach good news to the poor...to proclaim freedom for the prisoners...recovery of sight for the blind, to release the oppressed' (Lk 4:18). 'He went around doing good and healing all who were under the power of the devil, because God was with him' (Acts 10:38).

(iii) He died the cruel death of an innocent, abused victim: scourged, mocked, humiliated, in agony—for me (Mk 15:15–37).

(iv) The power of God raised him from the dead—a power which is available to all who believe and trust in Jesus (Rom 8:11).

(v) He ascended into heaven where he has gone to prepare a place for all who follow Jesus; a place where there is no more pain, suffering or evil spirits and where the activity of heaven is affirmation, that is, worship (Rev 21:1–8).

(vi) One day Jesus will come again as Judge. Every eye will see him, justice will be done and 'creation itself will be liberated from its bondage to decay and brought into the glorious freedom of the children of God' (Rom 8:21).

This is our God. He hates oppression and releases captives. The person who has suffered domination will often understand why God chooses to limit his power and allow angels and humans to have freedom and responsibility. God does not force others to be loving! Those who have been physically abused and beaten may find they can trust the God who came to earth and died painfully in a humiliating and abused fashion for them. Those whose spirits have been crushed through oppression may gain new hope from the power of God and the promise of eternal life without domination, pain and suffering. Those who can receive the gospel of Jesus Christ in faith will then know God as he really is, and be open to receive his love as he comes into their experience.

2. How do you *feel about what happened?*

Most Christian counsellors know the importance and value of forgiving those who have sinned against us just as God's word decrees (Eph 4:32; Col 3:13), but there is a tendency among some Christians who have lived reasonably sheltered lives to try and get there too soon.

A person who has suffered much but is required to forgive his tormentors instantly feels, 'I'm being told that what happened to me is unimportant. I'm being asked to approve of what they did to me. Nobody cares about how I feel or what I've been through. In the midst of a lifetime of hell I am informed that the only way out is to forgive and forget as if it never happened. But it did happen. It does hurt. And I want you to know that.'

The pain and feeling of injustice are too deep to move straight from identification to forgiveness, without expression. When someone has been deeply hurt, learning to forgive normally needs to be progressive.

As we start on the road of forgiving someone who has badly sinned against us we need to know exactly what God is requiring from us. He does not want us to say that sin is all right or acceptable. God asks us to hate the sin but forgive the sinner. Expressing anger against the sin which was done to us is a right and proper Christian activity. It is often the way to get rid of the hatred within and to clear the way for us to forgive.[10]

If a person has been punched on the nose, for example, I try to encourage him to express all the different emotions he experienced. He may have felt angry, frightened, picked on, unjustly treated and humiliated in front of others. I try and help him to talk about each felt emotion by gently asking how it felt whenever there is a lull in the conversation. After he has expressed what he felt at the time I may then ask how he feels now, and which negative feelings have remained. If someone comes up to him threatening to punch him on the nose today, does anger, fear or humiliation come to the surface?

Once the feelings have been expressed—staying for as long as possible on areas where strong feelings are exhibited—I then turn our thoughts to the sin itself. What does he feel about nose-punching? What does God feel about it? If he is clear that this is sin and that God hates it, he hates it and as a Christian he is allowed to hate it for the rest of his life, then I turn to the person who did it.

God hates nose-punching. What does he therefore feel about punching the man back on the nose? God would hate that too. To hate nose-punching is to hate it done to me and to hate it done to anyone else, even the one who hurt me. If I punch him back on the nose I do not hate nose-punching, I hate the person who did it, and this is sin.

I try to encourage a person wherever possible to express his anger against the sin but without sinning himself. My aim is to help the person to declare his hatred for the sin but not for the person. If an opposing player in a football match punches me on the nose and I punch him back, we are both sent off. We have both sinned. It may be necessary for me to lead the victim in a prayer of repentance for his own sinful response to the sinner before I move on to the next question.

3. Can you now forgive?

Often when a person has spent time telling me how it felt and feels to be badly sinned against, and can be assured and believe that the crucified Christ feels the same, he can then sometimes find it in his heart to forgive. Occasionally we need to go over the ground several times and maybe only deal with one incident out of many in any one session, but frequently when this is done, coupled with meditation upon the gospel of Jesus Christ, a person will say: 'As long as I can be sure God knows how I felt and know he feels the same way I do, then yes I can forgive. I hate what happened to me, but I forgive the person who did it.' Sometimes there is a need to forgive ourselves as well.

Jesus told us to love our neighbours as ourselves (Mt 19:19), but sadly I know many Christians who would be arrested if they did. They are so angry with themselves that if they responded to their neighbour in the same way it could result in criminal activity. There often appears to be civil war going on inside and this causes as much damage as any other abuse. It does not matter who sins against us—even if it is ourselves. Sin always brings hurt and needs to be forgiven.

Our aim as Christians is to see as Jesus sees, to love what he loves and to hate what he hates. He sees us as we are. He loves us, but hates our sin. He wants us to do the same. I have found working on three particular areas to be helpful in seeking to do this.

Truth

It is common for those who were abused as little children or raped as adults to blame themselves. The feeling of being violated and left unclean also brings with it a sense of shame and guilt. It is illogical but often felt.

Similarly many who were not affirmed as children frequently blame themselves when something goes wrong, even if it is not their fault. Some were brought up in homes where 'See what you made me do!' was a common cry.

In both situations this is seeing ourselves as Satan sees us. He accused Job while he was suffering when he was not guilty of sin, and he tries to do the same to us. The solution can often be found in renouncing false guilt, declaring the truth about what happened as God sees it and then praying, 'Come, Holy Spirit,' so that what is believed with our minds may be experienced in our spirits and felt in our emotions.[11]

Pride

Sometimes people claim to hate themselves when it is not really the case. 'I hate myself. My nose is too large; my legs are too short; my teeth look like tombstones.' But if I really hated someone I would, in fact, be pleased if his nose, legs and teeth did not match the Hollywood image. The truth is not that I hate myself but that I am full of pride. I am in rebellion against God for the way I am made. I love the wrong me in a wrong, vain kind of way.

Similarly, if I struggle to forgive myself for not having done better, I am struggling to accept myself as a sinner. I am seeing myself as better than I am. 'I ought not to have behaved so badly' means 'I am not really that bad'. In other words I am not seeing my sin as Jesus sees it: I am too proud to see myself as I am, to acknowledge my sin, accept God's forgiveness and forgive myself. I would rather think I am better than that. Repentance is necessary if I am to stop damaging myself through my own pride.

Mercy

Sadly there are times when a person's sin causes irreparable harm to another person, and then forgiving self can be very difficult. I know someone whose child was killed by a drunken driver. God offers forgiveness, the Christian parents were reported in the newspaper as offering forgiveness, but could the driver forgive himself?

I am not sure there are any words which can help someone in such a situation. Once a person has repented of such sin, it is only the coming of the Holy Spirit in forgiving power through the cross of Christ which can enable a person to receive the forgiveness of God and forgive himself.

I attended a conference at Swanwick several years ago which was organised by the staff of St Andrew's Chorleywood. Mary Pytches spoke about forgiveness and then her friend and colleague Prue Bedwell invited the Holy Spirit to come upon us. As he came she suggested we let God show us whom we needed to forgive.[12]

I went through my usual list: Dad, Mum, sister, friends, school teachers and church members, but no one rang any loud bells. I forgave them all anyway, just in case. Then in the stillness I sensed God speaking to me.

'Now forgive the one person who has hurt you most,' he seemed to say.

In my mind I saw a full length mirror before me and a clear image of myself looking in need of forgiveness. God said, 'Minister to him as you would to anyone else.'

I put my hand through the mirror and laid it gently on his forehead. 'Peter,' I said, 'God loves you very much and forgives you all your sins. I love you too and choose freely to forgive you.' Never before had I known the full depth of the person's sins to whom I now ministered God's grace. The picture faded. Power, love, acceptance and forgiveness came upon me. If I hadn't been British I might have wept.

When God comes in power and mercy he longs to affirm us and replace any negative experience we have suffered with the positive experience of his love. Sometimes his coming reveals deep pains to us, and then Christian counsellors filled with his love may be used by him to help us to forgive. Once this is done, the Holy Spirit is then given the necessary permission to come into our scars and heal them. He can forgive us our sins as we have forgiven those who have sinned against us and he can restore our damaged emotions. Whenever a person has been able to forgive those who hurt him we then pray, 'Come, Holy Spirit,' and prepare him to receive God's love once more. As God's forgiveness comes upon his own forgiving spirit he often begins to feel much better.

There are times during worship on Sundays when I look at some of the people in our church who have been able to forgive. Their arms are raised, their faces beam, their hearts are full of praise. I am ashamed sometimes to see those who have been hurt in ways I could never even begin to understand or imagine, loving God far better than I do. Because I know their stories I can at least testify to the measure of God's grace which has been poured upon them. I am now convinced it is possible, in the power of the Holy Spirit, to be crucified and yet pray, 'Father, forgive,' and by so doing allow God to heal our deepest wounds.

Notes

1. Dr Frank Lake was the founder of 'Clinical Theology'. He was based in Nottingham while I was at St John's Theological College. As a Christian psychiatrist he came to college from time to time to give lectures.
2. 'Restoring Personal Wholeness Through Healing Prayer', Swanwick.
3. Leanne Payne, *The Healing Presence* (Kingsway Publications: Eastbourne, 1989), pp 39–40.
4. John L. Sandford, *Why Some Christians Commit Adultery* (Victory House Inc: Tulsa OK, 1989).
5. In her book *Set My People Free* Mary Pytches argues against in-depth counselling being left in the hands of ordained staff. She writes, 'It limits church growth by using the valuable time of a few which would be better spent on leading the whole flock.' She gives the example of a church which stopped growing in 'the year the vicar started ministering inner healing'. These days I try to do enough praying with individuals to 'keep my hand in', but not so much that I become bogged down or stop being leader of the church (*Set My People Free* [Hodder & Stoughton: London, 1987], p 62).
6. Graham Powell, *Fear Free* (Sovereign World Ltd: Chichester, 1987).
7. Don Maclean, 'Crossroads' from 'The American Pie Album' by United Artists Records.
8. Dietrich Bonhoeffer, *The Cost of Discipleship* (SCM Press Ltd: London, 1959), p 15.

9. C. S. Lewis has written a popular book exploring this subject entitled *The Problem of Pain* (Collins Fontana Books: London, 1957). A more detailed historical and philosophical examination of the subject can be found in John Hick's book *Evil and the God of Love* (Collins Fontana Library: London, 1968).

10. Some counsellors major on helping people to express anger which has been suppressed, sometimes even offering it as a solution. In my experience it is only something which needs to be done to help us forgive, so that we may then be filled with the Holy Spirit. It is a way of dealing with sin which cuts us off from God's love. Francis MacNutt writes:

> ...to me it seems significant that anger seldom seems to surface when people are resting in the Spirit. When we consider that one of the purposes of counseling is to surface repressed anger, we might expect a lot of it to come bursting forth. But it just doesn't seem to happen that way.
>
> Perhaps this is because anger is not the root emotion, but comes as a result of a far deeper experience of hurt and pain, and it is these roots that Jesus wants to heal (Francis MacNutt, *Overcome by the Spirit* [Eagle, Inter Publishing Service (IPS) Ltd: Guildford, 1990], p 81).

11. Dr William Backus and Marie Chapian have written a most helpful book which not only analyses the problem of believing wrong things about ourselves, but gives practical help towards achieving a solution (*Telling Yourself the Truth* [Bethany House Publishers: Minneapolis, 1990]).

William Backus is a clinical psychologist and associate pastor in a large church. He has also written two other helpful books on truth-telling: *Telling*

Each Other the Truth (Bethany House Publishers: Minneapolis, 1985) and *Telling the Truth to Troubled People* (Bethany House Publishers: Minneapolis, 1985).

12. 'Come, Holy Spirit' conference at the Hayes Conference Centre in Swanwick, Derbyshire, 1987.

Mary Pytches has written four helpful books, mostly dealing with emotional healing: *Set My People Free* (Hodder & Stoughton: London, 1987), *A Healing Fellowship* (Hodder & Stoughton: London, 1988), *Yesterday's Child* (Hodder & Stoughton: London, 1990) and *A Child No More* (Hodder & Stoughton: London, 1991).

7

Healing the Demonised

Whenever I go to Kensington impressions from child-hood cause an air of expectancy and excitement to rise within me. It always feels like a very special place. I remember the museums crammed to overflowing with real trains, boats and planes, and towering elephants and giraffes which a little boy could stand under fearlessly, courtesy of the taxidermist. I recall being taken into Harrods to observe a different world inhabited by a dif-ferent class of people, where dreams but not purchases were permitted. I once dared to push open the door of the Oratory and step inside, though not for long. The atmosphere of this magnificent Roman Catholic church was too austere and holy for a small child to do anything but tiptoe around for a few seconds.

I never knew Holy Trinity existed. It is well hidden behind and between so that only the faithful can find it. In July 1990 I went there with Carol my wife, Roger our lay reader and a thousand other invited guests. The same air of expectancy and excitement was with me. The prophets had come to town.[1]

The sun shone all week so I brought my knees out into the open. We enjoyed summer on the lawns of Ken-sington, armed with sandwiches and surrounded by Christian friends chatting merrily about the stimulating talks and challenging ministry we had received. I began to feel very good. That is, until Mervyn came along.[2]

'I was hoping to meet you,' he said, 'after reading what you wrote about the demon of Antichrist in your book.[3] I think I've got it and I wondered if you'd get rid of it for me.'

I couldn't help thinking there were a thousand people close at hand far better qualified for this task than I, but failing to hear a 'no' from God I gave a 'yes' to Mervyn. With permission, and the establishment's blessing, we climbed some spiral staircases to the tiny audio-visual room. I say 'we' because if I was going, then all my friends were coming with me. Carol, Roger and Mike, who was putting us up for the week, Mervyn and I piled into a small area full of worktops covered with bits and pieces of recording equipment and material.

We prayed, 'Come, Holy Spirit.'

Almost immediately distressed facial manifestations began to appear on Mervyn's countenance and physical sensations of cold came from him in my direction.

'This is not Antichrist,' I said, a little surprised at the authoritative way it came out. We waited a little while longer until it became obvious from Mervyn's trembling on a warm, summer's day that fear was present.

Mike said, 'I'm getting the word "murder",' which seemed a direct communication from God. My own reaction was based rather more on experience gained from seeing similar manifestations before. 'Yes,' I said, 'I think it may be child sacrifice.'

Mervyn said later he knew at once something specific had been touched, because he felt as I said it a strange combination of dread and expectation within himself, accompanied by a tingling sensation. As we paused I shared a few thoughts.

Mervyn was a mature Christian who had had no association with such activities himself whatsoever. The root of this problem was clearly ancestral. Demons are legalists and when demonic rites have been enacted in the past, linking families and blood lines through sacrifice to Satan, then they claim the right to pass on at conception and death to other members of the family until those legal claims have been undone through the precious blood of Jesus. Becoming a Christian rarely seems to be sufficient to cleanse the whole temple. The old strongholds have to be pulled down and cast out. If a lady becomes a Christian but her husband does not, she is still married to a non-Christian. The same seems to be true when a family line has been wedded to Satan through sacrifice. When a member becomes a Christian the demons still claim rights to remain until 'divorce' and expulsion have taken place. This is why Jesus commanded his disciples to proclaim the kingdom *and* to cast out demons.

Mervyn had previously said prayers of renouncement and repentance on behalf of his ancestors and I suspect this is what caused the demonic presence to be revealed so quickly. Now we needed to go for divorce. Mike led us: 'In the name of Jesus we divorce Satan and his demons from this blood line. We undo the covenant made between this family and Satan through blood sacrifice. We renounce it, and break it, and render it powerless through the blood sacrifice of Jesus, which we accept fully. Satan, we divorce you. Jesus, we accept your offer to be married to us, and claim freedom from the sin of our ancestors as brides of Christ.'

Mervyn was quite suddenly and literally overwhelmed by what he described as a mixture of the most powerful grief and the acutest terror he had ever experienced. He crouched on the floor, buried his head down as hard as he could and tried to escape inside from what was taking place. He said later that the deep sobs and cries seemed all too insufficient to express the pain he felt. It appeared to us that the Holy Spirit was allowing him to grieve over the dead child, although Mervyn thought he was also experiencing and being released from some of the feelings which the child himself had felt. I think the Lord concealed further details from him which may have been too much to bear at the time.

Just as suddenly as they had come, the negative feelings lifted, leaving behind a seared emotional memory. We talked about Jesus' forgiveness. Mervyn reacted with feelings of self-condemnation and guilt as though he wanted to pay the price of his family's shame. This was a big battle. Jesus had paid the price and wanted Mervyn simply to receive forgiveness, but it was quite an effort for him to do this.

Mike began going through some central aspects of the Christian faith with him, to 'undo' what had been done. There was no major reaction to the cross, but at the mention of Holy Communion Mervyn cried out, 'Oh no, no, no... it's the meal, it's the meal!' Horror and revulsion engulfed him. He felt completely unclean as though his whole body had been polluted by nourishment from this spiritual meal. The immediate trauma passed quite quickly, although Mervyn was left very shaken.

Jesus said, 'Unless you eat the flesh of the Son of Man and drink his blood, you have no life in you. Whoever eats my flesh and drinks my blood has eternal life' (Jn 6:53–54). I slipped out to try and find some bread and wine. It seemed right for us to have Communion together. It was for us a way of accepting Jesus' sacrifice made once for all; a way of sealing the New Covenant made available through Jesus' blood, and a way of nailing our colours to the cross in the presence of God, one another and the demons. I explained the situation to a member of Holy Trinity, who kindly supplied all our needs.

Mike had just been ordained Priest in the Church of

England, but had not yet presided at a Eucharist. This became his first, memorable celebration as a priest. Mervyn struggled to receive the elements, especially the wine, but succeeded eventually as we all knelt in a circle. As he did so he screwed up his face, fell to his knees and began coughing and retching. Roger found an empty ice-cream carton in the room to use as a receptacle, which Mervyn crumpled angrily, empowered by the outrage of an exposed demon.

Mervyn returned to his seat and it now seemed the right moment to tackle the head demon. Mike had received a word from God earlier and I had used a little previous experience, but this time our method was trial and error. We threw out a number of words like 'dagger', 'high priest', 'witchcraft' and so on, but the demonic manifestation reacted most markedly to 'black mass'.

For a brief moment Mervyn felt despair: *It won't go—I haven't enough faith—I'm not clean enough.* But Jesus was there in the power of his Holy Spirit. As we commanded it to leave, Mervyn was projected from his seat full length across the floor and he knew instantly it had gone as peace descended upon him.

After a few more prayers, asking God to bless and protect, we all went out for a meal together. Some time later Mervyn wrote this to me:

Apart from having to stand against general attacks of fear, horror and sadness, I came under a very strong fear for my own children. This was only lifted some time later when the Lord put his finger on the need for me to forgive my ancestors who had been involved. I found this very hard, feeling, I think, that it could not be right to forgive what was to me the blackest act imaginable. The Lord showed me that the forgiveness of which I stood in need was not of a different order to the forgiveness I was denying to another. In accepting that God's mercy extended below this worst thing, and in forgiving, I found release—no longer me and my all-too-small God over against the most dreadful sin, but God in his astounding love and mercy through the cross encompassing even me and that sin. The fear had lost its power.

There will, I'm sure, be many different reactions to this brief account. The hardest thing for some to accept may well be the truth that Mervyn is a Christian. He is in fact an evangelical clergyman, born again, baptised in the Holy Spirit and a mature, dedicated Christian serving the Lord in a full-time capacity, worshipping regularly as a leader in the community of believers. Others, I know, have difficulty believing that punishment for the sins of the fathers can be visited on subsequent generations. We need to look at these two views.

Can Christians be demonised?

It saddens me greatly that the New International Version of the Bible speaks of being 'possessed' by demons, when there is no such word in the original Greek. This follows the pattern of the Authorised Version. A Christian cannot be 'possessed' by demons, as possession implies ownership, and Christians belong to Jesus Christ. But demons are not owners, they are squatters.[4] I believe the NIV is wrong to use the misleading word 'possessed' when it is not in the original.

The point can be simply made by looking at one example from the New Testament. John 8:49 is translated in the New International Version, 'I am not possessed by a demon.' The Greek says *Ego* (I) *daimonion* (demon) *ouk* (not) *ecko* (have): 'I do not have a demon.' I can only wonder where the translators found the word 'possessed'! It certainly isn't in Scripture. The word *daimonizomai*, used thirteen times in the New Testament, is the one often translated 'demon-possessed' (Mt 4:24; 8:16,28;

9:32; 12:22) and I believe it is more correctly rendered 'demonised'.

The Bible is not specific on the subject of Christians and demonisation, but the following references are worth considering:

The family of Job, a righteous man, suffers death, disease and destruction at the hand of Satan.

A man in the synagogue is delivered from evil spirits (Mk 1:23; Lk 4:33).

A daughter of Abraham had been bound by Satan for eighteen long years (Lk 13:16).

Satan entered Judas (Lk 22:3; Jn 13:27), a man who had been given power and authority to proclaim the kingdom, heal the sick and cast out demons (Mt 10:1,7–8).

'Jesus turned and said to Peter, "Out of my sight, Satan!" ' (Mt 16:23).

' "Simon, Simon, Satan has asked to sift you as wheat. But I have prayed for you" ' (Lk 22:31–32).

'Even as he spoke, many put their faith in him. To the Jews who had believed him, Jesus said, ". . . You belong to your father, the devil" ' (Jn 8:30–31,44).

The letters to the Christian churches found in the New Testament Epistles and the Book of Revelation do not indicate sin- or demon-free fellowships.

It is possible to argue against each reference individually, but cumulatively I consider them to be worth noting.

When demons in people speak the truth, it is a fair indication that the person also believes in that truth. We find these interesting statements on the lips of those who were demonised prior to their deliverance:

' "I know who you are—the Holy One of God!" ' (Mk 1:23).

' "What do you want with me, Jesus, Son of the Most High God?" ' (Mk 5:7).

' "These men are servants of the Most High God, who are telling you the way to be saved" ' (Acts 16:17).

The Gadarene demoniac responded to Jesus in this way: 'And when he saw Jesus from afar, he ran and worshipped him' (Mk 5:6, Revised Standard Version).

The parents of both demonised children mentioned in the New Testament also expressed belief in Jesus. Of the Canaanite woman whose daughter Jesus set free, Jesus said, ' "Woman, you have great faith! Your request is granted" ' (Mt 15:28). 'Immediately the boy's father exclaimed, "I do believe" ' (Mk 9:24).

I cannot myself believe that every one of these references is about unbelievers.

Jesus told the Twelve to proclaim the kingdom and cast out demons. In Mark 16 they are told to preach the good news and they will also drive out demons.[5] In Acts 5 people with faith laid the sick and demonised in Peter's shadow and they were healed, and in Acts 19:12 faithful people similarly took handkerchiefs and aprons to Paul, and evil spirits departed.

Surely if demons left people when they became Christians, the disciples would not have proclaimed the kingdom and cast out demons, and Jesus would not have told them to do both?

And we can go further than this. In Luke 11:24–26 (see also Matthew 12:43–45), following a passage where God's children are encouraged by Jesus to ask for the Holy Spirit, Jesus teaches against casting demons out of a man and putting nothing in their place. At the very least this is normally taken to mean the Holy Spirit. As unbelievers cannot be filled with the Holy Spirit, it can be argued that Jesus is saying we should not cast demons out of non-Christians. If he told his disciples not to cast demons out of those who do not have the Holy Spirit, I wonder whom he expected them to set free?

The practical implications of believing that Christians

cannot be demonised are frightening. Let us suppose a man manifests demons, as in the synagogue when Jesus preached, and we take him into a side room. Then what do we do? If he says he's a Christian, are we to believe he's lying because Christians can't have demons? If he says he's not a Christian, we then lead him to make a commitment because if we don't put the Holy Spirit in the place of a demon he'll be worse off than before. He is now a Christian, so what do we do? Christians can't have demons. If he manifests again do we tell him he hasn't really become a Christian, that he's a liar, or do we call an ambulance?

We then have to ask, 'Out of whom do we cast demons?' We shouldn't cast them out of non-Christians because they'll be worse off as they do not have the Holy Spirit, and we can't cast them out of Christians because they don't have any. So why was the early church casting out demons?

I can't help thinking somebody is trying to deceive the church! Maybe the real problem is the stigma: 'I like to believe Christians cannot have demons because this means I can't have them.' It also means that as a church leader I do not have to bother with them. In our experience demons are much more likely to be discovered after a person has become a Christian and received the Holy Spirit than before.

One evening Graham Turner, a nearby vicar, invited me to help him with Laura who jumped from chair to chair making unhelpful-sounding noises whenever he prayed, 'Come, Holy Spirit.' A couple of years ago her husband, Derek, had died in his thirties, leaving her with one young son.

At the funeral Laura heard a voice in her head saying he was Derek. He told her not to worry; that he would stay close, guiding and protecting her. From then on she regularly conversed with this inner voice called 'Derek' and everything seemed fine—until she decided to become a Christian. 'Derek' was very much against this, but she went ahead and asked Jesus into her life, using the prayer set out in Norman Warren's booklet *Journey into Life*.[6] Others prayed for her to be filled with the Holy Spirit.

Shortly afterwards the insistent voice of 'Derek' came while Laura, at a low ebb, was alone in the home with her son Adam: 'It is time to come and join me,' said 'Derek'. 'Set fire to the house, then you, Adam and I will be reunited.'

Laura had a go. She lit her copy of *Journey into Life* with a match and tried to use it to set fire to the house. Eventually, all attempts having failed, she came to her senses and realised what she'd tried to do. She came to Graham for help.

It was an enormous battle. We struggled all the time to convince her that the voice was not that of her husband Derek, but of a demon—probably one which had resided in Derek until his death and then transferred to her. That way it would know a lot about him and have no trouble convincing her of this falsehood. At times we seemed to be winning and then suddenly forces within her appeared to take over as she argued violently against us. Whenever we prayed over her—with permission—she jumped about, which meant we were praying over a moving target. We were not very good at it, but we were keen to persevere, bearing in mind the seriousness of the problem.

Very late at night Graham's wife Rosie suggested I played the piano and sang a Christian song. My piano playing is ordinary (Roger Jones says it's very ordinary) and my singing has been described by another qualified musician, gifted with words, as sounding like a cat with its head stuck in a dustbin.[7] But it worked. It was obviously too much for the demon.

Laura calmed down, gently worshipped God, agreed the demon was a demon which she no longer wanted to keep, and allowed us to command it to leave in the name of Jesus. There was a violent struggle, a sudden release of tension and pressure, and peace came over her. Subsequent ministry appeared to confirm the departure of 'Derek', and there was no more attempted arson.

It was after Laura became a Christian and was filled with the Holy Spirit that the demon of 'Derek' was seen and identified in its true light. Coming to terms with Christians being demonised can often be easier when we realise that the root and entry point of demons for many Christians is ancestral sin.

The problem of ancestral sin

As I see it the problem of ancestral sin is a far more complex issue than Christians being demonised. On the one hand God says, 'He punishes the children and their children for the sin of the fathers to the third and fourth generation' (Ex 34:7), but then prophesies through Jeremiah and Ezekiel it will not always be so: 'In those days people will no longer say, "The fathers have eaten sour grapes, and the children's teeth are set on edge." Instead everyone will die for his own sin; whoever eats sour grapes, his own teeth will be set on edge' (Jer 31:29–30).

Ezekiel comments on the same proverb in chapter 18 and says, 'The soul who sins is the one who will die. The son will not share the guilt of the father, nor will the father share the guilt of the son' (Ezek 18:20).

Because Jeremiah 31 is also about the promise of a New Covenant which was fulfilled in Jesus, and Ezekiel speaks about God's Spirit coming and bringing a new heart (Ezek 36:26–27) as he did at Pentecost, some have argued that the sins of the fathers no longer affect their children when they become Christians.

In addressing this problem it is interesting to see how God carries out his own laws and fulfils his promises. Neither curses in the Old Testament nor blessings in the New Testament are automatic and irreversible. When the children of Israel chose not to enter the promised land, and disobeyed God, Moses interceded for them (Num 14:17–19). As a result God did not punish the children for the sin of the fathers to the third and fourth generation. All but the first generation were allowed to enter Canaan.

Daniel and Nehemiah confessed, repented and renounced the sins of their fathers, and the children of Israel returned from their punishment in Babylon and rebuilt the city of Jerusalem (Dan 9; Neh 1). When Moses, Daniel and Nehemiah stood in the breach the consequences of ancestral sin were revoked.

Jesus for ever lives to intercede for us and has paid the price for our sins on the cross. This has set up a New Covenant. Through the cross of Christ we can be assured of forgiveness in a way which was never certain for Moses, Daniel or Nehemiah, but confession and repentance is still required. Ezekiel told people to repent (Ezek 18:21), John the Baptist told people to repent (Mt 3:2), Jesus told people to repent (Mt 4:17) and Peter on the Day of Pentecost told the people to repent (Acts 2:38). The principles have not changed under the New Covenant, just the assurance of the result. In Christ not even the first generation will be punished for their own sin if they repent.

To my mind the Bible makes an important distinction between the consequences of sin and the responsibility for sin. Ezekiel says, 'The son will not share the guilt of the father, nor will the father share the guilt of the son' (Ezek 18:20). But in Ezekiel 21:4–5 God says through the prophet, 'I am going to cut off the righteous and the wicked, my sword will be unsheathed against everyone from south to north. Then all people will know that I the Lord have drawn my sword from its scabbard.' Both Jeremiah and Ezekiel were taken into exile and suffered from the consequences of their ancestors' sins despite their own faithfulness. If my father sinned I may be affected by it, but I am not to blame for it. This makes logical and theological sense.

God says that the consequences of the fathers' sins will be visited on the children to the third and fourth generations. If the children repeat those sins the cycle begins again. On the other hand, if we confess, repent and renounce those sins, receive the New Covenant promises by faith in Christ and apply them to those consequences, the cycle will be broken. Our own teeth will no longer be set on edge.

It seems to me it is right and proper as Christians to confess, repent and renounce the sins of those who went before us. To confess means to see something the same way as God sees it. If I confess the sins of my ancestors I acknowledge before God that I see their sin the same way as he does. If I repent of their sin, then I turn from it myself, determined not to do what they did. If I renounce their sin, then I agree to stand against such sin and to oppose it whenever I come across it. Breaking the curse in the name of Jesus, and blessing those who caused it, will then often bring release, though demons may still have to be cast out.

In our experience demons appear to enter through sin and claim the right to remain until that sin is tackled. When specific sin is not approached with confession and repentance, accompanying demons will pass from generation to generation. I believe many people today are still suffering in Babylon because they have never confessed and repented of their ancestors' sins which still affect them, or asked Christian friends to remove the associated demons. Old Testament laws still apply until the New Testament remedy is applied.

In practice we do not go looking for our ancestors' sins or begin quizzing parents or grandparents about their private lives. We wait for the Holy Spirit to identify a problem and its root cause, and then we tackle it.

Our six o'clock service on a Sunday evening is traditional Evening Prayer with a robed choir and a robed vicar. When Felicity first came to our church she found hatred welling up inside her towards me at the six o'clock service but noticed it subsiding during the eight o'clock informal service at which I do not wear clerical robes. This was a regular feature for her on Sunday evenings.

One day Judy prayed, 'Come, Holy Spirit,' over Felicity who then saw a picture of a gravestone engraved 'Mary Elizabeth, 1602'. They asked the Lord to show them what it meant and the details 'Sigmund 1597' flashed across Felicity's mind as she began seeing and experiencing some of the distress of a girl being raped by a priest in robes. Confessing, repenting, renouncing and cutting free in the name of Jesus then enabled Judy to cast out the demon which called itself 'Mary Elizabeth'.[8] The struggle with physical manifestations of distress came to an end when tension rose up through Felicity's body and out through her mouth with coughing and spluttering— an indication the demon had gone.

A strange story perhaps, but she and her family have worshipped happily in our church now for several years where I wear cassock and surplice every Sunday and the irrational fear of clergy robes has never returned. Felicity now sings in the robed choir.

Preparation

Once we have accepted the possibility that Christians can be demonised, we need to be prepared for demons to be exposed by the Holy Spirit when he comes. The same steps we take when we become Christians and are filled with the Holy Spirit are the same as those which protect us from evil spirits:

1. We believe and trust in Jesus.
2. We confess and repent of our sins.
3. We ask him to come to us by his Spirit.

I recommend that everyone who is offering or receiving ministry learns to do this every time before they begin any type of ministry. Here are a few practical tips I often share with team members:[9]

1. We minister in pairs, always with someone of the same sex as the counsellee present. The Gadarene demoniac cast off his clothes and we have found demons which tempt people to do the same. We met one lady like that and no matter how much she wanted me to minister, we kept it to ladies only.

2. Wandering eyes can be a problem for some men when ministering to ladies, and demons will make use of this. We also need to recognise that sometimes people find themselves adopting undignified positions during ministry sessions. Although jogging suits zipped up to the neck may not be very feminine attire, they are very sensible when tackling deliverance.

3. Some large people brought up in violent homes can manifest quite physically and be difficult to handle. We have found that if they fast, missing at least lunch and tea before an evening session, their manifestations are much smaller and quieter.

4. We never encourage anyone to try to cast demons out of non-Christians. Very rarely God may initiate this for evangelism purposes, but we do not initiate it ourselves. When non-Christians come to us for help we

invariably suggest they worship with us regularly for six months before we see them privately. We see deliverance as part of the whole Christian package, and healing as part of salvation. As Christians we do not offer ministry apart from Jesus.

5. Demons can easily transfer when ungodly soul-ties are established between counsellor and counsellee. Ungodly soul-ties are formed whenever we allow domination, manipulation and control to take place between those present. This can mean not allowing a person in need to dictate to us or to blackmail us emotionally, just as much as we do not try to put their lives right for them. It is often important to say prayers cutting us off from each other at the end of every session.

6. We do not look for demons or address them until the Holy Spirit has brought them to the surface and revealed them to us. Our aim, as in any counselling situation, is to pray, 'Come, Holy Spirit,' and let God dictate proceedings. Just because demons are in a person does not mean God's next step for us is always to try to evict them.

Diane became ill in her twenties and after several hospital tests was informed she had a serious illness. Friends suggested she try acupuncture. After failing to bring much relief or healing, the acupuncturist suggested spiritual healing, which eventually led her deeper and deeper into occult practices. Diane's condition deteriorated and in desperation she went to a church for help. In due course they referred her to us.

Despite several failed attempts to cast demons out of her, Diane surprisingly became a Christian and remained firm in her beliefs. We continued to try to help her. One Saturday morning three of us met with her again in a room at the back of the church. This time we were determined to let God have his way among us. We prayed, 'Come, Holy Spirit.'

Immediately Diane's teeth began to chatter, fear spread over her face and from time to time as she saw things in her mind she screamed very loudly. We pressed on, frequently praying words like, 'Holy Spirit, help Diane to see Jesus. Bring Jesus into the picture to sort out the problem.' God enabled her to see graphically the demonic forces which were influencing the people who had offered to help her and to see the seriousness of what she had done. The whole incident took about three hours with a break in the middle, and this is Diane's account of what happened:

When we asked the Holy Spirit to come and minister to us my teeth started to chatter and my body shook. Feelings of extreme terror poured into me to an almost overwhelming level. Then in my mind I found myself in the room of a lady who was an alternative medicine eyes specialist, who had been recommended to me. I looked into a machine that produced coloured rays of light before moving to sit in a chair at the side of the room where she came and stood behind me. I could see her hands running over my face while she was giving me spiritual healing and as I glanced up at her I knew why I was so frightened. She had the head of a demon and I was her prey.

But fear turned to hope as the door opened and Jesus walked in. He put out his arm and rebuked her. She cringed and slowly retreated into the furthest corner of the room, spitting and hissing as her tongue flicked in and out like that of a reptile. Jesus took the position she had occupied and stood behind me. He placed his hands over my face and eyes, took my hand and led me out of the room where he made long strokes with his hand, up and down and all around my body, saying, 'I cut you off. I cut you off from this influence.' The terror lifted and a feeling of peace and soothing descended upon me. I felt my head going to the side as though I was resting on something.

But only a few seconds passed before mounting fear was clutching at my heart again. I saw myself in the room of another lady to whom I had been going for spiritual healing.

I was lying on a couch in the middle of the room with her by my side. She too had the head of a demon and there were many other demons sitting around the couch. Her hands were webbed between the fingers which had sharp, hooked nails like a bird. She proceeded to lay them on me. I looked on at myself and knew I was powerless to do anything. I was in terrible anguish when the door opened and in walked Jesus. As he did so the demons all backed off, hissing and spitting. Jesus took my arm and led me out of the room. Once again he cut me off from all influence and this brought peace for a few more seconds.

There was precious little time to recover before I saw myself in the room of a man who was giving me spiritual healing. He too looked like a demon and I was quaking with fear. Jesus, as before, came in and cut me off from his influence.

I saw the spiritualist church I had attended and the healers in their white coats who likewise were all demons, and I left with Jesus.

The scene changed once more as I saw myself at home with my companion. We were using a pendulum and there were two demons in the room, laughing at us and mocking. Jesus came in, told them to hop it and ordered all demons out of the house, claiming it back for himself. I saw my companion and myself go down on our knees and kiss his hands.

I felt very relieved, but I knew it was not over, for the fear came back again overwhelmingly. I saw myself in the home of the clairvoyant I had visited. The atmosphere weighed me down as I sat at the table opposite a really vile demon. Then the door opened. Jesus walked straight over to the table, smashed his fist down in the middle of it, and said very aggressively, 'This must stop!' He took me out of the room and severely reprimanded me, telling me never to do this again. I looked back at the room where I had been and the clairvoyant was standing in the doorway feverishly trying to lure me back in.

Under the power of the Holy Spirit I eventually saw myself talking with the acupuncturist, the place where it had all begun. Although it was the same man I had seen, he had a massive black head. He led me over to his couch where I lay down and he began to put needles into me. A black substance oozed into me through the needles and my whole body began to turn black. I was in a terrible panic by this stage and I couldn't see Jesus anywhere. I seemed to be there for ages while these black creatures continued their wicked art. Then suddenly I saw Jesus standing right in the background of the room with his arms folded. I heard myself appealing to him, but he remained unmoved. Into my head came the fact that I had at one time intended to go into some form of alternative medicine if I recovered my own health. I repented of this and asked forgiveness for having received acupuncture. Only then did Jesus walk slowly and deliberately to the couch and pull the needles out of me. The black creatures moved out of his way, hissing and spitting, but they were clearly powerless to stop him. Jesus took my hand and helped me down from the couch. As he did so, the blackness left me and I returned to my normal colour. Outside, he told me that if I ever did anything like that again, far worse would befall me. He said I would be his disciple, proclaim the gospel and be obedient to him. He then walked away.

This decisive exit of Jesus indicated that the ministry for the day was over and that the episodes covered had been dealt with completely. It still amazes me to think that all we really did was to pray, 'Come, Holy Spirit,' and sit with Diane for about three hours while Jesus revealed her sins, convicted her of them and helped her to repent. Diane had not been totally convinced acupuncture was wrong prior to this moment.[10] For those who doubt the validity of this type of ministry it is worth recording that not only has Diane's life been changed by Jesus, but many members of her family have now become committed Christians.

Deliverance

Once we have all confessed and repented of our sins, declared our belief in Jesus, maybe worshipped and read a suitable passage of Scripture—none of which need take more than half an hour in a two-hour interview—we invite the Holy Spirit to come. If a demon then comes to the surface and the person is happy for deliverance to take place, the simple procedure I often adopt is as follows:[11]

'Demon of Satan, in the name of Jesus I command you to tell me your name.' The demon may speak or the person may say something like, 'I think it is "anger".' Then I would say, 'Demon of anger, in the name of Jesus I command you to go to Jesus, to the place appointed by him, and never return. Out! In the name of Jesus.' Like putting a naughty child to bed, evil spirits do not always leave at the first command, but if one seems to be moving I persist confidently without shouting.

A cough, a yawn, a flickering of the eyes, a sudden release of pressure, or something more dramatic may be an indication to those present when it has left. The person normally knows himself when it has gone. We then pray, 'Come, Holy Spirit,' once more and look to see what the Father is doing. If another demon appears we repeat the process. If the person receives blessing and peace we minister as for blessing.

Sometimes there appear to be many demons and if they come up quickly and go easily it often speeds things up to command the head demon to come to the surface and tell us its name. Once this has taken place I may use words like, 'Demon of Beelzebub, I command you in the name of Jesus to release every demon under your authority!' We might then see a mass exodus in a short time. This seems to have happened biblically in the case of Legion. Jesus addressed the head demon Legion, even though there were many demons present, and everything appeared to leave at once (Mk 5:1–20). We then command 'Beelzebub', or whatever the head demon is called, to leave in Jesus' name. If this does not work there may simply be too many for our level of faith, so we return to doing them one by one.

If demons continue to come up and leave, it is probably right in the last quarter of an hour to bind any that are left in the name of Jesus, and command them to be silent. We then ask the Lord to bring blessing and peace. For those undergoing deliverance who have difficulty in sleeping, we have found saying 'Compline' together can be a great help.[12]

In conclusion, we say prayers, cutting ourselves off from one another and anything we have seen and heard which is better forgotten, and we pray a blessing on all who have been present.

Sometimes, though, manifesting demons do not leave when commanded to do so.

If demons do not leave

If we remove the ground on which demons stand they will normally leave when commanded to do so in the name of Jesus. If a demon does not leave it means there is more work to be done on the ground. I sometimes picture it like this: If twenty policemen come to a house to evict three squatters, they have all the power and all the authority to remove them, unless the owner of the house gives the squatters permission to stay. Through Jesus, Christians have the power of the Holy Spirit and the authority of God the Father to remove demons, unless the owner of the house gives them permission to stay.

In that situation a counsellor can easily become frustrated, start shouting and continue ministering beyond the anointing of God, causing himself and others all kinds of problems. I know; I've done it. A lady who has been abused by men will not be helped by another man shouting at her. If demons do not go comfortably we stop and talk. If something manifests which seems to have no root in the person's own life, as in the case of Mervyn, then we seek to undo whatever was done in the past, in the name of Jesus. We cut off, divorce, confess, repent and renounce in relation to ancestors' sin; we honour, forgive and bless the good things about them. With sin done to us, we express our hatred of the sin, agree with God's hatred of the sin, and forgive the sinner. With sins we have committed, we identify them, confess, repent and renounce them, and receive God's absolution granted to us through the blood of Jesus and made effective in our lives by the Holy Spirit. We see our own lives as God sees them through Jesus and forgive ourselves. This usually removes the ground on which demons stand.

One of the most effective sessions of deliverance I have so far witnessed took place at Ellel Grange.[13] Two experienced counsellors, Madeleine and Edwin, spent a couple of days ministering to a clergyman who at the time had known the Lord in a personal and committed way for twenty-eight years. They had already seen him previously for two or three sessions on a three-day healing retreat, at which time some demons had apparently left.

In the morning the clergyman shared about a recent bereavement and his participation in several powerful sessions of ministry in the Holy Spirit at his church over the weekend, during which time he had suffered headaches followed by bouts of yawning and coughing, which he had interpreted as demons leaving. But most of the morning was spent talking about dying to self and the problems he still faced with the need to achieve and the desire to be liked.

Lunch came and went and the session continued. Nobody seemed to be in any great hurry to talk about demons or to address them. Problems at the church and the difficulties of other members were as readily talked about as the clergyman's own struggles towards holiness. As the situation of one church person was shared, so the counsellee realised his own wrongful attitude, but otherwise some of the talking and sharing seemed quite irrelevant to the job in hand. Edwin and Madeleine listened sensitively, encouraged where necessary and only occasionally offered words of analysis or ideas of their own.

Time went by. Approaching afternoon tea-time, a major issue appeared to be clarified. Driven to achieve and be successful as a child by reprimands from Father and teachers, especially at school report times, the image of God as a schoolmaster with a cane emerged from the discussion. Naturally the counsellee, with his years of Bible reading and training, knew in his mind that 'there is now no condemnation for those who are in Christ Jesus' (Rom 8:1), but there was a credibility gap between head and feelings. Madeleine spoke of the difference between the conscience which condemns (Rom 2:15,27) and the Holy Spirit who convicts (Jn 16:8). The clergyman struggled with this teaching for a while, but it was eventually obvious to all that whenever he sinned he felt condemned rather than convicted.

After a brief cup of tea Edwin felt prompted to ask about a friend who had died which led into discussions concerning certain other relationships. It was thought—perhaps just to make sure—that the counsellee should be cut off from certain people where ungodly soul-ties might have been formed. By now it was five to six and the evening meal was due at half past. Everything seemed to be progressing decently and in order: a bit of cutting off, maybe cast out a troublesome demon or two, an evening meal and a relaxed time in front of the log fire with a good book.

But the cutting off was delayed. Madeleine suddenly challenged the clergyman: did he, would he in all circumstances, trust the Lord? Would he, for example, be prepared to jump off the top of Ellel Grange into the arms of Jesus? The clergyman struggled to answer the question, using his verbal skills until Edwin came in. 'That's just words,' he said. 'You know what the real answer is.'

The atmosphere changed. A pleasant day's discussion and quiet relaxation in an armchair flew out of the window. The clergyman seemed to undergo a personality change. The tone of his voice altered. Madeleine and Edwin were no longer his friends. Rejection and anger were showing themselves. 'We are no longer talking to the same person,' said Madeleine.

The evening meal was delayed and the clergyman struggled to stay in the room in what now appeared to be a hostile environment. 'This is a demon of control,' asserted Madeleine. 'I think we need to stay and deal with it.' Once the real enemy was perceived as demonic rather than human, some tension was relieved and ministry was able to begin.

Curses from the past were broken and demons appeared to leave through yawning and coughing. The spirit of mind control was identified as 'Antichrist' and left on command after the clergyman confessed to a wrong image of Christ within himself. When the spirit of death manifested, the face became pale and the right hand cold and clammy. As it was challenged the left hand also became like a dead man's hand until the demon left in a burst of coughing. Almost immediately the face regained its colour and both hands heated up considerably as the Holy Spirit brought blessing and confirmation of 'death's' departure. The ministry continued until bed-time.

In the middle of the night the clergyman woke up feeling emotionally drained but different. So many thoughts and inner voices seemed to have gone and a new loving, affirming Christ appeared centrally in his mind.

After a day's rest there was a further morning of talk and an afternoon of deliverance before the clergyman returned home tired but feeling like a new creation. His wife instantly knew the difference. His congregation gradually began to comment on the welcome change. The materialists will doubt it all. The liberals will fit these people's experience into their own worldview. The sceptics may ask me how I know the ministry to the clergyman was really authentic, effective and validated by the test of time. I can answer them quite simply, 'It was me.'

Notes

1. The Kansas City Prophets assisted John Wimber and Mike Bickle in a conference on 'Prophecy' held at Holy Trinity Church in July 1990.

2. All counsellees' names in this chapter have been changed.

3. Peter H. Lawrence, *The Hot Line* (Kingsway Publications: Eastbourne, 1990), p 277.

4. Noel and Phyl Gibson have written a helpful book entitled *Evicting Demonic Squatters & Breaking Bondages* (Freedom in Christ Ministries Trust: Drummoyne, NSW, Australia, 1987).

   Their book *Deliver Our Children from the Evil One* is also worth reading, especially for parents and youth leaders. (Same publisher, 1989.)

5. Some scholars argue that the longer ending of Mark was not in the earliest manuscripts, but even if this is so, it nevertheless reflects the practice and experience of the early church, and is worth noting.

6. Norman Warren, *Journey into Life* (Falcon Books, Kingsway Publications: Eastbourne, 1964), p 13.

7. Roger Jones, formerly director of music at Christ Church, is our lay reader. Composer of twelve Christian musicals, he now works full time for Christian Music Ministries, 325 Bromford Road, Birmingham B36 8ET. He is the same Roger who helped me minister to Mervyn.

8. A demon calling itself 'Mary Elizabeth', just like the demon of 'Derek' in the preceding illustration, must never be confused with the human spirits of Mary Elizabeth and Derek. These are merely demons who have assumed such identities for themselves because of their association with those people in the past.

9. Each denomination differs greatly about who may tackle deliverance. The Eastern Church allows 'charismatic' lay people (male or female) or monastics who are popularly recognised as being able to perform such a function. On the other hand, the Church of Scotland in 1976 received a report which suggested, 'There is no place in the Reformed Scottish tradition for such a rite to be devised.'

In the book *Deliverance* the Christian Exorcism Study Group suggests the following in keeping with Roman Catholic tradition: 'Minor exorcism, that is a prayer to God in the name of Christ, directed against the powers of evil, can be carried out by any baptized Christian.' In contrast 'major exorcism' carried out on a 'possessed' person must have a member of the Diocesan advisory team present. (*Deliverance* edited by Michael Perry [SPCK: London, 1987].)

As I see it neither 'exorcism' nor 'possession' are biblical words. 'Deliverance' seems to come between 'minor' and 'major' exorcism in practice and our assistant bishop has given me permission for this as long as I keep him informed of what we are doing, and everything done at Christ Church happens with my knowledge and under my authority. Each church and denomination will have to decide for themselves how to proceed, but it seems right to me always to come under godly authority.

10. Most Christian ministers who are experienced in deliverance include acupuncture on their lists of occult-related practices, but by no means all Christians are agreed on this analysis. A reasonably objective airing of most of the relevant issues can be found in Samuel Pfeifer's book, *Healing at Any Price?* (Word UK Ltd: Milton Keynes, 1988).

11. My teaching on the way I tackle deliverance included in this chapter is not intended to encourage every Christian to have a go. I think it is important to share that we have found new Christians are not only more ineffective than mature Christians in deliverance but can in fact harm themselves or the counsellee through inexperience. We have also found it necessary to limit the activities of those who rejoice in the number of demons which leave rather than the names which are written in the book of life. We always advise inexperienced team members to accompany the more experienced at first and ensure everything is done under my authority and with my permission.

12. *The Office of Compline—an Alternative Order* compiled by the Revd R. D. Silk (Mowbray: London & Oxford, 1980).

13. Ellel Grange is a centre for training and ministry in Christian healing and counselling near Lancaster. As I write they are in the process of setting up a similar centre in the south at Glyndley Manor, near Eastbourne.

8

Physical Healing

Iris woke up one Wednesday morning and started to prepare for work. She had a peculiar feeling in her head and decided to go back to bed instead of going to work. She was sick once.

Not thinking anything was amiss, Jeff, her husband, went to work on Thursday. Iris' neighbour had a key to their house and, noticing that the curtains were still drawn at ten o'clock, she went in and found Iris still in bed. She phoned for Jeff to come home immediately and he called the doctor. Iris was admitted to East Birmingham Hospital on Friday and transferred to Smethwick Neurosurgical Unit on Saturday.

By Sunday afternoon information filtered through to me that Iris was critically ill, and we were asked to pray for her in church. Everyone was very concerned. The doctors had diagnosed an arachnoid haemorrhage and had told Jeff an operation was necessary, adding that the chances of success were only about fifty-fifty. Permission was duly granted for the operation to take place first thing on Monday morning. As soon as I heard this I was keen to visit that night and pray for her to be healed.

I asked God about it and sensed that he wanted me to go ahead, but I knew I needed help. At the six o'clock service in church I knelt before the congregation as some of them laid on hands and prayed for the Holy Spirit to come upon me. I sensed power and warmth as they asked specifically for God's anointing and the healing touch of Jesus for that night. I visited Iris after the service, quite late. Though delicate, she was conscious and pleased to see me. I held up my hand over her head, not wanting to cause any more discomfort by touching her, and prayed, 'Come, Holy Spirit.' I waited quietly for a couple of minutes and then withdrew my hand. It was short and quiet. Iris thanked me and I slipped away soon afterwards.

In the morning the specialist visited Iris and decided there was no longer any need to operate. To our delight she made a full recovery.

This was an emergency situation when prayer was all that was possible and all that was needed. I am sure much of the battle was won during our time of intercession at the six o'clock service, although I believe praying for God's anointing over me, followed by my doing the same with Iris, played an important part.

Sarah was also healed of a headache when people prayed for the Holy Spirit to come upon her. She wasn't suffering from a hob-nail boot experience, nor was there acute pain, but life would definitely have been more abundant without it. It came on Friday, was still there on Saturday and accompanied Sarah to church on Sunday evening. At our young people's meeting after the service two teenagers laid hands on Sarah very gently and prayed in the usual way. Slowly and quietly she went out in the Spirit, keeled over on the seat and came round five minutes later without the headache. Neat, simple, cheaper than aspirin, and no side effects. Sarah was very grateful to God for her healing.

Some headaches are the result of emotional stress or hurt. I prayed, 'Come, Holy Spirit,' in our own church at one of our courses. During the ministry time a lady developed a very bad headache and people began to pray with her. As they did so and laid on hands the headache became worse so they called me. There was obvious distress on her face so I immediately prayed, 'Holy Spirit, come and help Lucy to see Jesus.'

Quite suddenly Lucy began to see Jesus on the cross. It was a close-up of his face, showing something of the intense agony and suffering our Lord went through as he took our sin upon himself. Slowly Lucy began to see more of the picture, as if the camera were moving along the beam to where one of his hands was nailed. There, beneath the pierced flesh, fixed also to the cross by a nail, was a little bottle of tablets. Lucy's husband had suffered from heart trouble and the day he died suddenly of a heart attack Lucy could not remember giving him his pills.

Being a mature Christian, Lucy knew what God was saying, what needed to be done and what was causing the headache: Jesus had died for her sins on the cross, but she was still carrying false guilt in her own body and suffering from the scars. She gave it to Jesus, accepted his forgiveness, forgave herself and then, as God's Spirit continued to flow upon her, the headache went.

Sometimes headaches can be caused by demons. I asked the Holy Spirit to come in another church where I had been invited to speak and minister. It was very noticeable to several people by the end of the session that one lady was suffering from a very bad headache. It became worse as people tried to pray or lay on hands. In the privacy of a small back room I asked the Spirit to come on her again and commanded a demon to leave in the name of Jesus. The headache became worse, pressure in the head intensified, then suddenly there was an explosion in the mouth, a burp and the headache was gone.

Iris was healed bodily after many church friends had interceded for her and prayed for God's grace to flow through me. Sarah was very simply and neatly healed by God as he switched her tense mind off and then on again.

Lucy came to emotional wholeness by receiving God's forgiveness and forgiving herself, while the lady with the spiritual problem of a demon needed deliverance. Every one had a physical headache, but every one needed a different kind of healing, and every one's healing began when we prayed, 'Come, Holy Spirit.'

We try to keep it simple. I teach our ministry team members to pray, 'Come, Holy Spirit,' as soon as the sick person is prepared and at ease. In this way we let God make the diagnostic decision as to what needs attention. We avoid trying to make human decisions about the root of a person's problem until we have first asked God to come.[1]

With Iris there was no opportunity to talk first and with Sarah it was unnecessary; Lucy and the demonised lady found the root of their problems exposed by the Holy Spirit in seconds, and appropriate action was not difficult or lengthy. Once we have asked the Holy Spirit to come on a physically sick person we can then follow biblical procedures according to what God is doing or revealing to us.

If the Spirit does not appear to come on a person, we suggest he may need to repent of his sin towards God and especially his wrong image of God. If God comes and highlights emotional damage, we help him towards forgiving those who have caused it. We consider deliverance only after God has brought a demon to the surface. If it refuses to go, we try to help people receive God's forgiveness, forgive themselves, be sure of their forgiven status in Christ, and if necessary forgive others, including their ancestors. If God sovereignly comes and begins a work of healing, we co-operate with him and bless what he is doing, sometimes giving short commands such as Jesus did—be clean, be healed, be open—as applicable. It is amazing how many can be helped or healed by praying simply for the Holy Spirit to come and then waiting to see what the Father is doing.

The principles I have already outlined in earlier chapters for learning to pray, 'Come, Holy Spirit,' over others are sometimes sufficient for helping people to receive God's healing. Being aware, however, of the different ways God uses to bring a person to health and wholeness will often assist the ministry team member in co-operating with what God is doing, especially if healing is not instantaneous. Here are seven different approaches I have seen God use:

1. Organic healing

When Iris became ill and was rushed to hospital there was something organically wrong with her. There was no evidence to suggest her sickness was anything other than physical.

Jesus and his disciples 'saw a man blind from birth. His disciples asked him, "Rabbi, who sinned, this man or his parents, that he was born blind?" "Neither this man nor his parents sinned," said Jesus' (Jn 9:1–3). Why Jesus then proceeded to put mud on his eyes and tell him to wash it off is unclear. Whatever the reason was for the mud, the man was organically ill and organically healed.

Sometimes praying, 'Come, Holy Spirit,' is all that is necessary for a person to be organically healed by God.

Roger Jones invited the Holy Spirit to move among us at the conclusion of a performance of his musical *Mary Magdalene*, which we put on in church.[2] Seventy-seven-year-old Daisy had a badly swollen knee which was preventing her from visiting sick friends and relations. As the Spirit came, Daisy's left leg started swinging backwards and forwards. Team members gathered round to bless what the Father was doing and command the knee to be healed in Jesus' name. When the leg stopped moving, all the swelling had gone down and Daisy was able to go visiting again.

2. Spiritual healing

We all have to face the practical fact of non-physical healing at times when ministering to others. Sometimes when prayer for physical healing is not successful, there can still be great spiritual blessings received.

There were three people recorded in the Gospels who died and were raised from the dead by Jesus (Mk 5:41; Lk 7:14–15; Jn 11:43–44). There were another three people recorded in the Gospels whom Jesus did not heal nor rescue from death. One of them asked Jesus to heal him before he died; one of them asked Jesus to save him before he died; one of them asked God not to let him die. All three died on Good Friday nailed to wooden crosses. Admittedly the circumstances were somewhat abnormal, but even so the principles found in the story are frequently applicable to more common situations.

One of the criminals who hung there hurled insults at him: 'Aren't you the Christ? Save yourself and us!' (Lk 23:39). In his unbelief the man sinned against God, received no healing and no blessing from Jesus. When the Holy Spirit does not manifest upon a sick person and he receives no healing and no blessing then he may need to repent of his sin towards God.

The other criminal said, ' "Jesus, remember me when you come into your kingdom." Jesus answered him, "I tell you the truth, today you will be with me in paradise" ' (Lk 23:42–43).

There was no physical healing for the repentant criminal who believed in Jesus, but there was a considerable degree of spiritual healing. It could be argued that he was far better off at the end of Good Friday than Barabbas.

Sometimes God's Holy Spirit comes on a sick person to give him a spiritual blessing rather than physical healing.

If the Spirit comes on a person who is ill, we bless what the Father is doing and at an appropriate moment, often when power and heat are felt in the affected area, we command the sickness to be healed in Jesus' name. If we are not sure of the situation, it is normally possible to find out what God is doing by asking the person at intervals what is happening. If the sick person senses physical power or improvement, we continue to speak healing in Jesus' name to the sickness. If not physically healed, the person will probably still receive blessing, and if this process is repeated several times it may be that faith will grow each time until full healing is received. If after some time nothing physical is happening but God is still coming in power, we bless what God is doing or minister to distress as described in Chapter 3. There are times when an encounter with the living God may well be sufficient for the hour.[3]

Bob developed cancer in his early forties, apparently due to industrial contamination through working with blue asbestos. His wife Janet shared this with me so I visited them several times in their home. Strange as it may sound to those unfamiliar with ministering to the seriously ill, I considered it a rare privilege to visit this family. As the illness advanced Janet and Bob shared more and more intimately, their faith in Christ deepened and they stared the final enemy of death firmly in the face without any 'let's pretend' games.

On one visit I pushed Bob hard to make sure he knew Christ personally. I wanted to be sure that he had dealt with his sins, had experienced the assurance of God's forgiveness and believed Jesus was preparing a place for him in heaven. Unless I sense God telling me otherwise I invariably consider the assurance of salvation through Christ to have greater priority than physical healing.

Feeling satisfied on the first score, we then talked freely together about healing. I offered no guarantees, but laid on hands and prayed, 'Come, Holy Spirit,' each time I visited. Always he received blessing, sometimes the pain was alleviated, but there were no signs of long-term remission or healing.

One day, as I paused outside the house to pray, I thought God was saying to me, 'This is the last time you will see Bob.'

'So how shall I minister, Lord?' I asked.

'Nothing special,' was the reply. 'Love him and pray for him as normal.'

This I did, laying-on hands towards the end of our meeting, inviting the Holy Spirit to come and do all he wanted to do. Power came upon him as the peace of God registered upon his face and eventually I became more comfortable about leaving him in the hands of God.

The following week I went into hospital myself for a minor operation and afterwards was told to take three weeks' rest from work. The day I returned to work was a Sunday and very early, before the first service, I received a phone call. 'It's Janet here,' the voice said. 'Bob died this morning.'

I had planned to visit first thing the following morning, so I did. At the funeral I was able to share with Janet and the family the story of what I thought God had said to me—a small confirmation that Bob was now in the presence of his Lord. God did not do what we had hoped he would do, but there is no doubt in my mind that he blessed Bob and prepared him for death in a beautiful way.

All ministry team members have to cope with people who are not healed. We can theologise and philosophise on the reasons until the Lord comes again, but in the meantime we have to help those who remain infirm. It is my opinion that every believer can be filled with the

Holy Spirit and receive some form of blessing when loving Christians lay-on hands and pray, 'Come, Holy Spirit,' even if we do not see everyone being physically healed. We all have to die at some time.[4]

In practice I am often more concerned with those who feel nothing ever happens to them than those who are not physically healed. We pray daily for more power, more healing, more love and more of Jesus, but we are learning to leave the big 'Why?' and 'Why not?' questions to him. It is comforting to know that Jesus could have called on legions of angels to heal the three who died on Good Friday, but he chose not to do so.

3. Healing the sceptic

Being the only Christian at work is never easy, but in times of trouble a faithful witness given over years can bear fruit. Invitations to healing services will often be accepted by unbelievers who are unwell.

One young lady worked in a very posh house where a member of the family discovered he was suffering from an incurable disease. The young lady was not confident in praying for the sick herself, but she had great confidence in someone else she knew who had been used of God to heal people before. Accordingly, she recommended him at an appropriate moment and the very sick man agreed to see him.

After a lengthy journey the patient arrived with a few friends at the lowly religious establishment—tired, irritable and far from well. He knocked at the door and a member of the staff answered it.

'He's too busy to see you right now,' the man said when he knew their business, 'but he says go take a bath in the river down the road and you will be healed.'

The posh, important, wealthy man nearly exploded. Never in his life had Naaman been treated like this, but before he could remonstrate the door was closed firmly in his face.

I have always felt sorry for the commander of King Aram's army who had leprosy (2 Kings 5). On the recommendation of his wife's maid he travelled with his entourage from one king to another until he arrived at Elisha's house, only to be given a message from his servant. Dipping seven times in the Jordan in front of his servants might have seemed demeaning, but what a result!

Jesus said, 'There were many in Israel with leprosy in the time of Elisha the prophet, yet not one of them was cleansed—only Naaman the Syrian' (Lk 4:27). Despite his scepticism the commander still obeyed the word of the Lord and was healed.

There are times when praying, 'Come, Holy Spirit,' can also bring healing to the sceptic if he is willing to give God a try.

Philip is a policeman who, according to his own testimony, was brought against his better judgement to one of our meetings. This is what he wrote afterwards:

Peter called on the Holy Spirit to come down upon us. We stood in silence, but nothing in particular happened to me. Peter encouraged people to relax and let the Holy Spirit work, and not to worry if they didn't feel any different. At this stage I did feel different—if you hold your arms out long enough the blood will drain from them and they'll go cold!

I did my best to concentrate, but my belief was stretched to the limit...I remember thinking to myself, 'Oh well, I'm not going anywhere. I might just as well put my brain into neutral and see what happens.' We must have been standing there for quarter of an hour before Peter had finished. Nothing happened.

The following morning, however, I felt different. I wasn't quite sure why, but I definitely felt different. It slowly dawned on me that I hadn't got backache! I had been diagnosed as having a slipped disc about seven years earlier, and over the years I had gradually become accustomed to a nagging pain. The pain was gone. I couldn't fathom it out, and kept it to myself just in case it was a temporary reprieve. I hesitantly told my wife that afternoon that I thought my back was better.

I was so exhilarated I set about a task I had long avoided—replacing a rotten old back door. Ironically this work gave me backache, but I was overjoyed. It was the kind of backache caused by heavy work stretching little-used muscles, something I hadn't felt for years. I then realised I had been avoiding that sort of exertion because of my bad back. That evening I was surprised to hear my knees crack as I got into the bath—my bad back meant I had been carefully lowering myself in without bending, but now I could sit straight down in the water without a second thought.

About six months later I had to have a full medical check-up in connection with my work. At the end I asked the doctor to have another look at my back. After some bending exercises and feeling my back, she said there wasn't any sign of anything wrong.

The healing experience has turned out to be something more than physical healing. I have learned a great deal from it, because I know it was God's way of opening my eyes to the power of the Holy Spirit. What is remarkable is that the Bible is full of examples of the Holy Spirit working through Jesus and his disciples, but I must have glossed over the bits which didn't make sense. Now I know better.

When Naaman was healed of his leprosy he became a believer in God (2 Kings 5:15). When Philip's back was healed he became a believer in the presence of the Holy Spirit for today. Sometimes when the power of God moves on a sceptic who is willing to taste and see, he is healed in body and in spirit and finds peace in his soul.

4. Healing and evangelism

When people are healed by Jesus they often tell their friends about him, then instead of inviting the sceptic to a meeting, the healed person goes out into the world to share the good news with others.

A man with leprosy met Jesus and was healed. Despite instruction to the contrary, 'he went out and began to talk freely, spreading the news' (Mk 1:45).

In the region of the Gerasenes Jesus freed one of the most demonised men in the Bible. Following this, 'the man went away and began to tell in the Decapolis how much Jesus had done for him. And all the people were amazed' (Mk 5:20).

Some people brought a deaf and mute man to Jesus and he healed him. 'Jesus commanded them not to tell anyone. But the more he did so, the more they kept talking about it' (Mk 7:36).

Whenever people meet Jesus and are healed it seems they cannot stop themselves from telling others about it.

Sister Christine Morris is a friend who works in the next-door parish, and sometimes we help one another when ministering to individuals. She kindly wrote this down for me:

> Ann, the lady who comes to clean my house, had a bad viral infection of the chest and so before she began work Mary, Margaret and I laid hands on her. (Well, I didn't want her collapsing before she had done the housework!) I had never prayed for her before and so we explained she was to try and picture Jesus, and relax. She was very soon engaged by the Spirit and began to give a running commentary on what was happening.
>
> She was on a mountain with trees, flowers and sunshine, breathing in the fresh mountain air, when she saw Jesus coming towards her, dressed as a shepherd, with a lamb in his arms. At this point she began waving her arms in front of her and told us that Jesus had come up to

her and she wanted to hug him. We encouraged her to go along with what the Spirit was doing and so she hugged him and he hugged her back. When she finally came back to my sitting room from the mountain-top she could breathe clearly and had no further problems. She did the housework and went home running up the road, absolutely thrilled at what God had done for her, telling everyone she met.

When we pray, 'Come, Holy Spirit,' people sometimes meet Jesus, are healed and cannot stop telling their friends all about it.

5. Forgiving self

'When Jesus saw their faith, he said to the paralytic, "Son, your sins are forgiven" ' (Mk 2:5).

The paralytic would have known the Old Testament well. In the Book of Exodus we read how the Egyptians sinned against God's people, refused God's request to let them go and worship, and as a result suffered many plagues including death. Whenever the people of Israel sinned in the desert disease and death came upon them as well. Much of the teaching in the Old Testament links disease with sin. The exception is the Book of Job.

The sick man who was lowered through the roof was a sinner. Maybe his own sin had caused his disability. More likely, 'Job's comforters' had kept telling him he must be a bad sinner to be so seriously crippled. He needed forgiveness. He needed to accept his own forgiveness. He needed to forgive himself before he could receive God's power to heal him. Jesus helped him in this way by assuring him his sins were forgiven. Forgiving self is often one of the most important and yet hardest things to do when seeking healing.

One of the clergy wives in Malawi asked to see me. She had suffered severe pain in the abdomen for several years and no one was able to help her. Some suggested going to the local 'healers', but she told me they normally prescribed all kinds of evil methods using chicken entrails and, being a Christian, she was not prepared to do this. I encouraged her to stay away from such 'healers' at all costs.

This lady attended several of our sessions when I invited the Holy Spirit to come, but nothing eased her abdominal pain so I asked her what was happening in her life when the pain first started. Progress was slow through an interpreter, but this is what she told me: For a few days she was delighted to be asked to look after her first grandchild. Children are greatly loved, treasured and affirmed in Malawi. During this time she and her husband attended a meeting and asked a friend to look after the grandchild for a few hours. While she was away the child became ill, was rushed to hospital but died there. No one was to blame. The child-minder did everything right. Grandma could not have done any more, but she was unable to forgive herself.

With this in mind I prayed, 'Come, Holy Spirit,' once more. I asked God to help the lady in the area of her bereavement and she saw the child in her mind running to Jesus and going off very happily with him, hand in hand. We then led her through a short time of accepting God's forgiveness and forgiving herself, before asking the Holy Spirit once more to come on the stomach pain. This time heat and blessing came in the affected area, the pain left and she felt much better. Receiving forgiveness and feeling forgiven can be very important steps to being healed.

6. Forgiving others

Jesus saw a man by a pool who had been an invalid for thirty-eight years. 'He asked him, "Do you want to get well?" ' (Jn 5:6). The man did not answer Jesus' question but blamed others for not getting well. ' "Sir," the invalid replied, "I have no-one to help me into the pool when the water is stirred. While I am trying to get in, someone else goes down ahead of me" ' (Jn 5:7).

From the brief account in John 5 it appears we have a man who regularly blamed others. After Jesus had healed him the former invalid was accused of breaking the Sabbath laws by picking up his mat and walking. He replied, 'The man who made me well said to me, "Pick up your mat and walk" ' (Jn 5:11).

Jesus then delivered a stern warning, telling him that if he did not change his ways he would become even more seriously ill (Jn 5:14). Instead of blaming others, the man needed to begin forgiving others if he was to remain whole. We have found forgiving others is often an important factor in being healed and staying healed.

Marie was very seriously sexually abused from the age of eighteen months to fourteen years. Her mother said she didn't want her before she was born and she didn't want her after she was born, and she often beat her. Marie always blamed her mother for knowing what was going on and doing nothing about it.

After she left home Marie fed on the hatred she felt for her mother. I remember her saying to me, 'Peter, you've no idea how good it tastes to hate when you've suffered as I have.' All I could do was stand there passively. I cannot possibly know what it is like to suffer in this way.

By the time she was middle-aged Marie was riddled from head to toe with arthritis. One day the power of the Holy Spirit came upon her and she knew God was telling her to go and see her mother and forgive her. Marie pictured it in her mind. There was no way she could see it working. Her mother would reject her as she always had done.

Even so, she obeyed what she thought God was saying. Her mother answered the door and Marie fell into her arms as they both experienced reconciliation and forgiveness. As they sat and talked her mother felt able to relate experiences from her own childhood which she had never shared with anyone before. Marie's mother had been a victim of sexual abuse herself. Marie was then able to wrap her arms around her and bring comfort as her mother was released from a tremendous life-long burden at the age of seventy.

Marie did not notice it at first, but later she realised her pains had all gone. Interestingly, one little area in her big toe joint still caused some trouble, so she saw a doctor. No, he said, that was not arthritis. It was caused by a genetic fault in the ankle. Over three years later the arthritic pains have not returned. Every day Marie asks for God to send his forgiving love to her mother.

7. Demons and sickness

'A man who was demon-possessed [demonised] and could not talk was brought to Jesus. And when the demon was driven out, the man who had been dumb spoke' (Mt 9:32–33).

Sometimes a demon is the problem and when it is cast out the problem goes. I prayed for one teenage lad who could not see very well, and almost immediately his face contorted as a venomous-sounding, unrecognisable language poured out of him. I challenged the demon in Jesus' name. There was a brief struggle, a bout of coughing and then peace registered on his face. When he opened his eyes he could see clearly. The whole episode took less than five minutes. There was no need to pray for healing as his sight was restored the moment the demon departed.

Sometimes a demon causes the problem and then healing

becomes a two-stage process. It is rather like squatters doing damage to the house. When the squatters have been evicted the damage remains and restoration work becomes necessary.

Jesus healed a woman 'who had been crippled by a spirit for eighteen years' (Lk 13:11). First Jesus said to her, ' "Woman, you are set free from your infirmity." Then he put his hands on her, and immediately she straightened up and praised God' (Lk 13:12–13).

It is not absolutely clear what Jesus was doing, but it is possible the word may have removed a demon and the touch healed her back.

Our most dramatic case involved a mother and her son. I am not too sure how demons in parents affect children, but we do know that parents' faith in Jesus can bring deliverance to their children (Mt 15:21–28; Mk 9:14–29). A five-year-old boy had a tumour in his neck which could not be removed surgically because of its position. His non-Christian parents asked us to help. He was not expected to live for much more than a year. During several visits the mother repented of her sins, became a Christian, received the Holy Spirit, spoke in tongues and was delivered of several very big and difficult demons. We then laid hands on the boy's neck and prayed, 'Come, Holy Spirit.' The day after we prayed an X-ray showed the tumour had gone down more than fifty per cent, and in due course it went completely. Five years later he has been officially classified as cured by the hospital, and he is doing well at school. Maybe this is an example of the way the sins of the parents which are visited on the children can be healed through their parents' repentance.

I am sure a failure to take demons seriously will reduce our effectiveness in healing the sick.

Staying well

' "See, you are well again. Stop sinning or something worse may happen to you" ' (Jn 5:14).

When God heals people of organic illnesses which are not attached to emotional or demonic roots I would expect them to remain permanently healed in that area for the rest of their lives. On the other hand, if the Holy Spirit has exposed other causes than the presenting symptoms in the process of bringing healing, the need to change lifestyle and beliefs becomes imperative if they are to stay well. When most people talk about healing they mean, 'Put me back to where I was,' but 'where I was' is invariably the place where I became sick. Healing or wholeness in the Bible is much more a case of going on to become what God wants me to be in Christ rather than going back.

It is very common in churches where hands are regularly laid on the sick to find that people who are healed on a Sunday report that their symptoms have returned by Wednesday. The basic problem is often that the root cause has not been put right; it is much easier to be a Christian in church than in the High Street.

If unforgiveness is the root of my illness I not only need to forgive on the Sunday to be healed, but I need to go on forgiving on the Wednesday to remain healed. I do not have to be perfect to stay whole, but I do need to know how to deal with sin if it occurs.

If I find my symptoms returning or anger rising up in me against the person I have already forgiven, then I probably need to do some more work on repenting and forgiving as soon as I can. Marie reported to me that the first six months after she had forgiven her mother and been healed it felt like intense spiritual warfare. During this time the old lifestyle of hate was gradually pulled down and replaced by the new lifestyle of forgiveness, but it was a daily battle. After the first six months, Marie said, the struggle lessened considerably and she began to feel peace and healing had come to stay. Instant, permanent healing is not always a realistic expectation when physical sickness is related to deep problems, but persistent prayer and faith will often bring its rewards.

It is considerably easier remaining in an attitude of forgiveness towards someone who has died or with whom we no longer live than to deal with the kind of problems a regularly battered or abused wife faces. Someone like myself who has never experienced violence in the home may at times be too quick to suggest separation. It is amazing what some people can survive by the grace of God, but they will often need much prayer and support. To see someone who has just been healed walking out of church and back into the place of pain is one of the hardest burdens in God's healing ministry. I think it is usually right to let the person decide for herself when enough is enough.

With someone like Lucy who experienced physical ailments due to bereavement, guilt or false guilt, healing can sometimes be a complicated process.

I prayed for one lady who was in constant agony. She couldn't sit, stand or lie down in any position without pain. Doctors had prescribed painkillers which were having little effect. The problem was diagnosed as trapped sciatic nerves down one side.

'How long have you had the pain?' I asked as a conversation-starter.

'Since my sister died,' she said instantly, without thinking about it. Her eldest sister had died at a good old age, as a Christian, in the sure and certain hope she was going to be with her Lord. Every week the two of them went shopping together in town and saw each other quite regularly. They were very fond of each other and had a good relationship. But this was the first one of her

brothers and sisters to die, and somehow irrational feelings had taken her over. 'If only I'd done this. I wish I'd
done that. Maybe if....'

I asked the Holy Spirit to come on the bereavement,
and her pain became much worse. I cut her off from her
sister, broke the power of false guilt, released her
departed sister to the Lord, and the pain began to ease,
but this process went on for several weeks. When false
guilt assumed the upper hand the pain became worse, but
when she released her sister into the hands of Jesus the
pain eased.

I find it is helpful to try and see bereavement or any
other psychosomatic problem as Jesus sees it. As a simple
process I find that when we see things as Satan sees them
we normally suffer, but when we see them as Jesus sees
them healing often comes and stays.

When Jesus was bereaved he wept. It is normal to
weep when we are hurt or sad; this is why God has given
us tears. Crying also helps us to come to terms with the
reality of death. My friend or relative is dead; this is why
I weep. For the Christian this sadness can sometimes be
more bearable because of the promise of life after death.
To give thanks for the life of the deceased or to celebrate
their promotion to glory may be right according to individual circumstances. To weep for our loss is right. But
to try and live for them, to live as though they were not
dead, or to try and contact them is wrong. To blame
ourselves for their failures or to try and pay or compen-
sate for their death is to listen to Satan. He is the accuser
of the brethren. He wants us to pay for that which Christ
has already paid, causing us suffering and denying the
effectiveness of the cross of Christ. When emotional
trauma hits us we may need Christian friends to help us
see as Jesus sees and be healed.[5]

There is also a strange question we occasionally need
to ask those who lose their healing. Jesus said to the sick

man, 'Do you want to get well?' (Jn 5:6). To be well
means to have no more excuses. 'I'm not a well man, you
know' can avoid a multitude of responsibilities. It sometimes costs to be well.

I remember as a child frequently catching cold and
going to bed for the day. I had a little bell to ring if I
needed anything. I had Lucozade to drink, a comic to
read and the radio to play. If I did not have a cold I had to
go to the school I disliked, and work hard. I found this to
be at the root of the many colds I suffered as an adult
when the pressure of work became too great. I have
needed to repent of a wrong attitude and really desire
health and wholeness when cold symptoms come, in
order to fight off germs and stay well. Since discovering
this and responding appropriately I have noticed a
marked improvement.

As part of the Jesus lifestyle which brings wholeness, I
believe we need to concentrate on worship, Scripture,
prayer and holiness which overflows into loving our
neighbour as ourselves. Giving thanks to God in all circumstances is, I think, particularly important (Eph 5:20; 1
Thess 5:18). It allows the free flow of God's affirming
love and keeps demons at bay; they cannot stand being
present when God is thanked and Jesus is praised. It is
good to declare God's healing power and minister in his
name to all who are sick, but it is also good to thank him
when we are well.

If a person with cancer is miraculously healed by God a
whole church will rightly give thanks and praise to the
Lord. If ninety-nine Christians come to worship the
Lord, are fit and well, do not have cancer and do not need
a miracle, then it is surely just as right to give God thanks
and praise for wholeness and health. We give thanks to
God in all circumstances and this, I am sure, will help us
to keep our healing.

At present we do not find a large percentage of people

being organically healed when we pray for them. We do, however, find many root causes being brought to light and many people receiving spiritual blessings. I have heard doctors say seventy, eighty or even ninety per cent of physical sickness in our country may be due to psychosomatic causes. Many of these are related to sin. I pray daily to receive more faith, more power and see more miracles, but in the meantime there is still much work which can be done. If these doctors are right, then Holy Spirit-filled Christians living a Jesus lifestyle ought to see seventy, eighty or even ninety per cent of physical sicknesses being healed, even if it takes time. Learning to pray, 'Come, Holy Spirit,' over everyone who is sick is the best way I have found of moving towards that goal.

Notes

1. This is a simplified version of the 'Wimber model' found in *Power Healing* and explained well by Ken Blue in *Authority to Heal*. In their approaches an interview is conducted first to try to find out if there is a root cause. I always advise chatting to a person first, but find praying, 'Come, Holy Spirit,' before coming to any decision about root causes is an easier method for our team members to follow. (John Wimber with Kevin Springer, *Power Healing* [Hodder & Stoughton: London, 1986]. Ken Blue, *Authority to Heal* [Monarch Publications: Eastbourne, 1989].)

2. Roger Jones, *Mary Magdalene* (Anfield Music Ltd: Birmingham, 1990).

3. In *The Prayer that Heals* Francis MacNutt writes, 'One of the great discoveries in my life has been that when a short prayer doesn't seem to help a "soaking" prayer often brings the healing we are looking for.' I don't think we ought to be too concerned if praying for healing takes us longer than it took Jesus. (Francis

MacNutt, *The Prayer that Heals* [Hodder & Stoughton: London, 1982], p 57.)

4. I have found the 'Eleven Reasons Why People Are Not Healed' in Francis MacNutt's book *Healing* to be one of the most practically helpful discussions on this subject. ([Ave Maria Press: Notre Dame, Indiana, 1974], pp 248–261.)

5. An interesting, maybe slightly controversial, but helpful book on bereavement is *Requiem Healing* by Michael Mitton and Russ Parker. In it they say, 'It is perfectly acceptable to love our dead. Consequently we need to be sensitive to people undergoing bereavement and not hurry them through the experience. The time for full letting go must be approached without undue pressure or strain.' Loving our dead while letting them go and not trying to pay for them seems to me a healthy aim in Christ. ([Daybreak: Darton, Longman & Todd Ltd: London, 1991], p 140.)

9

Leading a Congregation into Renewal

On the evening of Wednesday 12th November 1985 ten
faithful souls huddled together around a solitary fire in
the side chapel of Christ Church, Burney Lane. We sat in
a circle on hard wooden chairs, protected by a few flimsy
curtains from the icy cold temperature of the nave. I
prayed, 'Come, Holy Spirit.'

Nothing happened. I stared out at nine blank faces
frozen into expressions of tolerance and blandness. Having encouraged folk not to bow their heads, I shut up.
Panic was resisted with determination, but I received no
apparent reward for my efforts. Not a muscle seemed to
twitch; no obvious blessing or distress; no thunderbolt
from the sky or rustling in the leaves of the trees outside;
no sound or movement or visible sign of invisible grace.

Slowly the apathy gave way to a restless discomfort
and I knew I needed to say something.

'Right,' I interrupted breezily, 'who's got anything to
share?'

More silence.

'OK, let's go round the room. John, what were you
getting?'

'Nothing,' he offered apologetically, a response
echoed seven more times with varying degrees of embarrassment.

The last person in the circle was the church warden. I

had started so I finished. I looked in his direction as words by now seemed unnecessary.

'It was amazing,' said Peter, 'absolutely amazing.'

'Go on,' I said, trying not to sound too cynical, but grateful for anything at this point.

'When you prayed, "Come, Holy Spirit," ' he continued, 'this bright light hit me—right here.' He pointed to the spot. I looked at his bald head just above the right eye, but failed to detect anything.

'Eventually the light faded,' continued Peter, 'but now the area is red hot.'

Oh dear, I thought, *I haven't read about one of those*. Fortunately, a useful question formed in my mind. 'Would you say it was a good light or a bad light?' I asked rather simplistically, a little worried about masquerading as an angel of light and other such related complications (2 Cor 11:14).

'Oh, definitely good,' Peter answered. 'It was as though all the tensions and pressures of the day melted away.' And then, as if to add further confirmation, he said, 'Feel it; it's still hot.'

Gingerly I laid a hand on the spot. It was boiling! I think we could have fried an egg on it. I laid hands on the area and blessed what the Father was doing. Eventually the heat faded, we joined together in saying the grace and went home, grateful to God, albeit a shade puzzled.

This particular group of adults met fortnightly and everyone came back again for more. It was the first time I had tried this in a small adult group and as I prayed, 'Come, Holy Spirit,' at each subsequent meeting I repeatedly felt a similar measure of awkwardness, fear and apprehension. I was worried God would fail to show up and nothing would happen, and they were worried God would show up and something would happen—to them. And yet none of us could stay away.

I had already tried praying, 'Come, Holy Spirit,' in

two large church meetings, with disastrous consequences. Nothing at all happened and everyone was highly embarrassed, so I restricted it after that for a whole year to the small home-group-sized meeting. It was still very nerve-racking. It is not very easy, even among friends we know and trust, to spend fifteen to thirty minutes standing expectantly and waiting for God to come when no one has ever seen or heard of it being done before. My thoughts and prayers continued to focus on the ministry time whenever the day of such a meeting drew near. Would I get through? Would I look an idiot? Would God show up yet again and do something supernatural? Each time we met, something positive from God did occur and yet at each new meeting I wondered if anything would happen.

On Sunday 2nd February 1986 Sister Mary from the Anglican Community of St John the Divine approached me after the service in a hush-hush, secretive, 'I'm not going to tell you, but if...' kind of a way. 'Come on,' I said. 'What are you trying to say?'

'If God tells you anything about me before Wednesday night's meeting, will you let me know?'

I tried. I really did try. I prayed daily for wisdom and guidance and communication. I thought at one stage God was saying something about Sister Mary's natural sister, but nothing startling to bother her about.

On the Wednesday snow fell steadily throughout the day. If I had been sitting by a blazing log fire gazing through frost-tinted glass at the gentle snowflakes covering the weeds in my garden with a white carpet I might have responded with aesthetic approval in my soul—but I wasn't—and I didn't. As I went foot-slogging around the parish with moisture seeping into every part of my being I began to dread the inevitable cry I knew would be awaiting my return: 'Daddy. Build us a snowman!' I bravely carried on. I managed to see some sick people in the afternoon, and in the course of one visit to an elderly lady her daughter thrust a piece of paper into my hand. 'I thought the Lord was giving me this for you tonight,' she said. I put it in my trouser pocket without reading it, continued on my way and duly forgot about it in the excitement of fixing coal eyes, a carrot nose and my golf hat to the abominable creature now standing on the lawn.

By evening the snow was three feet thick in places, but as I contemplated ringing round to cancel the meeting I remembered Sister Mary's words and the note in my back pocket. It was a little soggy but still decipherable. This is what it said:

> Praise and exalt me when you fellowship tonight for I will reveal myself in a special way to those who have been doubting that the gifts of the Spirit are for them to claim and operate. I will reveal myself to those who have not yet sought me in this way and I will baptise them in the Spirit if they step out in faith and believe that I am a God with whom all things are possible.

As a result of reading this I decided to wait and see if anyone trekked through the snow to church; as I lived next door it was no great problem to me, once I'd dried out.

When Sister Mary announced to the other sisters of St John's House her intention of attending the mid-week meeting in church, there was an unusually cold response. At seventy-four a mile slog through antarctic conditions just to attend her several thousandth church meeting, even if she did look like a penguin in her habit, did seem a little excessive.

But no one else knew what Sister Mary thought God had said to her. For over twenty years she had desired spiritual gifts, especially speaking in tongues, and nothing ever seemed to come her way. Much of her time was spent serving the Lord in Namibia and Malawi (occasionally in the presence of charismatically gifted pastors) and yet her requests and prayers went unrewarded. She therefore resigned herself to the possibility of spiritual gifts not being for her. Now maybe tonight the answer lay at the end of a mile-long path of deep snow.

Despite the atrocious conditions Sister Mary arrived early for the meeting. 'Somebody handed me this,' I said casually, 'while I was on my rounds this afternoon.' As she read it excitement and anticipation spread across her face until she resembled a child on Christmas Eve. 'I thought God said he would give me the gift of tongues tonight,' she blurted out, 'but I didn't dare tell anyone till now. I received this picture of myself kneeling in the middle of the group as you laid hands on my head and prayed for me.'

It was difficult to contain her after that. As I tried to begin the meeting there were five of us present altogether, but I kept being interrupted.

'Now?' asked Sister Mary after the first song. 'Shall I kneel down now?'

'No, Sister Mary, not yet,' I replied. 'We haven't finished worshipping yet.'

'Now?' asked Sister Mary after the second song. 'Shall I kneel now?'

'No,' I said as seriously as I could manage, 'we haven't read the Bible yet.'

'I can't wait,' she said. 'I can't wait.' And down on her knees she went in front of us all. I decided not to put off the moment any longer.

We laid on hands and prayed for the Holy Spirit to come on Sister Mary and give her the gift of speaking in tongues. We saw nothing, heard nothing, but after a while Sister Mary sat down in her chair again, reasonably content something had happened, and the meeting continued.

The next day Sister Mary went into chapel alone to

pray. 'I began to pray in tongues,' she told me afterwards. 'I was only there two minutes, but when I looked at my watch half an hour had gone by.' This was just the beginning of a number of experiences Sister Mary continued to have in the power of the Holy Spirit, which encouraged the faithful few at Burney Lane.

Peter was sixty-five and Sister Mary seventy-four when the Spirit of God touched them in a special way in our little meetings. There were others too in this older age bracket. One day Daisy, well into her seventies, insisted on seeing me after the early morning Sunday service. I wondered what was coming. 'Peter,' she said, 'what happened to me at the meeting last week was absolutely marvellous.'

'Oh?' I said, taken aback, not used to hearing good things from people who want to see me 'for a word' after a service. 'I'm pleased you enjoyed it.'

'No,' she said, 'you don't understand. It was wonderful.' The Spirit had come powerfully on Daisy and drenched her in his love in a way she had never experienced before. Daisy's life has been a sacrificial one, spent in caring for others, and it was encouraging to hear of God coming to her in such an affirming way.

Anne, also in her seventies, seemed to be a gift to our fellowship for a season. When anyone laid hands on her and prayed, 'Come, Holy Spirit,' she would heat up instantly like a kettle. Anne worried a lot about others, especially friends and family. It was worry that always led into prayer and action, but we never quite managed to stop her anxiety. So God seemed to come powerfully on her every week, take away the excess worry and fill her up again.

At regular intervals more members of our congregation were encouraged to lay hands on others for the first time. Some were very apprehensive about it. 'I don't think I could. I'd be too worried nothing would happen. I haven't got the faith,' they might say.

'Oh, I'm sure you'll be all right,' I would reply. 'Why not go and lay hands on Anne over there?'

Tentatively, sometimes simply because the vicar suggested it, the person would creep up to Anne, put a hand on her head and pray, 'Come, Holy Spirit.' Fifteen minutes later the nervous, totally unsure, lacking-in-faith, but obedient servant would come back looking radiant. 'You'll never guess what happened!' the reluctant 'minister' would begin.

'Go on,' I'd reply with enthusiasm, 'tell me all about it.'

Every story would contain the words 'heat' and 'power'. We were careful not to overdo it, but God used Anne several times in helping people begin to minister. From there they often moved on to minister to others with greater faith and confidence.

Anne herself received her first direct word from God just a few days before she died. It did our church no harm at all to see things of the Spirit happening to people in our midst who were past retiring age.

Follow me

The Good Shepherd said to his sheep who heard and recognised his voice, 'Follow me,' and they did. He led them to green pastures and still waters. He taught them to eat living bread and drink living water, and showed them how an overflow of the Spirit was meant to affect the world. They watched him proclaim the kingdom, heal the sick, raise the dead and cast out demons, and they learned to follow in his path (Mt 10:5–8).

When Jesus called Peter to be a shepherd, to feed his lambs (Jn 21:15) and take care of his sheep (Jn 21:16), he repeated his initial command to 'follow me' twice more

(Jn 21:19,22). Peter, filled with the Spirit of Jesus, followed him. He received words from God which enabled him to proclaim Jesus as King (Acts 2), heal the sick (Acts 3), raise the dead (Acts 9:36–43) and cast out demons (Acts 5:16). In due course the new converts led by Peter and the other apostles also followed the Jesus way (Acts 6:1–8; 8:4–8).

When I became a vicar in 1979 I tried to be a British shepherd. I walked behind the sheep, poking, prodding, encouraging and shouting, in the hope that they would go first and find green pastures and still waters. They were hungry and thirsty, but often they failed to find food and drink.

In 1985 when I returned from a signs and wonders conference I was inspired to believe that I could be an Israeli shepherd and lead from the front.[1] I had been to many other conferences, heard many other Spirit-filled speakers, and come away believing they could do it. For the first time in my life I now believed I could do it. I really did think with practice I could learn to pray, 'Come, Holy Spirit,' and shut up. In my three days at the conference I decided to move from the back of the flock to the front and have a go. It wasn't as easy as I had hoped it might be, but in time the gifts and fruits of the Spirit began to appear. I am now convinced that those who are called by God to lead are called to lead—from the front.

It seemed right, once I had started, to make sure nothing was done behind locked doors. In the early church Peter and Paul frequently ministered in public, and in the presence of King Agrippa Paul told Festus that what they did 'was not done in a corner' (Acts 26:26). Although we restricted the praying of 'Come, Holy Spirit' to our small groups initially, I made sure everyone heard about church warden Peter, Sister Mary, Daisy and Anne. I used them as illustrations in sermons when I preached about the ministry of Jesus and his disciples in the power of the Holy Spirit. Most of my monthly letters in the church magazine were on a similar theme, so that everyone knew what was going on and everyone was invited to join us. We tried not to do anything in a corner, even though it meant those who wanted to stay put were worried the forest fire was coming nearer.

One year after I'd begun to pray, 'Come, Holy Spirit,' in our small groups I sensed it was right to try again in our main Sunday morning service.

I stood in the pulpit and looked out over our congregation. I prayed, 'Come, Holy Spirit,' and waited. Bang! Almost immediately an elderly lady crashed to the ground, knocking into three others as she fell. One never came again. A second decided to attend our earlier service instead. A third just about coped. The lady came up beaming, claiming God had greatly blessed her, but rumblings spread around the congregation. Some were not very happy.

In our evening house-group meetings people began going over in the power of the Spirit and remaining on the ground for fifteen to thirty minutes. Their testimonies were invariably of love, assurance, power and blessing. Other manifestations such as shaking, rocking and eyelids fluttering also occurred. By now we had learned to stand rather than sit when we prayed, 'Come, Holy Spirit,' and more seemed to happen. But not everything was received as positively by spectator as participant. At one large meeting in our church a visitor screamed very loudly for a short while and one relative newcomer to our church, who was visibly upset, never returned. We visited her, but to no avail. There were some who took this as evidence to use against us. They wanted to put out the fire before it was too late.

Facing the opposition

A meeting was called. I duplicated some notes on 'Come, Holy Spirit' and circulated them beforehand. In response, others duplicated some notes entitled 'Stay where you are, Holy Spirit' and distributed those. In the end there were very few who voted against us, and I think these are some of the reasons:

Biblical authority

I belong to a denomination whose articles of belief rest on the authority of the Bible. The Old Testament and New Testament alone are given canonical authority. 'In the name of the holy Scripture we do understand those canonical Books of the Old and New Testament, of whose authority was never any doubt in the Church' (Article VI). The three creeds 'ought thoroughly to be received and believed: for they may be proved by most certain warrants of holy Scripture' (Article VIII). 'And yet it is not lawful for the Church to ordain anything that is contrary to God's Word written' (Article XX). To put it in more modern English the beliefs and doctrines of the Church of England must be taken only from the Bible.

Some of my free church and house church friends wonder why I stay in the Church of England when odd statements from some of the more liberal hierarchy are frequently quoted in the press. My thinking is quite straightforward. Whenever anyone contradicts or goes against Scripture, it is they who depart from the basic beliefs of the Church of England, not the Church of England which is at fault. The media are always willing to quote unorthodox or controversial figures, but many of the leading figures in the Anglican church are orthodox, Bible-based believers, teachers and preachers. I was lectured on the Bible by Archbishop George Carey, Bishop Colin Buchanan and Canon Michael Green when I was at theological college and I am very proud of it. I similarly try to preach and teach the Bible and appeal to its pages in all questions of authority just as they taught me.

Even if those who attended our church meeting did not like it, they all knew that shaking (Acts 4:31), falling (Acts 9:4) and shrieking (Acts 8:7) are all recorded in the New Testament as phenomena occurring when the Spirit came. No one was able to argue against it from Scripture.

History

The history of revivals such as the Quakers, John Wesley, the various American Awakenings and the Welsh Revival, all record things happening similar to those we had witnessed. I was now glad I had done some homework and often illustrated my biblical preaching with stories from the historical revivals.

Since our debate took place Francis MacNutt has written an excellent book entitled *Overcome by the Spirit*, which looks particularly at the phenomenon of falling or resting in the Spirit.[2] As well as looking at the biblical evidence and modern-day testimonies, he also outlines the experiences of people like Teresa of Avila, John Tauler, Ignatius of Loyola, John Wesley, Jonathan Edwards, George Whitefield, Bishop Francis Asbury and Charles Finney. We certainly could not be accused of introducing 'new' doctrines or experiences but rather reintroducing very old teachings. It is comforting to have many of our own experiences in the power of the Holy Spirit confirmed by the Bible and history.

Liturgy

The Anglican services allow in certain places for 'other suitable prayers' to be said and 'silence' to be kept. In the Eucharistic Prayers phrases like 'Renew us by your Spirit' and 'Send the Holy Spirit on your people' are incorporated.[3] Similarly, our traditional hymn books contain words like, 'Come down, O Love Divine'; 'Breathe on me, Breath of God'; 'O Breath of Life, come sweeping through us'.[4]

Presumably 'Come, Holy Spirit' is therefore a 'suitable prayer', allowed by the Church of England services. In places where even that may raise objections, to sing together, 'Spirit of the Living God, fall afresh on me,' and then wait in silence may be a more appropriate way of welcoming God to do what he wants to do.[5]

Testimony

To have Peter, the church warden aged sixty-five, Sister Mary in blue habit aged seventy-four, and Daisy and Anne in their seventies giving testimony of changed lives did us no harm at all.

Practice

What we did was to worship God, listen to his word, and then ask him to come among us. I said, 'Come, Holy Spirit,' from the pulpit. No one touched the lady who fell over or the one who shrieked. It was very difficult to argue against the practice, even if people did not like the results.

In the end I believe one family and two or three individuals left the church, but many more were added to us. We received a mandate from the meeting to pray, 'Come, Holy Spirit,' at any service whenever the leader of the service felt led of the Lord to do so. A summary of how things began in our church may be helpful:

(a) We prayed, 'Come, Holy Spirit,' in small home groups and mid-week church meetings among people who were prepared to learn and try new things.

(b) We preached the Bible, including what is taught about the Holy Spirit.

(c) We illustrated Bible truths with stories from historical revivals and testimonies from our small groups whenever possible.

(d) When enough people became familiar with this ministry in small groups and we sensed it was right, we introduced it into the main services.

(e) We armed ourselves with good biblical, traditional and liturgical reasons for praying, 'Come, Holy Spirit.' This meant being able to answer verbally and in writing such questions as, 'Is it biblical to pray, "Come, Holy Spirit"?' and, 'Why ask him to come when he is already here?' (see Chapter 2, pp 34–60).

(f) 'Occult' means 'hidden'. We tried not to do anything in a corner, and when disputes arose we held open meetings to air problems, discuss our feelings and re-examine the Scriptures.

(g) Undergirding all of this was constant prayer by individuals and groups, asking God to come and do whatever he wanted to do in his church. We asked for wisdom and discernment to hear his voice, and courage to obey his word.

Learning together

In the early stages I took as many people as I could to training days and conferences. A number of us went to the regular teaching and ministry days held at St Thomas' Crookes, Sheffield[6] and St Andrews, Chorleywood[7] and attended the John Wimber conferences.[8] Events were also arranged with local churches and we invited a number of people with more experience than ourselves to come and teach and minister to us. Sometimes we learned as much from others' mistakes as anything else.

One Saturday night a group of us attended a meeting in central Birmingham. It began with joyful but sensitive worship, enabling us to relax quickly into an atmosphere of praise, especially as we knew all the songs. The word given was informative and uplifting, so when the coffee break came we approached it communally with a considerable degree of well-being. The warm, dry room made the thought of a drink all the more welcome, despite the limited menu. We were offered coffee or coffee. Christine chose coffee. She would have preferred tea, but parched gaspers imbibe what they can. It was the start of the least agreeable part of the meeting for Christine as something in the coffee disagreed with something in her and sought an early exit.

'We stand to welcome the Holy Spirit,' announced the leader, and Christine dutifully became upright. As she did the room began to swim, the centre of gravity to shift and her feet to move towards the door. *I've got to get out of here*, she thought to herself.

'Come, Holy Spirit,' prayed the minister, and immediately Christine lost consciousness and crashed to the floor. 'Bless you, Lord. Thank you for what you are doing,' he commented as local team members gathered round and laid on hands. They were thrilled to be a part of what appeared to all of us as the work of the Holy Spirit so early in the proceedings. Slowly, Christine returned from whence she had been and became aware of voices: 'It's all right. Stay where you are. The Lord's blessing you.'

'No he's not! I want to be sick. It's the coffee. Where's the loo?'

Presuppositions can sometimes be difficult to shift in spiritually-minded Christians, but eventually common sense prevailed. The ladies followed Christine to 'the Ladies', prayed for her to be healed and she was, as a result of vomiting.[9] In due course the feeling of well-being returned.

We learned a new truth from this experience: falling to the ground after someone has prayed, 'Come, Holy Spirit,' may be due to coffee. More seriously we discovered the danger of presuppositions, the importance of common sense and the value of being able to laugh at ourselves.

Birmingham is very centrally placed for travelling and we are very fortunate in being able to hear and experience the teaching and ministry of many gifted and experienced leaders. My friends who live east of Cambridge, west of Exeter and north of Carlisle are not so fortunate as we are, but I know of one church who equipped themselves with many of the excellent tapes which are now available.[10] They met each week in small groups, worshipped together, played a teaching tape and then prayed, 'Come, Holy Spirit.' After six months they felt God saying to them, 'Now do it yourselves,' which they did and never looked back. In our day and age tapes and videos are so readily available we really have little excuse for not having a go.

Training a ministry team

Once the ministry sessions move from small intimate groups to larger public meetings it becomes necessary to train and prepare authorised ministry team members who will assist the leaders.

In Great Britain there are two kinds of people who are allowed to drive a car on the public highways: (a) those who have been taught and trained and have reached a certain degree of competence; and (b) those who are being taught and trained and have not yet reached the required degree of competence. One is allowed to drive alone and the other only with a competent instructor. Someone driving alone who has not yet reached the stipulated degree of competence is driving illegally and may be fined, banned or, if necessary, imprisoned. We do not give a driving licence to someone because he is a nice chap, a mature Christian or even because he's been driving a long time. Safety on the roads is too important for that. We give a driving licence to those who have proved themselves to be competent. A learner driver normally sees others driving first, then has a go while others watch and instruct, and finally is allowed to drive alone. The model is this: I do it, you watch; you do it, I watch; you do it. Jesus followed a similar model when teaching his disciples how to minister.

In our teaching and training sessions we worship, teach and then frequently divide the group into two for ministry, following the pattern I outlined in Chapter 3. Occasionally I may pray for someone publicly first, giving everyone present a chance to observe. I then invite God to send his Holy Spirit on half of the group while the others watch and prepare to take part. In church services I usually ask the Holy Spirit to come on the whole congregation, making me the only one who ever sees what is happening. By dividing into two for training, everyone can see what God is doing some of the time.

As one group watches I normally comment on what is to be seen and at appropriate moments encourage individuals to go and minister to others, while I try to keep my eye on them. If possible I encourage those who have been receiving to share afterwards with those praying for them, whatever has been helpful or unhelpful. As well as being teaching and training sessions these are also real ministry days during which we have learned to expect the unexpected.

On one memorable occasion I asked God to send his Spirit on half of those present while the others watched prior to laying-on hands. During the coffee break between sessions a man said to me, 'Nothing ever happens to me. After coffee can I switch sides and have another go?' Having been in the receiving group he was now due to be in the ministering group. The coffee must have been all right this time because I gave him permission. I couldn't help noticing him after the break, and again nothing seemed to be happening to him.

In the middle of the session Tony, who was receiving,

suddenly held out both his arms in a sleep-walking posture and began walking towards the church door with his eyes closed. There is a main road outside the church so I was a little concerned. I went up to Tony, tapped him on the shoulder and asked, 'Tony, what is happening?'

'The Lord's told me to walk until I find someone to lay hands on,' he said. 'He wants me to minister to them.'

'Right,' I said, knowing Tony quite well, 'I'll come with you,' and hoped we didn't end up in the local pub.

Tony's eyes were closed throughout the sleep-walking episode. He walked down the aisle, away from the people, towards the main door with me at his shoulder. There he turned round and walked back again, eventually stopping right in front of the man who had changed sides—something which Tony knew nothing about. He put out his hands, found a head and prayed in the power of the Spirit. The testimony afterwards was of power, love and assurance coming on the recipient. At last something happened to him.

After several of these general sessions we move towards the driving test.

This, I find, is best done in smaller groups of about ten, each with an experienced leader. The leader puts people in pairs, prays, 'Come, Holy Spirit,' and watches while one lays hands on the other. After a break the process is reversed. Rather like the driving lesson in a car when the person is actually driving on the road, these valuable teaching and training sessions are also times of real anointing, blessing and healing. Whenever a leader considers an individual to be ministering well and competently, I normally try to have a look, and in due course may invite such a person to be a member of our team. They receive a badge to wear for authorisation and identification and the others are invited to pray alongside badged people until they receive one for themselves.

Invariably my criteria at this stage are simple: do they

get in God's way, or do they help people to receive what God is doing? It must also be said we have normally by now been able to observe the person receive ministry as well as praying for others, and to check out that they are Bible-believing, born-again Christians.

Licensing the team

In our *Supplement to The Alternative Service Book authorised for use in the Diocese of Birmingham* we have a short 'Order for Commissioning Pastoral Assistants or Lay Elders'.[11] With the minimum of adaptation we were able to use it in the middle of our main service for licensing our first ministry team members, which we did with the bishop's blessing. I laid hands on each one, prayed for them publicly and gave them a badge. We began with twelve and since then have added to their number regularly.

At the service I suggested the rest of the church offered themselves for experimental purposes and everyone with a twinge, sore throat, sick relative or unwell budgerigar came forward for the laying-on of hands. In a service of about sixty adults thirty people sought ministry from the newly-authorised twelve and this publicly sealed and affirmed the new appointments. Every team member prayed for two or three people on their first official day, and even though I cannot remember anything dramatic taking place we were now up and running.

James 5:14 says, 'Is any one of you sick? He should call the elders of the church to pray over him and anoint him with oil in the name of the Lord.' I wrote about this passage in the parish magazine and listed the names and phone numbers of the newly-licensed twelve. I encouraged those who were sick at home to ring one of these people whom I now considered as 'elders' authorised to visit and pray for others. They were taught to go in twos, to lay-on hands, ask the Holy Spirit to come, and whenever it seemed appropriate to address physical complaints in the name of Jesus and anoint with oil.

I think doing all this publicly and officially enabled us to proclaim and safeguard the ministry of the Holy Spirit at Burney Lane.

Using the team

If I pray, 'Come, Holy Spirit,' at the end of a service or meeting, I believe it is my responsibility to ensure I have enough trained people available, or a good follow-up system, to cope with whatever happens. The more open people are, the more help will normally be required. The size of the gathering may also determine the way we proceed. In a congregation of fifty or less I can normally see what is happening to most people, and even allow people to lay hands on each other. In such situations a few trained helpers may be all that is necessary. But once numbers increase beyond fifty, the team will need to be larger (at least ten per cent of the gathering) and the controls stricter.

Our church has the problem of being long and narrow, so I advise the team to sit scattered among the congregation, preferably in end seats. This means they can turn unobtrusively during ministry times to observe what is happening. I also like to use a 'floor manager'. It is very important on these occasions, especially if slightly distressing manifestations occur, for me to be seen at all times by all people to be in charge at the front. I therefore remain in the pulpit by the microphone until the official closing of the meeting. At present we have three teams of fifteen, each with two co-leaders, who are on duty once every three weeks. The other two teams can be called upon when it is not officially their turn if demand exceeds supply.

The primary responsibility of the 'floor manager' and members of the team when we begin a session is to deal with emergencies. When Jesus taught in the synagogue in Capernaum a man cried out (Mk 1:24). On rare occasions the leader at the front may feel it right to tackle such a problem publicly as Jesus did, but as a general rule it seems more appropriate for the floor manager to arrange for someone to take people out for private ministry if they disturb the session early on.

It must be said that this does not happen every time and we found in our early days it never happened at all. In the beginning God seemed to come on us with waves of blessing and gentleness until we learned more about problems and coping with them, but it is always reassuring to the person leading, and to the congregation, to know someone is available to take people out if necessary. A no-nonsense, straightforward shake will bring most people back to their senses and is usually quicker than engaging publicly in spiritual warfare, or trying to cope where they are. We normally prefer to help those exhibiting severe signs of distress privately, for the sake of their own dignity and comfort.

Unless an emergency arises, I encourage the team first to watch what the Father is doing and not to interfere. Team members clambering all over seats will not help people to receive, and some take a long time to let go and let God. Normally, when I consider it right, I will ask the team: 'Now go and minister,' and this is also the time they can come to me with words from God, or I can give others, perhaps received before the meeting.

When to pray, 'Come, Holy Spirit'

I prayed, 'Come, Holy Spirit,' in the middle of our main morning Communion service, soon after our ministry team was licensed. Unfortunately, the robed choir was then unable to sing the anthem after 'the peace' because most of them were still sprawled out on the floor.[12] Clearly if this is likely to occur the ministry is better done on a regular basis at the end of the service. This is our present pattern for Sunday services:

We have a short, said Holy Communion service at nine o'clock and from time to time we offer the laying-on of hands after the service at the altar rail.

During our main Holy Communion service at eleven o'clock we always offer individual ministry in the side chapel. People are encouraged to receive communion first and then go to the team in the side chapel afterwards. If necessary this can continue after the service has finished. The preacher is always given permission to pray, 'Come, Holy Spirit,' over the whole congregation after the sermon if it seems right and this happens occasionally. When it does we choose a suitable moment to continue the service and those still engaged by the Holy Spirit join in with the rest of us when God has finished. It is normally quite gentle these days and all anthems are sung before the sermon.

At six o'clock once a month we have a special service or healing service. This tends to start with 'Evening Prayer (Shorter Form)'.[13] It can at times be evangelistic and we normally ask God to come and do what he wants once the sermon is over. The usual six o'clock service is more formal, though individuals frequently chat afterwards or minister to one another while waiting for the later service to begin. When it is Holy Communion the same procedure is followed as at eleven o'clock.

At eight o'clock we welcome people from other churches, worship for half an hour, have a thirty-minute address and then normally pray, 'Come, Holy Spirit.' This is often the time when more visible things occur.

Our aim is to give God a chance to come and do what he wants to do at every service whenever practically possible. It is interesting that our most dramatic healing of former church warden Peter occurred after the nine o'clock Holy Communion service, which is very quiet and formal.[14]

Sustaining renewal

The trail-blazer cuts away enough of the jungle to make a path for himself and his friends as they press on towards their destination. Soon after he has gone the jungle grows back as it was and his efforts benefit no one who follows.

The pioneer cuts his path, clears an area of jungle around it and then builds a settlement of huts and houses so that many others may benefit from what has been achieved. Although 'green' people would prefer trail-blazers, as a spiritual illustration the pioneer is to be preferred for enabling willing followers to join him.

It saddens me greatly that many who move in renewal, charismatic gifts and signs and wonders have become trail-blazers rather than pioneers. They share with others in talks, tapes and books the great new places they have discovered and explored, and we are greatly impressed. The Christian world loves Christian superstars, and they certainly brighten up a dull weekend, but I wonder if some of them are in danger of putting so much distance between themselves and the ordinary church or Christian that the kingdom of God hardly benefits at all.

I believe there are two things we need to do in our local churches to be pioneers rather than trail-blazers and to sustain renewal: (a) stay within the anointing of God; and (b) keep giving it away.

(a) The anointing of God

When Moses and the Israelites left Egypt to go to the promised land 'the Lord went ahead of them in a pillar of cloud to guide them on their way and by night in a pillar of fire' (Ex 13:21). When the cloud or fire moved they moved; where the cloud went they went; when the fire stayed still they all parked for the night. God also gave them Moses as a leader who could hear God's voice: 'With him I speak face to face' (Num 12:8). And yet when God told them to enter the promised land they refused, and God withdrew his anointing. The people mourned and said, 'We will go up to the place the Lord promised' (Num 14:40), but God was no longer in it. They tried in their own strength and failed.

I am sure if we keep making room in our meetings for God to come and do what he wants to do we shall recognise his anointing, see what he is doing and hear his voice. If we stop asking him to come, we shall move when we want to move and stay put when we choose to do so. Then we may find ourselves outside the anointing of God where renewal will not be sustained because we are trying to do what God is not doing.

It is important that we do not equate God's anointing just with excitement and signs and wonders. For everything there is a season and sometimes doing God's will can seem very ordinary. There came a time in our church when there was a danger of complacency and boredom setting in. We had seen people shaking and failing, demons leaving and people being saved and healed. What else was there? It is then when obedience needs to be preached and eyes turned upon God rather than his works; to seek his face more than his hands; to offer ourselves in praise and service rather than ask for more. Someone who comes to our church for the first time who is unsaved or sick does not want to hear that we did salvation and healing last year and are now bored with it. It is the moment when the shepherd needs to hear the words, 'Do you love me?... Feed my sheep' (Jn 21:17). If we continue to ask the Holy Spirit to come, however 'routine' it may have become, I believe we have much more chance of discovering what God is doing and wanting to do than if we just stick to our own plans. Doing what God is doing will then help us to stay within his anointing and be renewed on the inside. Sustaining renewal does not mean continually doing new things but being renewed in our spirits by his Spirit to do whatever he wants us to do, even if we have done it before.

(b) Giving it away

On the Day of Pentecost the believers gathered together in one place and the Holy Spirit came powerfully upon them (Acts 2). A crowd then gathered, so Peter preached and explained how those who had come to see what was happening might also receive the Holy Spirit. The rest of the Acts of the Apostles relates how this good news spread. The more they received the more they gave away, and the more they gave away the more they received. God's love is like that.

Recently I went with a weary team of ten from our church to Stoke-on-Trent for a weekend. Many of us had been ministering long hours to others. Quite a few were in need of help themselves. Most of us would rather have been relaxing at home.

We had been through times when dramatic things were happening, but not recently. We all drove over in muted style, not expecting much, feeling tired and somewhat unprepared. But the church at Stoke-on-Trent had been preparing for months and holding prayer meetings every day in anticipation of our arrival. Our quarter-of-an-hour prayer time before we left put us to shame when we discovered the amount of regular prayer to which our hosts had been committed regularly for several months.

I gave the same old talks with the same old jokes and received the same old groans from our own people, who had heard it all before. And yet—God came powerfully and dramatically every time. On the Saturday afternoon about thirty people came—the inner core. We divided them into two groups, encouraged them to minister to one another and virtually everyone ended up flat on their backs with big smiles on their faces. In the evening more fringe people came and stayed for a session in church. Many of them crashed over, a few wept, some laughed, others smiled and all were encouraged. On the Sunday morning the regular congregation experienced the same thing and in the evening God released accurate words for many people through some of our folk who do not often give them. The Lord's love, power and presence were experienced everywhere, and once again many ended up on the floor. Some had come to the church for the very first time that Sunday and had never before seen anything like it.

Our intention in going to Stoke had been to give, but we came away excited and thrilled, having received great blessings and renewed hearts from God. It was good to have been there. I am convinced that we were helped to sustain renewal in our church by their preparation and prayers, and our commitment to give away what God had given to us. God always seems to give us more, the more we seek to give away (Lk 6:38).

Throughout the eighties the battle cry of many priests, preachers and prophets was, 'God wants his church back.' Our aim in praying, 'Come, Holy Spirit,' in many of our meetings and services is just that. When God is allowed to come and do whatever he wants to do he invariably responds positively and begins leading his people where he wants them to go. I am sure the secret of leading a church into renewal is to give God the reins and let him reign.

Notes

1. Signs and Wonders Part I conference held in October 1985 at Sheffield Town Hall.
2. Francis MacNutt, *Overcome by the Spirit* (Eagle, Inter Publishing Service [IPS] Ltd: Guildford, 1991).
3. *The Alternative Service Book 1980* (Collins Liturgical Publications: London, 1980), pp 132, 138.
4. *Hymns Ancient & Modern Revised* (William Clowes & Sons Ltd: London), nos 235 & 236.
   Mission Praise (Marshall Morgan & Scott: Basingstoke, 1983), no 164.
5. Paul Armstrong, copyright © Restoration Music Ltd/Lifestyle Music Ltd 1984 in *Songs of Fellowship* (Kingsway Music: Eastbourne, 1991), no 511.
6. Details of courses and tapes can be obtained from St Thomas' Church, Nairn Street, Crookes, Sheffield, S. Yorkshire.
7. Details of courses, videos, and audio tapes can be obtained from St Andrew's Church, Quickley Lane, Chorleywood, Herts WD3 5AE.
8. Details of John Wimber conferences and tapes can be obtained from Vineyard Ministries International (UK), PO Box 163, London SW20 8BX.
9. This was purely a physical problem solved physically.
10. For tapes on renewal and healing I would recommend the three addresses above (notes 6, 7 and 8).

    For tapes on emotional healing we have used Gloria Thompson's 'Free to Be' course which is particularly helpful for ladies. This is available from Christian Life Training, PO Box 7182, Orange, CA 92613-7182, USA.

    Ellel Grange now have a considerable library of videos and tapes on all aspects of healing, including deliverance, and are well worth considering. They also have material by Tom Marshall, Bill Subritzky and Harold Dewberry which I have found useful. Their address is Ellel Ministries, Ellel Grange, Ellel, Lancaster LA2 0HN.

11. *Supplement to The Alternative Service Book* (Diocese of Birmingham: 1984), 'Order for Commissioning Pastoral Assistants or Lay Elders', pp 8-9.

12. In *The Alternative Service Book* Communion we share the peace of God with one another before the Eucharistic Prayer and the sharing of bread and wine.

13. *The Alternative Service Book* (Collins Liturgical Publications: London, 1980), p 82.

14. Peter H. Lawrence, *The Hot Line* (Kingsway Publications: Eastbourne, 1990), p 69.

10

Leading the Minister into Renewal

'Hello! Peter here. Ringing to find out about the healing service this Sunday.'

'Oh yes. Peter. Thank you for ringing. We're looking forward to your visit. What do you need to know?'

'How long may I speak? And what kind of ministry can we do?'

'About twenty minutes—thirty at the most. Anglican service. We like to do things decently and in order. After the blessing we normally invite individuals to come forward and kneel at the altar rail for the laying-on of hands.'

(Pause for breath. The altar rail is presented as the usual hurdle.) 'Twenty to thirty minutes is fine.' *(Need to be careful with the next bit.)* 'I thought it may be right to invite everyone to stand while I ask the Holy Spirit to come to them.'

(Another pause. This time for him to take a breath.) 'I don't know about that,' he says slowly, implying that he knows all about *that*. 'It sounds a bit "Wimberish" to me. Our folk are not ready for that yet; it wouldn't work.'

(An even deeper breath.) 'I'll tell you what: if it's a fiasco; if they don't like it; if nothing happens, blame it all on me. You can't be blamed for what I do. If it's helpful and a blessing you can praise God and take it on from there.'

(I sense the British culture struggling to come out of its strait-jacket at the other end of the line.)

'It won't work,' he repeats, 'they really are not ready yet.' *(This is far less resistant in tone and yet it needs answering without domination or manipulation.)*

'Can I have a go then?' I asked directly.

'Do what you like,' he concludes, 'but don't blame me if nothing happens.'

'No. I'll take all the blame. Bless you! See you on Sunday....'

In the context of using spiritual gifts Paul wrote, 'Let all things be done decently and in order' (1 Cor 14:40, Authorised Version). I can't help thinking the Church of England has concentrated for too long on 'decently and in order', and not enough on 'see that all things are done'. This conversation was typical of many.

I spoke for thirty minutes, invited everyone to stand, and prayed, 'Come, Holy Spirit.' They were one of the most 'ready' congregations I have ever visited. Immediately one person crashed to the floor and no one else batted an eyelid until the Holy Spirit did it for them. Several others slumped into their chairs. Power was visible on perspiring brows and beaming faces. Hands shook, and towards the end a few demons manifested. This caused no problem. People stayed, prayed and praised God for the deliverance which followed.

Afterwards, over tea in the hall, an elderly lady approached me: 'I've never experienced anything like it,' she said. 'The love of God came all over me in great power and I couldn't stay on my feet. It was marvellous.'

I still remember with great affection the 'Signs and Wonders' conferences held in Britain from 1984 to 1986.[1] Since then I've met many clergy and friends who attended them.

'What did you think?' I invariably ask.

'Oh, marvellous! Found the teaching on the kingdom of God so helpful.'

'And the signs and wonders?' I ask.

'Impressive, weren't they? Never really seen healings or the power of God at work like that before.'

'And how are you getting on with it all?' I eventually ask. This frequently produces a pause. Sometimes during the silence the powerful clergyman and articulate theologian takes on the appearance of a little boy who has been found out.

'Yes, well. What works in America isn't always right for here. We're taking our time. Difficult situation where I am. Can't push our kind of folk.' There seems to be a problem. Good, godly, Bible-believing, theoretical charismatics who would love to see renewal in their own churches but....

There are reasons why ministers do not easily take risks, and those who would seek to help them may find it helpful to understand the pain of the pastorate.

When I came to Birmingham in 1976 as a raw, immature curate I was extremely fortunate in having Bishop Mark Green to oversee my post-ordination training. He is a kind, gentle, saintly man, marvellous at leading retreats, often able to impart deep spiritual truths and insights because of his love for the Lord. I could never imagine Mark Green having an enemy in the world.

But I will never forget his account of the first time he became an incumbent—the vicar of a parish. In those days it was necessary to do several curacies first. Everyone loves the curate. He learns his trade by visiting endless numbers of old ladies who love to mother him and give him cakes and tea. He often comes fresh from college, full of exciting new ideas, and giving only one sermon a month means he has time to prepare and excel. He is still young enough to kick a football around with the kids and take the teenagers away on boating holidays.

If he is single, the congregation, overstocked with spinsters, positively bristles and beams as he comes down the aisle in his flowing robes like a knight in white satin. But when he becomes a vicar....

Bishop Mark Green said his induction to the cure of souls made him arch-enemy number one for some people overnight. He was totally unprepared for it. His gentle, caring, sensitive nature was almost broken and, but for the grace of God, he might have left the ministry at that point. We bright-eyed and bushy-tailed curates needed to hear this and so do those who would seek to lead their minister into renewal. The clergyman is often very difficult to lead into renewal because he lives his life under siege. Moving into renewal involves taking risks, and people under siege do not easily take risks.

Clergy under siege

Persecution

Compared to the suffering of the early church and Christians in other parts of the world, the persecution of clergy in our country can only be described as minimal, and yet it is very real. The son of a kind and very gentle clergyman in the parish next door to us was bullied so much at school because he was the vicar's son, his father had to remove him and seek grants to pay for private education.

Our church has been flooded by vandals. Window guards have been ripped off, windows smashed, many items stolen, trees and fences broken down and graffiti sprayed on the walls. As we live on the same site as the church the trouble has also spread to our home and garden. I planted some conifers at the front as a windshield and one was burned down before the fire could be extinguished. My car was stolen three times in a year, and on one occasion I entered the local pub in my clerical collar only to have things thrown at me.

Those who built our home put the main electricity switch in the garage and gave us a big, heavy wooden door. If ever we leave the door open youngsters from the next-door school come in and switch the electricity off. Sometimes I have been using my computer to write a chapter and I have lost it. In such circumstances I leap to my feet, run out in my slippers and chase the offenders up the lane. Since they are fourteen and I'm over forty, they always win—not that I would know what to do if I caught one. I think they enjoy being chased by a clapped-out vicar more than switching off the electricity.

Other ministerial friends living in rougher areas than I do have far worse tales to tell. Many social workers and probation officers who work in difficult areas go home in the evening to the suburbs. The clergyman often lives in the middle of it and needs our support and understanding. Having said that, the worst attacks, and those often hardest to face and understand, commonly come from within the church, not the outside world.

People's expectations

When the vicar leaves a parish the Church Council meets to discuss the kind of person they would like to replace him. This is then made into a document and sent to the bishop. Most churches, when looking for a new minister, normally want the Archangel Michael. This reveals a fundamental problem: a dependent church. There seems to be a theological view held by many of the laity which sees ministers as having funnels in their heads, through which God pours all his blessings. He then squirts the blessing wherever he goes, and solves everyone else's problems.

In practice, the Archangel is not normally available. Every member of the Council has made sure his or her expectations are included on the list of requirements and all members of the church, even if they are not asked

what they think, have their own firm views. Even
though the appointing committee is aware of the new
man's limitations, the people's expectations of what the
leader should do and be able to do have not changed. A
gifted teacher arrives, but some wanted a gifted pastor, so
they continually moan, groan and criticise him for not
being what he is not, has never claimed to be, is not called
by God to be, and has no desire of ever becoming. He
may even find himself haunted by the imaginary ghost of
his predecessor, who was a gifted pastor and who will
have become a much more gifted pastor in the eyes of the
flock since he left.

Richard W. De Haan is the son of a pastor and in his
booklet *Your Pastor and You* he writes with some feeling
and insight about people's expectations:[2]

> In many churches today it seems that the pastor just
> cannot do anything right. No matter how sincere he may
> be or how hard he tries, there are always some who stand
> ready to find fault and to criticize. Someone has expressed
> the situation in this way:
>
> If the pastor is young, they say he lacks experience;
> If his hair is gray, he's too old for the young people.
>
> If he has five or six children, he has too many;
> If he has no children, he's setting a bad example.
>
> If he preaches from notes, he has canned sermons, and is
>   dry;
> If his messages are extemporaneous, he is not deep.
>
> If he is attentive to the poor people in the church, they
>   claim that he is playing to the grandstand;
> If he pays attention to the wealthy, he is trying to be an
>   aristocrat.
>
> If he uses too many illustrations, he neglects the Bible;
> If he doesn't use enough stories, he isn't clear.
>
> If he condemns wrong, he's cranky;

If he doesn't preach against sin, they say he's a compromiser.

If he preaches the truth, he's offensive;
If he doesn't preach the truth, he's a hypocrite.

If he fails to please everybody, he's hurting the church and ought to leave;
If he does please everybody, he has no convictions.

If he drives an old car, he shames his congregation;
If he drives a new car, he is setting his affection upon earthly things.

If he preaches all the time, the people get tired of hearing one man;
If he invites guest preachers, he's shirking his responsibility.

If he receives a large salary, he is mercenary;
If he receives a small salary, it proves he isn't worth much anyway.

It feels to many clergymen like being asked to judge a baby competition. If there are twenty entries, it matters not which baby he chooses: the judge makes one friend and nineteen enemies.

People's own problems

As the buck stops with the leader who makes the decisions, he often becomes the scapegoat for church members' own emotional problems. The minister of the church may well represent the father who beat me; the elder brother who tormented me; the teacher who scolded me; the boyfriend I never had; or the idol I worship. Consequently, when the vicar is firm with me, it feels like a beating; when he encourages me to follow him down a new, dangerous or dark path, I fear he will torture me; when he preaches repentance, I am doing poorly in my exams and receiving a critical school report;

when he affirms another woman, I am jealous; and if ever he sins, my world is shattered.

Such deep-rooted and often unrealised hurts from the past frequently cause church members to be antagonistic to a clergyman whom they genuinely admire and respect. I have encountered several church members who, for a while, criticised me to my face and praised me behind my back. It was reassuring to hear later about the praise, but it did not help very much at the time. Sometimes unjustified criticism can be demonic in nature.

On one occasion an angry young lady burst into my study. She had been to our church a few times. 'I can't stand you!' she screamed. 'You make me sick! Every time I look at you I want to vomit.' I prayed, 'Come, Holy Spirit,' and her wish was granted. Sometimes demons leave in that particular way. There can be little doubt that demonic forces, sometimes present in church members, will not want a minister to be led into renewal.

The goldfish bowl

It can be very hard being under attack in the office from nine till five, but being able to escape in the evenings or at the weekends has provided a life-line to many in difficult times. This life-line is not readily available to the average clergyman, especially the Anglican vicar and his wife who live in the vicarage beside the church.

In her Grove booklet, *Living with God at the Vicarage*, Wanda Nash has gathered together some interesting comments from clergy and their wives:[3]

The Women's Experience:

We are just about the only people left who are on 24-hour call to the public. The call may be trivial but it may be important. How can one tell? We can never not answer the phone or the door.

Our 'public' life gets mixed up with our 'private' life.

Because the office is in the house, other people's worries invade the kitchen, the sitting-room, they even come upstairs into the bedroom. I can't have a home of my own.

An ordinary Christian family with an Open Door approach can shut it when they want to. We can't.

My home is a fish bowl. We are so exposed.

The Men's Experience:

The interruptions! And I always have to take them lying down!

The 'parish' is a personal space-intruder, and a sexual space-invader.

The Vicarage, my work-place, my family base, is a gold-fish bowl.

I want to be popular, but I'm on a pedestal for criticism.

I want to be loved.

Friends or relatives who come to stay with us are often totally amazed at life in the vicarage and are sometimes pleased to be going home to rest and peace. When members of the parish live in the vicarage while the family and I are away on holiday, we find they are much more sensitive and sympathetic towards us when we return.

The answer to leading a minister who is under siege into renewal is not bombardment. To give him a book he must read, a tape he ought to hear, or a video he simply must watch will not normally pierce the defences of a man who, out of necessity, is now operating a well-fortified castle. If you go into almost any clergyman's study you may well notice a pile of books in one corner, each with a bookmark at page 10. These are books he has started and intends to read one day. Close by will be a guilt pile of letters and jobs to be done which always takes precedence over the books but never seems to become any smaller. After my first book came out I kept bumping into clergymen who all said the same thing, 'Hello Peter. My wife's reading your book.' Anyone who thinks they have *the* book which will change their minister's life would be well-advised to give it to his wife for her birthday.

Bombardment or attack in any form always speaks of opposition, and it frequently creates opposition from someone who is supposedly on the same side. The Acts of the Apostles gives us rather more positive approaches for helping the leader:

1. Love

In Acts 6 the twelve apostles gathered all the disciples together and said:

> It would not be right for us to neglect the ministry of the word of God in order to wait on tables. Brothers, choose seven men from among you who are known to be full of the Spirit and wisdom. We will turn this responsibility over to them and will give our attention to prayer and the ministry of the word (Acts 6:2–4).

The leaders of the church were relieved of menial tasks by seven men who were 'full of the Spirit'. Two of them, at least, were extremely powerful waiters: 'Now Stephen, a man full of God's grace and power, did great wonders and miraculous signs among the people' (Acts 6:8); 'When the crowds heard Philip and saw the miraculous signs he did, they all paid close attention to what he said. With shrieks, evil spirits came out of many, and many paralytics and cripples were healed' (Acts 8:6–7).

Sadly, in many of our churches, when the menial tasks need to be done it is the 'charismatics' who are sometimes most noticeably absent. The excitement and the thrill of experiencing free, unmerited spiritual gifts seem to cause some to stop short of bearing spiritual fruit. There is a Zulu proverb which says, 'I cannot hear what you say for the thunder of what you are.'[4] It is very difficult for clergy to hear what some of their flock are saying because of who they are.

Serving our church and our minister and coming under his authority will not lead him into renewal, and neither should we do it for that purpose; that would be manipulation. But genuine love casts out fear and takes down the walls of prejudice. In every church, drains need to be cleared, floors cleaned and maintenance carried out regularly. When those keen on spiritual gifts are the first to volunteer for such tasks, prove to be reliable, and love all other church members through him who first loved us, then their minister may be more willing to listen to them.

My colleague John Weller is a traditional clergyman whose father and brother also followed the same vocation. While serving the Lord in Zambia a former parishioner, for whom they had the greatest respect, wrote excitedly to them about how Michael Harper had led him and his family into renewal.[5] At about the same time the *Church Times* carried an article about a Fountain Trust rally in Guildford Cathedral. John's wife Jean felt that if something was bringing the Church of England to life it was worth finding out more about it.

As soon as they returned to England and settled into a Birmingham parish Jean attended a Fountain Trust Conference for herself. There she saw people who had something she knew was missing from her own life. As tactfully as possible Jean told John she thought he was a good priest, but maybe sometimes lacked a little 'bounce'. Jean left a copy of *Nine o'Clock in the Morning* lying around, just in case.[6]

When God is moving, letters, newspaper articles, conferences, books and right people at right times often follow one another in quick succession. John was assisted in his parish by an elderly priest who happened to mention how helpful he found praying in tongues with geriatric patients. Words, books and tapes offered by loving, respected colleagues at the right place and time rather than insensitive, charismatic 'keenies' may seem more like food to the hungry than bullets to the persecuted.

John is a quiet and cautious person, but having registered all this he privately sought and received the gift of tongues in church. From tongues he moved to healing and eventually began to experience blessings in a difficult parish where conventional pastoral methods had not seemed to work too well. Looking back, both John and Jean would say that their ministry before then was not an unmitigated failure and since then it certainly hasn't been an unmitigated success, but they can definitely see the changes the Holy Spirit has made in their lives and work for God.

Time and time again, whether it be conversion or seeking more of the Holy Spirit, people say, 'I saw something they had which I wanted.' Loving service in the power of the Holy Spirit will often help others to see something they are lacking. This has the effect of raising the portcullis and once this has occurred articles, books and conferences can enter the minister's fortress more easily, when prompted by the Holy Spirit.

2. Prayer

In Acts 12 we have a church leader under siege—in prison. James has just been executed by Herod, and Luke records this: 'So Peter was kept in prison, but the church was earnestly praying to God for him' (Acts 12:5). I believe we need to pray for our ministers. After the early church had prayed, Peter was freed by an angel, the guards were executed and Herod was eaten by worms. Who knows what may happen if we begin praying for our ministers?

When praying for someone who holds different views from myself I never feel it is right to pray that God will make him like me. It does not seem appropriate to try and pray away his free will, which is a gift from God in the first place. I normally advise praying in twos and threes for three things:

(a) We pray for God the Father through Jesus to send his Holy Spirit upon our minister. We have found in experience that when we pray, 'Come, Holy Spirit,' he comes. It may seem right to ask God to come in loving, affirming, renewing power.

From the cross Jesus prayed, 'Father, forgive them, for they do not know what they are doing' (Lk 23:34). He did not pray, 'Make them repent'; 'Change their attitude'; or even, 'Help them to see the truth.' His prayer was to ask Father God to send forgiving power in their direction.

It is my belief we can ask Father God, through Jesus, to send his Spirit on our minister.

(b) We pray, in the name of Jesus, against any satanic forces attacking our minister from outside or inside, that his eyes may be free to see Jesus.

Jesus said, 'Simon, Simon, Satan has asked to sift you as wheat. But I have prayed for you' (Lk 22:31–32).

We have found through deliverance ministry that we have power in Jesus' name over demons. When Daniel prayed, angels came and fought the satanic forces over Persia and Greece (Dan 9; 10:20).

It is my belief that when two or three agree together to come in prayer against demonic forces which affect our minister, the effect of those forces will be minimised (Mt 18:18–20).[7]

(c) We pray for the Holy Spirit to come upon us and change us, that we may be as Jesus to our minister. 'Lord, make me like Jesus,' sounds better to me than, 'Lord, make the minister like me.'

Jesus also prayed for himself: 'Father, the time has come. Glorify your Son, that your Son may glorify you' (Jn 17:1). Unlike Jesus, we also need to ask God to show us if there is anything wrong in our relationship with the minister from our side.

I believe we can ask the Holy Spirit to come upon us and help us to become more like Jesus.

Praying for the Holy Spirit to come upon our minister, praying in the power of the Holy Spirit against Satan's forces, and inviting the Holy Spirit to come upon us seem to me to be correct and helpful ways to pray. In effect we are praying for our minister to be freed to see the real Jesus. This is not asking God to take his free will away, but rather asking God to give him more freedom to see the truth and make up his own mind. If God comes powerfully upon him, the demons which blind his eyes are bound, and the members of his congregation are showing forth the love of Christ, and still he refuses to change or move forward, then I suspect there is little else which can be done other than to persist and not lose heart. I am convinced, however, that love, prayer and patience will help many ministers to take their first faltering steps towards renewal.

One day in 1967 'DG', who is now a Methodist minister, was walking past the church of St Martin's-within-Ludgate on Ludgate Hill when a compulsive urge came upon him to go inside. He tried to resist by walking past the door a few times, but eventually he entered. In the porch stood the Revd Francis Roy Jeremiah who was then the leader of the London Healing Mission. He was standing in for the vicar who was on holiday.

'Ah! There you are!' said Francis Roy. 'We knew you

were coming because the Lord told us so. It's over here.'
The 'it' was a prayer chapel and the 'we' consisted of
Francis and three elderly ladies belonging to his prayer
partnership.

Francis told DG that the Lord wanted him to pray for
him to be blessed with all needful things. DG refused. He
did not want to sit and allow Francis to place his hands
upon his head and pray in that way. It was one of those
moments when clinging on to faith in the silence can be
vital. Suddenly DG changed his mind and agreed to
receive prayer. Francis then prayed, and as he did so DG
agreed with the prayer, but found himself asking for its
fulfilment to come in three years' time. To this day DG
does not understand the reason for this. From that
moment he knew himself to be born again in the Spirit
and began to learn something of the significance of the
event.

There followed three very eventful, interest-packed
years. Whenever spiritual needs were identified someone
appeared at the right moment with the right teaching,
help or encouragement. This is what DG wrote to me:

> I began to be caught up in a much more committed way
> in the life of the church, but I was still very much aware
> there was something more yet. In 1970 without any real
> desire, or even any real understanding of the Person of the
> Holy Spirit, I became 'baptised in the Spirit' and this was,
> for me, in a way every bit as dramatic as Paul's Damascus
> Road experience and the 'third heaven' experience of
> 2 Corinthians 12:2–4. Ever since I have been a charismatic
> Christian.

I think we need to avoid thinking, feeling or saying,
'All we can do for our minister is to pray.' I believe it is
the best thing we can do for anyone. Those three ladies
who prayed with Francis Roy Jeremiah for DG are even
now indirectly influencing whole congregations through

their prayer. As with St Peter in prison, prayer was enough.

3. Taking the opportunity

If I knock on someone's door in our area and try to tell him about Jesus, there are times when I may receive a string of abuse. I will probably come away from such an encounter totally convinced this person will never be open to the gospel, no matter what I do. But suppose I went round the following week just as he had been told his wife had cancer. I might find myself presented with far greater opportunities.

In 1984 I was invited to attend the signs and wonders conference in Westminster and was not the least bit interested in going.[8] In 1985 my life hit rock bottom. I was depressed, disheartened, and a few major personal problems had come to the surface. In desperate need of help, I was invited to go to a similar conference, this time in Sheffield, and I went.[9] It was a life-changing experience for me.

In leading a minister into renewal, timing is essential, especially God's timing. Until that moment, love and prayer will often prepare the way, help us to recognise God's appointment when it comes, and hopefully give us the necessary discernment to choose which vehicle best suits the person and the moment. I needed a large, anonymous conference where I could sit by the exit and keep my options open. I doubt whether a book, tape, video or visit from another minister would have helped me at that time. For others, such approaches may be absolutely right. Some, despairing over their own congregations, may well say, 'If one of your charismatic friends can come and do anything with this lot, I'm prepared to listen.'

My lay reader, Roger Jones, goes to other churches

with the East Birmingham Renewal Group about once a month to lead seminars on worship and the Holy Spirit.[10] Many times when the minister sees what God can begin to do with his own folk, he begins to take tentative steps himself, sometimes quite dramatically.

Recently Roger led a weekend for a church and the vicar stood in the aisle, watching as people began falling to the floor all around him. He had to step out of the way to let ministry team members come to them. Quite late in the proceedings power came on the vicar himself and he also ended up on the floor. The timing was obviously right. Someone called out, 'Praise God! He's got the vicar.'

Sometimes an Anglican may need to see or hear a canon or a bishop in action before he is convinced. That is why we have often taken people to Sheffield to sit under the ministry of Canon Robert Warren,[11] or to Chorleywood to experience Bishop David Pytches in action.[12] There are many options these days, when the time is right.

Robert, a Baptist minister, said to me recently. 'The challenge of ministry itself drives me towards personal renewal because I am constantly aware of my inability to meet the task with the meagre human resources I have.' He found events organised by Post Green, John Wimber, Spring Harvest and Roger Jones to be a blessing. I would suggest that whenever our minister becomes aware of his 'inability to meet the task with...human resources', there may be an opportunity to take him along to the right event. If we continue to work on love and prayer, we are most likely to recognise that moment and be able to offer the right book, tape or conference to our leader when it is most appropriate.

When to leave

Inevitably there will be churches where faithful members have loved and prayed for their minister and waited, and waited, and nothing ever seems to happen. I am reluctant ever to suggest members should leave their churches. The day before Paul experienced his Damascus Road encounter with the living Lord, most Christians would have said, 'Have nothing to do with that man.' God can do miracles and change lives, and many renewed ministers will testify to the love, prayers and patience of faithful church members who helped them in their less fruitful days, and stayed with them. What the church of Christ most desperately wants today is evangelism, not recycling.

Even so, there may be times when God says, 'Move on,' and here are a few guidelines I often share with people to help them test God's call:

1. Does the minister stop me from doing what the Bible suggests I ought to be doing?

I know of one full-time worker in a church whose boss does not believe in miracles and demons, but never stops her from praying for the sick and casting out demons. The church as a whole may not come into renewal unless he changes or goes, but until then small groups of people and individuals are being greatly blessed. There seems to be no reason for leaving.

2. If the minister does stop me from doing what the Bible says, is he on the same road as me or a different track?

The key here is the Bible. Does he believe, preach and teach God's word? If he does, but has not yet fully appreciated the significance of spiritual gifts and ministering in the power of the Holy Spirit, then I would normally suggest staying. Love, prayer, patience and taking God-given opportunities may well change the situation in time. Few of us believe today everything we believed when we were converted. Most of us have learned more about God since then and have changed our views. People on the same biblical road will often come across the same truth about the Holy Spirit and spiritual gifts sooner or later.

One lady United Reformed Church minister I know was greatly affected through Bible study groups. It is very difficult to study the Gospels and Acts of the Apostles in homes with one another without noticing the sick being healed through Jesus or the disciples. It is even harder when there are sick among us not to lay hands on them and pray for their healing. She wrote to me recently about 'people who had only hours to live—with cancer or MS—who were healed'. If the leader of the church is a Bible-based minister, there will always be hope in Bible study groups because charismatic renewal is in the Bible.

Very often there are several home groups or Bible study groups operating in Bible-based churches, to which the minister does not come. It is quite possible in many places to obtain permission from the minister to meet with friends for Bible study and prayer. 'Come, Holy Spirit' is a valid prayer and when it follows the study of God's word and a time of worship, it is often a helpful way of leading a small group into renewal. Hopefully, there may be times when it is right to invite the minister to this, but even if he refuses to come, much can be achieved through God's grace as long as the leader gives his permission. I don't think it is ever right to be deceitful about it. We defeat Satan with God's weapons, not his own. If such a group is allowed to function there will probably be no need to leave the church, and hopefully, prayerfully, renewal may come and spread from such a meeting.

If the leader of the church does not believe, preach and teach God's word, and stops others from doing so, then it may prove impossible to stay, but occasionally the geographical situation may make a difference. My parents-in-law used to live in a village just outside York where there was a local service each Sunday morning. The clergyman who came did not appear to believe in the Bible, but they continued to attend for two reasons:

(a) They were still able to witness to local people living in the same village, some of whom became born-again Christians. The only service was held on a Sunday morning and provided the contact point, which was worth maintaining.

(b) They were able on a Sunday evening to drive into York and attend the Church of St Michael-le-Belfry which definitely did preach the gospel and feed them spiritually.

In Britain today there are few people who choose to become ministers of churches because it is a good job, has prestige and provides security. Maybe this was once the case, but in our largely secular society it no longer appears to be so. This means that nearly all the leaders of our churches believe in God and somehow, in some way feel he wants them to serve him as church leaders. There is hope in this. At the very least this offers a dimly-burning wick which love, prayer and patience may fan into flame.

I am convinced our own church is only moving forward into renewal because its blundering and impetuous vicar has been given permission to fail by a loving and patient congregation. We still need to learn to pray more, but the congregation's love for me and my family is sometimes overwhelming.

Recently on a church outing, my wife Carol fell into a hole, chipped a bone in her ankle and was in agony for weeks. Almost immediately a cooked meal began to appear at the vicarage at tea-times, accompanied with offers of baby-sitting. They certainly know of my limited culinary skills and their quickly organised food rota was a great help and blessing. To feel loved as a minister can often make the difference between going on with God or turning back.

I am sure that if lay members of churches, filled with the power of the Holy Spirit, seek to understand the problems their leaders face and then learn to help him tackle those problems with love and prayer, then opportunities will be given for leading the minister into renewal. Those who stay close to Jesus will be in the best place to recognise those opportunities and to know how best to offer practical help. Our churches and our country need more ministers to be renewed by the Holy Spirit and I believe we can win this battle through prayer and love. Jesus led eleven out of twelve most unlikely ministers into renewal and by his Spirit he is still with us today.

Notes

1. 'Signs and Wonders' conferences took place in England from 1984 to 1986 in London, Brighton, Sheffield and Harrogate.
2. Richard W. De Haan, *Your Pastor and You* (Radio Bible Class: Grand Rapids, 1973), Section 5.
3. Wanda Nash, *Living with God at the Vicarage* (Grove Books Ltd: Bramcote, 1990), pp 8–10.
4. Contributed by The Rt Revd Laurence Brown, then Bishop of Birmingham, to a compilation by John Pollock of favourite quotations from famous people, entitled *Dear John* (William Collins Sons & Co Ltd: London, 1976).
5. Michael Harper was the leader in the seventies of the Fountain Trust organisation, which organised a number of charismatic conferences in various parts of the country. In recent years he has been directing the work of Sharing Of Ministries Abroad.

6. Dennis Bennett, *Nine o'Clock in the Morning* (Kingsway Publications: Eastbourne, 1971).

7. Praying against principalities, powers and demonic forces has been given a helpful airing in the book edited by Peter Wagner entitled *Territorial Spirits* (Sovereign World Ltd: Chichester, 1991).

8. Conference entitled 'Third Wave', organised by Manna Ministries and held in Central Hall, Westminster in October 1984.

9. Signs and Wonders Part I conference held in October 1985 at Sheffield Town Hall.

10. East Birmingham Renewal Group is a small interdenominational fellowship of Christians working towards renewal in the church. Each member attends his or her own church on Sundays, but meets together mid-week for worship, teaching and ministry. The group prayerfully supports Roger Jones, one of its members, in his full-time, itinerant Christian work and ministers in teams in the power of the Holy Spirit when churches or communities invite them to do so.

11. Canon Robert Warren, Vicar of St Thomas' Church, Nairn Street, Crookes, Sheffield, S. Yorkshire.

12. Bishop David Pytches, Vicar of St Andrew's Church, Quickley Lane, Chorleywood, Herts.

11

More Power

On Friday 31st October 1985 we took some of the young
people from our church to a Roman Catholic mass at
Maltby in Yorkshire. One or two Catholic friends who
often attend our courses recommended it to me and I am
prepared to try anything once. We spent the afternoon
sampling the delights of the Derbyshire Dales. We wandered by meandering streams, played games in the roll-
ing hills, and ate chips out of a bag at the Matlock
Riviera.

Maltby is a uniformly constructed town made up of
identical rows of back-to-back terraced homes which
were built to house some of the workers from the South
Yorkshire coalfields. Unlike our part of Birmingham, the
small town felt like a community with its own very
definite identity. One type of housing on one site for one
kind of worker created a feeling of oneness. We sensed a
number of eyes were upon us as we, the obvious visitors,
entered the Church of St Mary Magdalene.

The simple Roman Catholic church was packed. To
the right the organ and piano were hidden by dust covers,
while in front of us was the high altar, with a lady chapel
to the right; the symbolic carved dove hovered over all.
Several musicians with strings and pipes were seated on
the very front row of the congregation as we took our
places a few rows behind them.

At half-past seven the elderly priest entered with his servers, and the mass was underway. A liturgy not unlike the modern Anglican Communion service was used, with responses led by lute, flute and voices from the front row. It made a pleasant change. We were welcomed for a blessing when the others received the consecrated bread. It was all over in an hour.

There followed a quarter of an hour's break before the Benediction began. I had never attended one before and wondered if I should stay, but having come a long way I decided to go for everything.

The priest took out a large wafer from a tin box on a stand in the corner, put it on the altar and everyone sang in tongues for twenty minutes. We were then invited to wait upon the Lord in silence and call out anything we thought he was saying. Some useful thoughts and phrases were shared, mostly of an encouraging nature.

'There will now be another fifteen minutes' break before the ministry,' said the priest, and retired once more to his vestry.

The 'ministry' was the main reason we had come, so we paced about for quarter of an hour, not being close enough to the loo queue to secure a place worth having. In due course the quietly-spoken, saintly-looking elderly priest came to the front of the congregation. For just two minutes he shared some helpful thoughts on the light of Christ, and then began giving some words he believed were from God.

'Is there somebody over here with a pain in the lower back?' he asked as he moved towards a group of people. He pointed to no more than four or five and someone's hand went up. 'Receive the light of Christ into your pain,' he said. 'Someone over here with tooth trouble?' he enquired gently, and a mother with babe in arms claimed the light of Christ for her little child. After five or six of these (all of which were claimed but not tested), he went behind the altar rail.

Everyone else seemed to be ready for this moment and formed a queue along the centre aisle. Thirty or forty knelt across the front of the church, some helpers stood behind them, and the priest went along the row laying hands on every person. He barely paused at each one, but they all fell backwards, were caught, laid down, and the catchers moved on swiftly. Those on the floor hardly had time to stagger to their feet before the next group moved in and fell over to take their place.

'Come on, Peter,' said our enthusiastic young people, 'it's our turn.'

'Oh yes, right. Carry on then,' I stuttered.

'No, you first. We'll follow.'

I turned white and felt red. I took my time. Maybe now was the right moment for the little room in the corner. For the first time that night there was no queue. The minstrels struck up. They had been up, down, up and back again and sounded very blessed.

I led the youngsters to the back of the line, grateful I was not wearing my clerical collar! I have experienced some nervous waiting moments before: the dentist, the operating theatre, my wedding day, the birth of my children. This was worse than any of those.

He's not going to push me over, I muttered to myself. *There's no way he's going to push me over.* On the other hand, I thought, *what if I'm the only one in the whole building who doesn't go over?* I admonished myself with a quick crash course in theology. *Falling over doesn't matter. It's receiving from the Lord whatever he wants. Outward signs are unimportant.*

I should have been convinced, but I wasn't. Pure, unadulterated fear dominated everything. *I'll roll over,* I thought. *No one will ever know.*

At least the dialogue was taking time while the number of those in front diminished and the time for the execution drew closer. At the last moment I made my decision: *Whatever you want, Lord. But he's not going to push me over.* I felt this covered all possible wrong motives.

I knelt on the step, hands clasped behind my back, like Thomas More in the tower. The saintly old priest drew nearer and nearer. Boing! Boing! Boing! Down they went. As he reached the one next to me I just had time to think, *He's not going to.* . . . one more time before his hand came within six inches of my head, and I was gone.

Pleasant power washed all over me. It felt beyond my control. I eventually opened my eyes and found myself giggling with holy joy. 'You can't stay there,' said a firm voice. 'The next lot are here already.' As I staggered back to my seat I was still giggling. The music stopped and the congregation began chanting 'Hail Marys'. I sat and giggled. My neighbour nudged me and said, 'Hey! You don't laugh during a Hail Mary.' I tried to giggle more quietly.

In no time at all it was over. We had fish and chips next door then a silent ride home in the middle of the night, during which I was alone with my thoughts.

'Lord, I feel strange. I'm still bubbling over with joy inside. You seem very close. Is it really you?' I asked in my mind.

'Yes, Peter,' he seemed to say, 'it is.'

'But Lord,' I argued, 'he's a Roman Catholic.'

'And I love him as much as I love you,' came the reply.

'Yes Lord, I understand that,' I continued, 'but he believes things which are wrong. His theology is unsound,' I remonstrated, expressing my deepest concern.

'Do you think,' the Lord appeared to be asking, 'that everything you believe is right? You've changed your views over infant baptism three times in the last month.

If I could only use people whose beliefs are one hundred per cent right. I wouldn't be able to do very much with you.'

I often notice how 'words' in my head which I think are from God never seem to comment on doctrine. God's words in the Bible in my experience are the only ones I have ever been able to use for clarifying doctrinal beliefs. For the moment I was happy to accept my experience of falling to the floor and bubbling over with joy as from the Lord. I certainly felt greatly loved and affirmed.

Afterwards I was helped enormously by Bill Subritzky's teaching on Roman Catholics.[1] He suggested that however unsound some of their superstructure may appear to some Protestants, they were acceptable as a Christian church because their base was Jesus Christ. This made much sense to me. Jehovah's Witnesses and Christadelphians are not acceptable to the World Council of Churches because of their inadequate beliefs about Jesus Christ. Often we spend hours arguing about the different superstructures of our many Christian denominations when in reality we are all one in Christ Jesus because we share the same cornerstone.

I became totally certain I had fallen to the floor under the power of the Holy Spirit, especially as I returned twice more and became more convinced each time of the kindness, sensitivity, and gentle Christian sincerity of the elderly priest who laid hands on me.

Jesus said to his disciples, 'You will receive power when the Holy Spirit comes on you' (Acts 1:8). Power came from the hand of the priest, even before it reached my head. He never did touch me. He certainly did not push me over. He had received power, which came on others as he ministered to them in Jesus' name; more power than I had previously experienced. For him there was no, 'Stand with your eyes closed, heads up, hands held out, and think of Jesus for fifteen minutes while I pray, "Come, Holy Spirit." ' He ministered much more in the same style as Jesus did.

Our aim is always to minister as Jesus did, but we have found the path towards this goal to be full of progressive steps and far from instantaneous. Jesus seems to have taken some of these steps himself. At the age of twelve he knew God as Father (Lk 2:49) and yet after that he continued to grow in 'wisdom and stature, and in favour with God and men' (Lk 2:52). This went on for eighteen years. He did not begin his ministry until he 'was about thirty years old' (Lk 3:23). He began after 'the Holy Spirit descended on him' (Lk 3:22) and after he had spent forty days alone in the desert. When he emerged to start his ministry Jesus was 'full of the Holy Spirit' (Lk 4:1–2). The assurance with which he did so was based on knowing God as Father from an early age and being filled with the power of the Holy Spirit.

The disciples spent three years with Jesus during which time he made the Father known to them (Jn 14:8–11). After this they waited several days in Jerusalem for the gift of the Holy Spirit and then had the privilege of beginning their ministry at a time when God was pouring out his Spirit in great miracle and revival power. I am not convinced that we can expect to start ministering where Jesus and the disciples finished.

I heard a story once about a young man who took over from an elderly and gifted pastor. At the farewell gathering he was introduced to his predecessor and tried to find encouraging words to say to him. 'I'll continue where you left off, sir,' he offered. The sagacious pastor thought for a moment and then replied kindly, 'No, you'll start where I started.'

We have found that if we start trying to minister in a bold and directive way, claiming everything we do or say is from God, we are very likely to mistake enthusiasm for faith, put people off and spoil God's agenda with our own. By asking God to come, waiting and watching, we discover the God who comes in a similar way to the early disciples who waited and watched Jesus. It is our first step on the path to more love, more power and more of Jesus in our lives. We begin by inviting God to send his Holy Spirit on Christians, confident in the knowledge that Jesus himself ministered mostly to believers.

Ministering in the power of the Holy Spirit to believers

In New Testament Greek, 'faith' is the noun and 'believe' is the verb of the same root word. To have faith is to be a believer. With this in mind I found these verses to be very reassuring.

'When Jesus heard this, he was astonished and said to those following him, "I tell you the truth, I have not found anyone in Israel with such great faith.... Go! It will be done just as you believed it would" ' (Mt 8:10,13).

'When Jesus saw their faith, he said to the paralytic... "Get up, take your mat and go home" ' (Mt 9:2,6).

'Jesus turned and saw her. "Take heart, daughter," he said, "your faith has healed you" ' (Mt 9:22).

'Then he touched their eyes and said, "According to your faith will it be done to you"; and their sight was restored' (Mt 9:29).

'Then Jesus answered, "Woman, you have great faith! Your request is granted" ' (Mt 15:28).

Jesus said, 'Everything is possible for him who believes' (Mk 9:23).

'Then he said to him, "Rise and go; your faith has made you well" ' (Lk 17:19).

'Jesus said to him, "Receive your sight; your faith has healed you" ' (Lk 18:42).

Even Legion, 'when he saw Jesus from a distance, he ran and fell on his knees in front of him' (Mk 5:6).

The corollary, seen when Jesus visited his home town, is perhaps even more persuasive. Jesus 'did not do many miracles' in Nazareth, 'because of their lack of faith' (Mt 13:58).

When the Holy Spirit was given to all believers there were still times when healing came in response to the faith of the sick person. 'Paul looked directly at him, saw that he had faith to be healed and called out, "Stand up on your feet!" ' (Acts 14:9–10; see also Acts 5:15–16).

Praying for believers does seem to be the right place to start. When Jesus sent out the Twelve among the people of God (Mt 10:6), to proclaim the kingdom, heal the sick and cast out demons he gave them these instructions:

> Whatever town or village you enter, search for some worthy person there and stay at his house until you leave. As you enter the home, give it your greeting. If the home is deserving, let your peace rest on it; if it is not, let your peace return to you. If anyone will not welcome you or listen to your words, shake the dust off your feet when you leave that home or town (Mt 10:11–14; see also Luke 10:8–11).

Those who respond to the preaching, as with the crippled man at Lystra (Acts 14:8–10), are to be healed and delivered. Those who do not receive the word are not to receive ministry. It is certainly much easier praying with those who have faith themselves.

I remember one service at Christ Church when, after thirty minutes' worship, I preached for about forty-five minutes and then invited the Holy Spirit to come among us. Quarter of an hour later I said a closing prayer and sat down in a chair at the front to recover. After a few minutes a man approached me.

'Nothing ever happens to me,' he said, 'but I believe that if you lay hands on me it will.'

I felt tired and faithless. It was the end of a long

Sunday and I was ready for my armchair, slippers and cornflakes. I did not want to be involved, but his display of faith encouraged me to say, 'Yes'. There was no further conversation. We both stood and I prayed, 'Come, Holy Spirit,' with my hand lightly on his forehead. Immediately there was a 'Maltby-type' reaction and he crashed to the floor. I still felt tired and faithless, so I summoned others to come and stay with him while I retired to my armchair.

The Lord continued to bless him, anoint him with power and show him many things concerned with evangelism into which he was calling him. It is easy and a great privilege to pray with someone when he has faith in Christ. I think most of those who have been healed when I prayed for them were healed by Jesus through their own faith in him, rather than mine.

Reflecting on our experience at Maltby, it is right to say one member of our group did not go over in the Spirit and did not receive a blessing. After the initial embarrassment and stigma had worn off, she tackled a number of problems as outlined in Chapter 5. Subsequently, she fell down in the power of the Holy Spirit at our church when others prayed for the Holy Spirit to come upon her, and she received considerable emotional healing. She also returned to Maltby where a similar thing happened. It seems right to say that power from God does not normally override our free will, even though there was more power coming on more people at Maltby than we normally witness at Christ Church.

On our journey of learning to minister as Jesus did with more power, we begin by asking God to come on believers. There is considerable biblical evidence to support and encourage us in doing this. After a while we may progress further along the path and begin doing things a little differently.

The Holy Spirit helps us to know God

I am told that when I ask the Holy Spirit to come on our congregation I do not do it the way I teach others to do it. I am not alone in this. When I was in South Africa I asked John Wimber to pray for my friend William, which he very graciously did, for some time. I could not help noticing he did not use the Wimber model as described in *Power Healing*.[2] Recently my wife confessed to me that she only ministers to individuals in the 'Lawrence way' when she is demonstrating my teaching publicly.

Basically, what has happened is that by ministering in the power of the Holy Spirit for some time we have begun to know the Holy Spirit as a person. Now, as well as asking him to come on the counsellee, we are also sensing his presence on our side of the fence. I have found that if I say to Christians, 'Listen to God and do whatever he tells you to do,' many of them never start ministering in the power of the Holy Spirit at all. They find it is very difficult to recognise someone's voice when they do not know the person. By encouraging them to be filled with the Holy Spirit themselves and to ask him to come on others, especially those with faith, it is amazing how many people learn to do what the Father is doing and begin to know the Holy Spirit as a person. Then they can start being more confident and directive; more assured they are speaking in God's name rather than their own.

St Peter spent three years following Jesus everywhere, seeing him minister as well as having a try himself. In Acts 3 Peter says to a man crippled from birth, 'Silver or gold I do not have, but what I have I give you. In the name of Jesus Christ of Nazareth, walk' (Acts 3:6). I know the Holy Spirit came powerfully upon Peter in Acts 2 and almost certainly filled him in a new way, but I can also sense his three years with Jesus playing an important part. It is as if he is walking in his Master's footsteps and knows exactly what Jesus would say and do in these circumstances. He speaks in the name of Jesus, filled with the Spirit of Jesus, with the confidence of one who knows Jesus personally. In speaking about the incident before the Sanhedrin Peter is in no doubt as to what has happened: 'It is by the name of Jesus Christ of Nazareth, whom you crucified but whom God raised from the dead, that this man stands before you completely healed' (Acts 4:10).

In some ways I think learning to be filled with the Holy Spirit and praying for the Holy Spirit to come upon others is rather like the 'experience' Peter had of Jesus ministering to others for three years. Through the Scriptures we have access to the same teachings Peter heard, and through the Holy Spirit we have access to the same experience of Jesus' ministry.

As we ask the Holy Spirit to come on believers, and as we wait and watch what he does and co-operate with him, so we come to know God in a personal way, as the disciples did by being with Jesus. Ministering in the power of the Holy Spirit is ministering from the position of a relationship. As we come to know more about God his image in us begins to change, our relationship deepens and we are in a better place to receive more power. It is important and comforting to see some of the mistakes Peter made in those first three years.

Peter was full of doubt and very little faith (Mt 14:28–31); dull (Mt 15:15–16); unforgiving (Mt 18:21); at times inspired by Satan and a stumbling-block to Jesus (Mt 16:23). He fell asleep when he was asked to 'watch and pray' (Mk 14:37–38); did not know what he was saying (Lk 9:33); argued with Jesus (Lk 8:45); tried to tell him what to do (Jn 13:8); and became violent (Jn 18:10). Finally he denied Jesus three times and called down curses on himself (Mt 26:74).

When Jesus called Peter to follow him, Peter was hardly an off-the-peg and ready-to-wear Christian; he was not even a rough, uncut diamond who required chiselling down and smoothing. He was much more a clay pot who needed to be smashed by the potter before he could start again. In fact when Peter first followed Jesus it is highly likely he followed the wrong Jesus for the wrong motives. His image of God was distorted by the oppression of his people.

Peter followed Jesus because of the testimony of his brother: 'The first thing Andrew did was to find his brother Simon and tell him, "We have found the Messiah" [that is, the Christ]' (Jn 1:41). 'Messiah' means 'anointed one'. We know what it meant to Jesus because we know the gospel story, but Peter's eyes at the start were covered with rather different shades. There had been other 'christs' before from whom he had gained his presuppositions.

King David was the anointed one who had defeated the Philistines. Before him Joshua had taken the land and Moses had led the people out of slavery in Egypt. King Cyrus of Persia is referred to as the anointed one in Isaiah 45:1 for setting Israel free from Babylon, and in Peter's day Judas Maccabbeus would be remembered as the one who defeated the Greeks and cleansed the land.

Peter's Messiah would be expected to set Israel free from the Romans. Jesus seemed to fit the bill. In every way he could be seen as the people's champion. He drew support from large crowds of ordinary people. They were his to command. As a teacher he held their attention, instructed them clearly and inspired them with zeal. Peter's Messiah was compassionate yet powerful in the face of opposition: he walked through crowds who wanted to kill him, and took on the scribes and Pharisees without flinching. In every sense he was the people's champion.

Jesus was also God's champion. The people were on his side and so was God. He healed the sick, raised the dead, fed five thousand, walked on the water and calmed the storm. Like Moses, Elisha and Isaiah before him, Jesus could do signs and wonders to confuse and defeat the enemy because God was with him. God's Messiah was expected to bring in the Day of the Lord when every eye would see Israel as God's chosen people. It would be a day of liberation and triumph. In every sense Jesus was God's champion.

So when Jesus said, 'Who do you say I am?' Peter had no problem: 'You are the Christ' (Messiah—anointed one), he replied promptly (Mt 16:15–16).

The title was right. Jesus affirmed him. The problem was the content. The problem was in going to Jerusalem to die. 'Peter took him aside and began to rebuke him. "Never, Lord!" he said. "This shall never happen to you!" ' (Mt 16:22).

Jesus' insistence brought confusion but obedience. If he had to fight and die for the liberation of Israel, so be it. Peter was no coward. He was there at the arrest with his sword. He struck the first blow for the freedom fighters, but it was also the last. Jesus healed the man and gave himself up for arrest, torture and death without any fight. This was not Peter's Messiah.

When Peter said three times, 'I don't know the man,' there was a sense in which he was telling the truth. That night Peter's wrong image of God died as he went outside and wept bitterly (Mt 26:69–75).

After the resurrection Jesus came publicly to Peter and asked him three times, 'Do you love me?' and we know the content of that love. 'When you were younger you... went where you wanted; but when you are old... someone else will... lead you where you do not want to go' (Jn 21:15–18).

This is the beginning of the right image of Jesus forming in Peter. By the Day of Pentecost the vessel had been broken and rebuilt, ready to be filled with the Holy

Spirit. Only Jesus-shaped vessels will hold the Holy Spirit and be able to cope with God's power. I always think it is ironical that Peter was the one led by the Holy Spirit to take the gospel of Jesus to the Romans; the ones Peter had wanted Jesus to help him kill (Acts 10).

I suspect nearly everyone comes to Jesus initially because of what they hope to receive from him. His normal response is, 'Follow me.' But I believe 'more power' will come to the Christian when he stops seeking what he can get and starts asking what he can give; when he learns to serve, obey and eventually to love the King of all glory, rather than try to use him for his own ends. 'If anyone would come after me, he must deny himself and take up his cross and follow me' (Mt 16:24).

When I first began praying for the Holy Spirit to come upon people I did so with enthusiasm and impatience. There was a kind of unspoken feeling that if God would only release more power in me I would change the world. I was much more like the Peter in the Gospels than the one in the Acts of the Apostles. But power for power's sake would be disastrous. Power without submission and obedience to the will of God would be satanic. The angels who follow Satan still have the power God gave them but, without submission and obedience to God, they have devastated our world, for a season.

Asking God to come and then waiting for him to do so often begins to deal with our impatience and own agendas. Until God is seen or felt to come nothing happens. When he does come it is not ourselves doing it, so we learn about God: what he does or may do in many and varied situations. The more we see him come and change these situations, the more our trust in God through faith in Jesus also begins to grow. I believe it is a style which also minimises the damage our mistakes can do to others and in learning about the real Messiah adds an important experience-dimension to the Scriptures.

As we learn about God through the Bible and our experience of him in the Holy Spirit, our need for change is exposed. The same Spirit flowing in us and through us can then begin to effect that change, put the right image of Jesus within us and start equipping us to lay hands on those without faith. This is our next step.

Ministering in the power of the Holy Spirit to unbelievers

There were a few occasions when Jesus, full of faith and power himself, brought healing to those with no expectation, hope or faith. In Luke 7:11–17 we have a record of Jesus visiting the town of Nain. As he approached the town gate a dead person was being carried out. The widowed mother of the dead man had not heard Jesus preach, she did not ask him for help, and there is no other reference in the New Testament to the town of Nain. Jesus, uninvited but with compassion, approached the coffin and spoke to the dead man, who was raised back to life.

In John 9 Jesus came across a man blind from birth who was not sick because of his parents' sin nor his own (Jn 9:3). Jesus put mud on his eyes and told him to wash it off. The man obeyed and received his sight. Obedience was present, but there was no request to be healed and no sign of faith.

In John 5 Jesus met a man who had been crippled for thirty-eight years. He asked him if he wanted to get well and the man responded with complaining. Even so Jesus told him to get up and walk, and the man obeyed. Afterwards when questioned, 'The man who was healed had no idea who it was' who healed him (Jn 5:13). He had heard no preaching and shown no faith. In fact Jesus described him as a sinner (Jn 5:14).

When Peter was used by God to heal the crippled

beggar in Acts 3 there also appears to be no evidence of faith in the sick man. He asked for alms and got legs. It seems there are times when God gives the faith and the power to the person ministering in his name.

One Sunday evening I persuaded Susan to lead our time of ministry with five or six young people in her parents' home. 'It's quite easy, Susan,' I said. 'All you do is pray, "Come, Holy Spirit," and then shut up. You watch to see who receives most, go and lay hands on them, and all will be fine.' Hesitantly Susan did as she was told. For once I was able to close my eyes and receive from God myself.

Almost immediately power came upon me and I saw a picture in my mind. A white figure was taking me by the hand. We ran along together and then took off into the air, just like Raymond Briggs' Snowman.[3] I don't know how, but I knew it was not Jesus. At first I thought we were going to fly round the area and learn a few things which might be helpful for our church. But rather too quickly for my liking, we started to leave the world behind and I became afraid. 'Where are we going?' I enquired from the figure in white.

'To heaven,' he said kindly, 'to see God.'

The fear of God came suddenly all over me. 'I'm not ready,' I said, 'I'll never cope. I don't feel at all prepared to die.'

He smiled. 'When we leave the world behind,' he informed me, 'we leave fear behind as well. Heaven is a place of love, not of fear.'

And he was right. The more we travelled and the higher we flew, the less afraid I became. If this was death then it was better than I thought it would be.

Eventually we landed in what seemed like a waiting room. Other figures in white were there, all very friendly and sincere. I knew they were all angels. I was asked to go into the throne room, where I saw a large seat from behind. A kind voice spoke to me: 'You must not see me from the front,' he said. 'When you do that you will not be going back. How can we help you?'

I thought for a moment. 'Could I take these angels back with me?' I asked. 'We need some help.'

God laughed. 'How many do you need?' he enquired rather rhetorically. 'One angel killed 185,000 men in a night' (2 Kings 19:35).

I realised there was no answer to such a comment, but God did not seem to expect one. 'I will give you the one who brought you here,' he continued, 'to be with you at all times; he will help you.'

Until then I had hardly noticed the angels in Scripture and never preached about them. 'How do I treat him?' I asked. It seemed a good offer, but I had no idea what to do with an angel. God was quite specific.

'You must never seek him or speak to him unless he speaks to you,' he replied. 'Then you may reply. You continue praying to me as before, but know that we are with you.'

I'm afraid I doubted the reality of what I was seeing in my own imagination. 'How may I know this is objectively true?' I ventured.

'In a few moments the picture will fade. When it does, open your eyes and look around for someone for whom nothing is happening at all. Go over and lay-on hands but say nothing.'

Very soon after that the picture went and I opened my eyes. Hesitantly, Susan was still looking for the one for whom most was happening. I took the opposite view. Instantly I spotted Donna. Nothing ever happened to Donna and tonight's 'nothing' was as obvious as all the others. I walked over, sat beside her and gently laid my hand on her head. As I did I saw flames with colours emanating from them over her head. Donna rolled over and lay on the floor as great power came upon her and blessed her.

Afterwards I asked what had happened. 'I don't know,' she said, a little bemused but overjoyed something had taken place at last. 'I felt great power and saw flames with colours in my mind. It was lovely.'

Susan was far from happy. 'Why did you go to Donna?' she demanded. 'Nothing was happening to Donna. I'm sure nothing was happening with Donna.' It seemed to Susan a question of 'do as I say, not as I do', but I did my best to explain.

A few days later Christine was suffering very badly from neuralgia on the left side of her face. I tried it again. I laid a hand on the side of her face and said nothing at all. Great heat came on the area and after fifteen minutes Christine said all the pain had gone. 'It was like an anaesthetic,' she commented, 'I lost all sensation in the side of my face for fifteen minutes.' This was some time ago and no neuralgia has returned.

A week later during a prayer time in our lounge Julia said, 'I can see Jesus; he's standing in a white robe behind Peter.'

Immediately Carol and I said together, 'Are you sure it is Jesus?'

'Hang on,' said Julia, and had another look. 'No,' she replied, 'it's not Jesus. It's a man in a white robe.'

From time to time others have seen a similar picture without knowing of the previous ones. I share this story for three reasons:

(a) It was the moment when I first believed God could work through me irrespective of the other person's faith.

(b) I believe this picture was not just meant as an encouragement for me but for all Christians. 'Are not all angels ministering spirits sent to serve those who will inherit salvation?' (Heb 1:14; see also Matthew 18:10 and Acts 12:15).

(c) I received this vision and affirmation when someone else prayed, 'Come, Holy Spirit,' over me.

As we invite the Holy Spirit to come on others and encourage them to receive whatever God wants to do, through faith in Jesus, we begin to know the Holy Spirit as a person. As we allow the word of God and the power of the Holy Spirit to make us more like Jesus, we may begin to experience his anointing on us for signs and wonders with believers and unbelievers. Then, I believe, it is the time to seek God for even more power to do his will.

More power

In Acts 2 Peter proclaimed the King and the kingdom, and 3,000 were saved. In Acts 5 Peter's shadow healed all who were tormented by evil spirits. In Acts 9 Peter, all alone, prayed and then raised Tabitha from the dead.

This is more power than I have ever seen, but the principles by which he operated are still the same. Peter received the authority of God the Father and the power of the Holy Spirit through faith in Jesus Christ. Jesus led him to an experiential knowledge of the 'God who speaks' and the 'God who comes'.[4] Once he had learned to lay aside his own thoughts and desires his faith in such a God led to more power flowing through him—and miracles did not end with the apostolic age. There have been others since Peter who have been used by God to do similar signs and wonders, even in the twentieth century.

In 1903 at Rock Island, Illinois Maria Woodworth-Etter held one of her large tent meetings. A seven-year-old boy was brought to her who had never walked and was born insane, blind, deaf and dumb. She prayed for him in the name of Jesus, after which he received a bright, intelligent mind, and could hear and see perfectly. For the rest of the campaign the congregation saw him every day laughing, playing and walking around in front of the pulpit.[5]

Shortly afterwards a member of Maria Woodworth-Etter's team visited a young girl in St Louis who was also born deaf and dumb. As a result of this infirmity she was run over by a street car, paralysed from the hips down and put into a plaster of Paris cast. The lady from the team went to pray for the girl and as she approached her in bed the Holy Spirit came upon her in a remarkable way. Not knowing one single letter of the deaf and dumb language, she found herself explaining to the young girl, in sign language, how to give herself to the Lord. The girl did this and then prayed for herself. At once she had a vision of Jesus and heard him saying, 'You can walk.' She saw him reaching out his hand and she took the tips of his fingers. She rose from her bed and the plaster cast broke and fell off her legs as she walked to her Father.

The next day a friend who had been crippled for sixteen years telephoned the family. She refused to believe she was now talking to a girl who was born deaf and dumb, and came round on her crutches to see for herself. As she did, she believed, was healed herself, and threw away her crutches.[6]

Smith Wigglesworth was an unschooled plumber from Bradford who died at the age of eighty-seven in 1947, the year I was born. It is claimed God used him to raise fourteen people from the dead.[7] One of these Smith Wigglesworth has recorded himself:

> Carrying the mother across the room I put her up against the wardrobe. I held her there. I said, 'In the Name of Jesus, death come out.' Like a fallen tree, leaf after leaf, her body begin moving—upright instead of lifeless. Her feet touched the floor. 'In Jesus' Name walk!' I said. She did, back to bed.[8]

The lady gave her own testimony later at one of his meetings.

The healing of Grant Packer in 1984 is a more recent story and God only healed him after the modern medical profession had done all they could, but failed. His crippling spinal disease was referred to an orthopaedic surgeon, then passed on to a neurologist and finally to a rheumatologist, all of whom were unable to help. Not only was he confined to a wheelchair, but the constant pain required powerful drugs, which took their toll on his body. He was given nine months to live.

Brian and Diane Packer were Christians, but did not believe in miracles until, out of sheer desperation, they took their son Grant to see Bill Subritzky. Bill prayed first for Diane, who fell over on the floor under the power of the Holy Spirit, and then for Brian, not wanting their attitudes to stop Grant from being healed. Finally he prayed for Grant, anointed him with oil and prayed for him again. As Grant sat in the wheelchair Bill said, 'I want you to stand up.' This he did, then walked and ultimately ran down the corridor. It took forty-five minutes, after which the floor needed mopping because of Brian's and Diane's tears. Dr Bruce Conyngham, a medical doctor, testified to Grant's complete healing.[9]

I was not alive when God was using Maria Woodworth-Etter and Smith Wigglesworth, but I have met Bill Subritzky and worked as a member of his team on two conferences. I have witnessed others being healed by the power of God at work through Bill, and have spoken to them afterwards. I believe the same power of God who raised Jesus from the dead is present in all Christians and can work signs and wonders through them. Just as with St Peter, we can receive the authority of God the Father and the power of the Holy Spirit through faith in Jesus Christ.

Jesus was used by God to heal seriously ill and disabled

people, and occasionally to raise the dead. Since praying, 'Come, Holy Spirit,' in our church we have seen the healing of quite a few minor ailments, and very occasionally something more serious.

When Jesus met the Gadarene demoniac he cast out 'many demons' with one command and left the man dressed and in his right mind. Since the Holy Spirit has brought demons to the surface in some of our congregation we have been able to cast them out a few at a time and most people have registered improvement in their walk with God.

As Jesus, full of the Holy Spirit, did signs and wonders in Galilee huge crowds followed him. After the Holy Spirit had done signs and wonders in Jerusalem through the apostles 5,000 were added to them very quickly. Since learning to minister in the power of the Holy Spirit at Christ Church, numbers have risen slightly in an area where some churches have lost people dramatically.

It is a beginning. We have found that by praying, 'Come, Holy Spirit,' weekly at Burney Lane God has empowered us to proclaim the kingdom, heal the sick and cast out demons as never before. But it is only a beginning. In Jack Hywel-Davies' story of Smith Wigglesworth he says: 'The secret of spiritual success is a hunger that persists. To Wigglesworth the worst that can come to any child of God is to be satisfied with his present spiritual attainments. "It is an awful condition," he would tell his hearers.'[10]

The classic little book, *In the Footprints of the Lamb*, written by G. Steinberger in 1915, says, 'We no longer draw the Word of God down to the level of our experience, as we so long have been doing. We permit the ideals and goals of Scripture to stand, and strive toward them.'[11]

We have not yet seen any cripples being healed, nor dead raised. Neither have we walked on the water. We have certainly not experienced any of the 'greater things'

Jesus promised to his followers (Jn 14:12), but we believe in the God who speaks and the God who comes. What we have seen has encouraged us to believe for more. We are praying for miracle power and revival, that the King of Glory may come in and be glorified in our church and in our nation. But we do not use praying for revival as an excuse for doing nothing else. It is our belief that those who are already proclaiming the King and the kingdom, healing the sick and casting out demons, as the early disciples had all done before the Day of Pentecost, are those who will be best equipped to cope with revival when it comes.

Until then we continue to pray, 'Come, Holy Spirit,' over many or few, in church or in house groups, at the office or by the hospital bed. As we encourage hope in others, receive faith ourselves and learn to minister more like Jesus in the power of the Holy Spirit, we meet the God who comes. Giving God his church back not only improves church management, but teaches us to trust in the God who stretches our horizons and takes us deeper into him. It is an uncomfortable path, but a sure and certain one. Our hope is not in our faith, but in a God who is faithful. Our security is not in what may happen, but in the unchangeable God who loves to do a new thing.

When we stand with heads up, hands out and hearts open to the Holy Spirit we are filled again and again with the source of all love and power, and come to know him. I can only believe that the more we invite him to come, and the more we welcome his coming, the more we shall be equipped to do what comes supernaturally in Jesus' name.

Notes

1. Bill Subritzky came to Birmingham twice before 'The Battle Belongs to the Lord' conference at Brighton during which time he shared his views on Roman Catholicism.
2. John Wimber with Kevin Springer, *Power Healing* (Hodder & Stoughton: London, 1986).
3. Raymond Briggs, *The Snowman* (Puffin Books: London, 1978).
4. In many ways my first book is about the 'God who speaks' and this one is about the 'God who comes'. Knowing God as both seems to me to be very important for anyone seeking to minister as Jesus did. (Peter H. Lawrence, *The Hot Line* [Kingsway Publications: Eastbourne, 1990].)
5. Marie Woodworth-Etter, *A Diary of Signs and Wonders* (Harrison House: Tulsa, Oklahoma, 1916), p 143.
6. *ibid*, p 149.
7. The claim that Smith Wigglesworth was used by God to raise fourteen people from the dead is made by Albert Hibbert in his book *Smith Wigglesworth: The Secret of his Power* (Sovereign World Ltd: Chichester, 1987).
8. Jack Hywel-Davies, *Baptised by Fire* (Hodder & Stoughton: London, 1987), p 90.
9. Bill Subritzky, *But I Don't Believe in Miracles* (Dove Ministries Ltd: Auckland, 1989).
10. Hywel-Davies, *op cit*, p 75.
11. G. Steinberger, *In the Footprints of the Lamb* (Bethany Fellowship Inc: Minneapolis, Minnesota, 1936), p 79.